POTTED ORCHARDS

Growing Fruit in Small Spaces

POTTED ORCHARDS

Growing Fruit in Small Spaces

ALAN F. SIMMONS

with drawings by Denys Baker
and diagrams by the author

DAVID & CHARLES
NEWTON ABBOT   LONDON
NORTH POMFRET (VT)   VANCOUVER

0 7153 6666 1

Set in 11 on 13 pt Imprint
and printed in Great Britain
by Ebenezer Baylis & Son Limited
The Trinity Press Worcester and London
for David & Charles (Holdings) Limited
South Devon House Newton Abbot Devon

Published in the United States of America
by David and Charles Inc   North Pomfret
Vermont 05053 USA

Published in Canada
by Douglas, David & Charles Limited
3645 McKechnie Drive West Vancouver BC

CONTENTS

		page
	Foreword	9
	Introduction	11
1	General Management	13
2	Training	21
3	The Orchard House	33
4	Outdoor Protection	37
5	Health and Welfare	41
6	Apples	48
7	Apricots	69
8	Black Currants	76
9	Blueberries	85
10	Cherries	92
11	Citrus Fruits	107
12	Figs	123
13	Gooseberries	131
14	Grapes	139
15	Mulberries	150
16	Peaches	152
17	Pears	169
18	Plums	181
19	Red and White Currants	193
20	Strawberries	200

ILLUSTRATIONS

	page
Tree forms—upright, arching, maiden and feathered maiden	22
Tree forms—single cordon, bush, double cordon and pyramid	23
Pyramid training	24
Bush training	25
Standard training	26
Delayed open-centre bush training	26
Single cordon, double cordon and triple cordon training	27
Espalier training	29
Fan training	30
Spindle bush training	31
Diagram indicating air drainage	39
Apples	49
Apple and pear fruit spurs	51
Apricots	71
Black currant and red currant propagation	77
Black currants	78
Blueberries	86
Fruits buds: cherry, plum, peach	93
Pruning of sweet and acid cherry	94
Cherries	100
Citrus water sprouts	109
Citrus fruits	111
Fruit development of the fig	125
Figs	128
Fruit spurs of the gooseberry and red and white currants	132

ILLUSTRATIONS

	page
Gooseberries	137
Grape training	141
Grapes	144
Mulberries	151
Peaches	154
Pears	176
Plums	182
Red and white currants	194
Strawberries	201
Strawberry varieties	208

FOREWORD

The ideas in this book can be adapted to suit the different circumstances of fruit growers, actual or would-be, wherever they may be in temperate regions of the world—the fruit grown and the methods of cultivation used varying, of course, from place to place depending on soil and climatic conditions.

While it is not possible to describe every variety of fruit grown, the most important ones are included here. A special chapter, 'Health and Welfare', deals with pests and diseases, the most common of which are described in the relevant fruit chapters.

The book is dedicated to the workers in the research and horticultural institutes throughout the world, including those at East Malling, Kent, England; the Connecticut Agricultural Experimental Station, USA; the Tatura Horticultural Research Station, Australia; the Research Institute, Stellenbosch, South Africa; the Danube–Tisza Agricultural Research Institute, Agled, Hungary; the Volkani Institute, Israel; and the National Research Centre, Dokki, Cairo, UAR. It is dedicated to them all in appreciation of their ever-readiness to impart newly acquired knowledge and so help to broaden the picture of fruit cultivation worldwide.

INTRODUCTION

WHY POTTED TREES?

Many people who would like to grow fruit think they cannot do so because they have not a big enough garden. Yet, by growing trees and bushes in pots it is possible to have a far wider variety of fruits in a small plot or yard than in an equal area where trees are planted out. Potted trees can also be grown on balconies, patios, terraces and roof-top gardens.

There are other advantages, too. When trees are planted out, the soil conditions may not be to their liking: some trees and plants, such as the stone fruits, prefer a little chalk in the soil, and others, such as the blueberries, like the soil to be peaty. With pot cultivation, it is usually possible to add any deficient ingredient—peat, sand, loam, brick rubble, chalk, etc—to whatever you have at hand.

When trees are potted they become mobile, and this is an asset. If there is a danger of frost at blossom time they can be moved temporarily into a shed or to some other protective place. If high winds occur, the trees can be moved behind a hedge or wall for shelter. Where a glass house is available, they can be moved into it at the time their fruit is ripening; thus choice fruit which has been thoroughly ripened on the tree will be obtained. Currants, blueberries, cherries and gooseberries can be moved into the glass house so that their fruits are protected from birds. The mobility of potted trees means they can be fully used for ornamental purposes when in blossom or in fruit, being brought temporarily indoors or placed in a part of the garden for special effect.

With the exception of the apple and pear grown on dwarfing rootstock, pot-grown trees are kept very much smaller than normal, so no ladders are required. This facilitates cultivation, such as pruning, and also harvesting—a particular bugbear with cherries. Potted orchards are, therefore, an advantage for the less agile.

In warm climates a veritable assortment of fruit can be grown outdoors in pots. The most delicate kinds, of course, require a suitable situation or climate, but in any cool, temperate climate, if a glass house is available, it is possible to include citrus fruits in your potted orchard. Potted trees normally come into bearing earlier than others, but a large quantity of fruit cannot be expected. The quality and flavour should be better, however; you will, in fact, be growing luxury fruit.

The main disadvantage with pot cultivation is that it necessitates more work than normal methods. A sound maxim is: the more limited the space in which your fruit grows, the greater the amount of work you will have to do. Success or failure with potted trees depends on correct management. Careful attention must be given to pruning and other general matters, but for those interested in fruit growing this only adds to the pleasure of it. Whether you decide to have only one tree or a collection to form a potted orchard, you will find it is a delightful and quite profitable hobby.

I

GENERAL MANAGEMENT

Many of the principles of fruit cultivation which are applicable to the open garden and plantation also apply to the potted orchard, but because of the restriction imposed on the roots by the pots some special treatment is necessary.

POTS

First, what kind of pot should be used? Provided it gives proper drainage and allows the tree or bush to be easily removed when required, any container, box or trough is suitable, but horticultural pots or tubs are usually more satisfactory. The pots can be made of clay or plastic. Some growers prefer the old-type clay pots because they not only encourage good growth but have a natural appearance. The appearance may not matter much when young stock are growing, but a mature tree gives a more attractive ornamental effect in a large clay pot, which can be obtained in various shapes, beside the standard design. The disadvantage of the clay pot is that it can be easily broken. Plastic pots are light and easy to carry—an important consideration. They are also warmer and keep slightly more heat in the compost than do clay pots. Plastic pots do not dry out like the clay ones and this makes watering easier. They are cheap to buy and easy to clean.

Whatever pot is used, it should not be larger than is necessary to take the plant's roots when they are properly spread out. The fibrous roots should be allowed to lie horizontally into the soil and, provided this is done, the smaller the pot the better. If the pot is larger than necessary the roots will immediately start spreading into the entire compost area, so that the effect of limiting the root system—and hence the top—is lost. It is desirable for the tree to go through a gradual succession of increasingly larger pots. Young trees can be given a larger sized container each time they are repotted, but as the trees get older this is not so necessary.

More mature trees can go back into their original pots, providing these have been cleaned, but will benefit from the freshness of other pots of the same size, if available. Trees may be kept up to thirty years in an 18in pot and some, especially figs, will make do with much smaller sizes.

SOILS

But the plants grow in something else besides the pot. This other thing is living soil which, in turn, provides further life. A brief look at this big subject will be sufficient to give some idea of the nature of soils. There is a characteristic type of plant with a corresponding soil type in each of the world's major climatic zones: arctic, cold temperate, maritime and continental warm temperate, desert, sub-tropical, tropical. All of the many soils of the world provide—in greater or lesser degree—air, water, food and support for plant roots. To a large extent a soil's ability to provide these things is governed by the size of the particles of which it is comprised.

Stones, obviously, are the largest particles, with gravel, sand, silt, clay and humus in descending size. There is also limestone, or chalk, the particles of which can be of variable size. The smaller the soil particles the more active they are chemically and physically, and both clay and humus, consisting of very small particles, have considerable effect on the character of any soil aggregate in which they are present. Sand, although providing air, is unable to retain moisture and dissolved plant food. Silt is not porous and is so fine that it can become compacted, preventing either air or water entering into it. Both clay and humus act as binding agents between larger particles in an aggregate, and also retain moisture.

In most areas soils are an aggregate of some, if not all, of the different soils. Usually an ordinary soil will grow a great variety of plants but it may not necessarily be the *best* for a particular plant. So, with some knowledge of both soil characteristics and the requirements of a particular fruit, it is possible in a potted orchard to go a long way to providing the best available.

Where sand and clay particles are well balanced the soil is called a loam. Sometimes this loam is described as 'light' or 'heavy'. A light loam will consist of many large particles (sand) and a heavy loam of many small particles (clay). A light, sandy loam, although offering good drainage, will dry out quickly, and a heavy, clay loam is cold and suffers from poor drainage. Light, sandy loams lack plant foods, and heavy loams, although often fairly rich in food, lack air between the very small particles, so that the plant starved of air cannot use the food. Everything in a soil aggregate that is not actual particle must be either air or moisture, and a lack of either of these two things will limit plant growth. A good soil, which will provide both air and moisture, is one with a soft granular or crumb-like texture.

All soils, with the exception of humus and chalk, have a mineral (inorganic) derivation. These small inorganic particles are composed of many elements, some of which, such as iron, magnesium and potassium, are required for plant nutrition; these elements either dissolve or are retained on the surface of clay or humus particles.

It has been said that a good balance of sand and clay makes a nice loam and also that humus particles are even smaller than those of clay. What is humus? It is the vehicle of life through which all the animals, plants and micro-organisms feed upon each other and continue in everlasting life. Humus can be recognised by its dark brown or black colour. Leaf mould and peat are two examples of humus. A soil with a dark colour will indicate the presence of humus and a high degree of productiveness—although some dark soils may be acidic or sour. Peat from coniferous forest and moorland has high acidity. A further characteristic is that with a forest soil the surface layer tends to be leached of the soluble nutrients, such as lime, potash and phosphate, whereas with a *natural* grassland soil the surface layer is richer in nutrients than the subsoil. This can be explained to some extent by the fact that forests occur in humid regions, where the annual amount of rainfall exceeds evaporation, so that movement of dissolved minerals is downwards, whereas *natural* grassland occurs in arid regions where evaporation exceeds rainfall and the movement of moisture tends to be upwards.

Amongst the cultivated fruits only the blueberry and cranberry like an acid soil, and others cannot make full use of the nutrients available unless there is also some calcium or alkalinity. Stone fruits, for example, prefer a chalky soil. Chalk helps to bind light soils together and makes heavy clay soils more workable. A too chalky soil lacks humus and also plant food; it is sticky when wet but soon lacks any moisture in a dry period.

FERTILISERS

The nutrients needed for healthy plant growth can be divided into three categories: the major elements (nitrogen, potassium and phosphorus); the lesser elements (calcium, magnesium and sulphur); the trace elements (boron, manganese, molybdenum, etc). All elements in order to be available to the plant must be soluble. In some cases, although an element is available in the soil, some plants cannot make use of it because of the presence of another element. An example of this is the blueberry, which may be unable to make use of iron in the soil because of an excess of calcium.

Humus contains most of the nutrients required and is also alive with micro-organisms and bacteria without which the soil would be dead. Humus can be in the form of farmyard manure, leaf mould, composted garden and kitchen waste, sewage sludge, spent hops, meat and bone meal, fish meal, seaweed. Well-rotted farmyard manure from cows and pigs is the best organic plant food. Liquid manure can be produced by suspending a sack with animal manure or soot in water for a few days. Sawdust in a well-rotted condition and pine needles make a very good mulch for blueberries. Balanced chemical fertilisers can be purchased; a general all-purpose fertiliser would consist of seven parts superphosphate, five parts ammonia, two parts sulphate of potash.

Different kinds of fruit require different proportions of the two very important elements: nitrogen and potassium. The main requirement of dessert apples, red currants and gooseberries is potassium; although nitrogen is necessary at certain periods in their lives they cannot make full use of it unless potassium is available at the same time. Pears also require potassium as a continuing food, but they will benefit from heavier applications of nitrogen than the fruits previously mentioned. Plums, peaches, apricots, cherries and black currants require nitrogen to enable them to provide a regular supply of annual plant growth. Nitrogen promotes vegetative growth and one of the symptoms of nitrogen starvation is a pale green colour to the leaf. Sulphate of ammonia is a commonly used inorganic fertiliser to provide nitrogen. Dried blood, soot and fish meal contain a high percentage of readily available nitrogen. Potassium helps to ripen fruit and to give flavour. Sulphate of potash is a good inorganic fertiliser to provide potassium. Wood-ash—provided this has not been exposed to rain and the potassium leached out—is the best organic source of the element. Phosphorus, the other major element, encourages flower and fruit production. Superphosphate of lime is a quick-acting inorganic fertiliser to provide phosphorus. Bone meal, also containing nitrogen, is slow acting and a very good organic manure.

The ideal ingredients for a really good compost for pots would consist of five parts turfy loam, one part leaf mould, one part coarse sand, one part chalk (in small lumps) or brick rubble, one part well-rotted farm manure, and a liberal dressing of bone meal. Failing this, a satisfactory alternative could be seven parts loam, three parts coarse sand, three parts peat and either a good dressing of bone meal or a little sulphate of potash.

STOCK

We can, if we wish, start with maidens (one-year-old trees) and train these ourselves to the form required. If we do not want this trouble and are anxious to get fruit as quickly as possible, we should start with three-year-old trees in the form required. For those who would like to train their own trees—and there is much to commend this as well as satisfying a creative desire—the subject is dealt with in chapter 2. Whether we start with maidens or three-year-olds, they should preferably all have been grown in pots from the beginning. Some nurserymen specialise in pot-grown trees. Apples, pears, cherries, plums, apricots are best grown in pyramid form, while peaches and nectarines can be grown as dwarf, open-centre bush trees. If, however, the aim is to grow the maximum number of different kinds or varieties of fruit, some of the trees can be grown as single cordons. Single cordons will give the maximum weight of fruit from the available space. Details of these and other forms to suit special circumstances are also given in chapter 2.

Before the stock is potted up, badly bruised or injured roots should be cleanly and neatly cut out and the tap root shortened by up to one third its length. The pots chosen for the trees should be thoroughly clean and, if they are of clay, the bottom holes covered with crocks to allow drainage. Compost should be firmly rammed into the bottom of the pot to a height which will enable the upper roots of the tree to be just covered with compost, and the level of this at least an inch from the top of the pot. When the tree is put into the pot its roots should be carefully spread out, the compost put in a few inches at a time, and rammed well down around the side of the pot. The top surface should then be lightly loosened to prevent an impervious crust being formed. The potted trees should be given a good watering and left to winter. If it is possible to provide an ash bed, the pots can be buried in this up to their rims. The ash helps to prevent the pots being cracked by frost and keeps worms from getting inside. If ash or small brick rubble is not available, the pots can be buried in ordinary soil and, in those areas subject to severe winters, they can be well covered with litter.

With the exception of the citrus, all the fruits dealt with in this book should be left outside to winter because the wood is ripened or matured by cold weather. Fruit trees like sunshine, fresh air and reasonable amounts of rain. Again, with the exception of citrus, all the trees are deciduous and need to rest. They do this in cold weather and so no heat is necessary. They can, if desired, be grown continually in the ash bed or moved, as required, to some other garden position, roof garden, or restricted place, provided

17

there is reasonable shelter. There are obvious advantages in having a glass house, and this subject is dealt with in chapter 3. Where a heated house is available, it is possible for tropical and sub-tropical fruits to be grown in potted orchards; details regarding their cultivation will be found in my book *Growing Unusual Fruit*.

PLANT CARE

Once the trees have been potted they will require little if any attention during the winter, except for pears and apples which need pruning. All potted trees need careful pruning and this, particularly in the case of the stone fruits, should preferably be done with a sharp knife as secateurs are liable to bruise the wood and such wounds do not heal very quickly. In general, all cuts should be made just above a wood bud, leaving no unnecessary length above a bud to die off. Wood buds are recognisable in spring as they tend to be pointed and long, while blossom buds are short and plump. The cut should start level with the bud at the opposite side of the shoot and be slanted upwards at 45°. Main branches should be pruned back to a wood bud pointing outwards, so that subsequent growth is outward and away from the centre of the tree. Any laterals (side branches) which will make the centre of the tree crowded, as well as any crossing another branch, should be completely removed. Strong-growing shoots should be pruned lightly—up to one-third of new growth. Those which are weak should be heavily pruned—up to two-thirds of new growth. An aim of pruning should be to maintain the balance and form of the tree; with small trees it is often possible to keep the shape by pinching out the side shoots at five or six leaves in summer and pruning the leading branches in winter.

As the trees grow on during the following years, the compost in the pots will require replenishment to enable the roots to continue to feed. The operation should be done in the autumn or commencement of leaf fall. By first removing a little of the compost around the edges below the rim of the pot, and then lying the tree on its side, the tree can be easily taken from the pot, with a ball of compost around its roots. Any long, woody roots should be cut back to about two-thirds of their length, but fibrous, hairy roots should, as far as possible, be untouched. With large roots it is better to tend to be severe because strong-growing trees, such as pears and apples, will soon become too big for pot culture if such roots are unchecked. Annual repotting is not always necessary; trees which are obviously healthy may only need the removal of the surface compost, or perhaps some of the sides of the root-ball. This can be done with a pointed stick, taking care not to injure the roots.

If the compost is fairly dry, it is easy to free the roots by placing the tree's root-ball on a board laid across a barrow, with its head pointing away from the handles of the barrow. Stand between the handles and with one hand hold the stem of the tree and with a stick carefully loosen the soil around the roots. This method is less likely to injure roots and fruit buds.

When repotting is necessary, use the next largest size. As the trees grow bigger the soil should be put in no higher than about 2in below the rim of the pot, to allow for top dressing and watering. When such top dressing has left little room for watering, a strip of zinc or tin about 6in wide can be bent around the inside of the rim and pressed into the soil. Watering can thus continue and the tree given more top dressing if necessary. During the summer, the trees will need plenty of water and, if available, a mulch of well-rotted manure is beneficial.

It is of the utmost importance to provide the trees with sufficient moisture; dryness is one of the chief causes of failure. It not only causes loss of flavour, but also prevents the fruit from reaching its full size and may cause it to drop prematurely. During really hot weather, the roots may need some protection, as they are more likely to be exposed to the direct rays of the sun than those of a tree with its roots in the ground. Straw or damp sacking may be placed around the pots at such times. Thorough watering should be given almost every day so that the moisture gets right down to the bottoms of the pots, and the foliage may be syringed.

At blossom time help can be given to pollination by dusting or stroking inside each individual flower with a camel hair brush during dry weather. If compatible pollinators are grown together, a heavy set of fruit is forthcoming. Remember, though, that the trees not only have to bear and ripen fruit during the current year; they also have to produce and mature or ripen new growth, as well as set fruit buds for the coming year. If a tree is overcropped it means a poor crop next year and, perhaps, even worse—a very sick tree. The trees will benefit from diluted liquid manure fed to them once a week from the time the fruit is beginning to swell, and this should be continued throughout the growing period. Thinning of fruit can be carried out at intervals, but the final thinning of stone fruits should be left until after the stone has formed. By correct thinning—and this applies to all fruit—larger specimens are obtained. Young, three-year-old peach, apple and pear trees can be allowed to carry about six large fruits and up to nine smaller ones. Plums should be limited to up to twenty on a three-year-old tree. Cherries do not require much thinning unless it is desired to obtain large fruits. As the trees grow in size over the years the crops can increase accordingly.

2

TRAINING

Training fruit trees into the shapes required, except for the simplest artificial forms, needs some skill. Even so, once the principles of training are understood, the skill can be acquired and, if you have patience to wait for the fruit, it is a creative and absorbing hobby. For one thing you will have a more intimate knowledge of your trees and hold them in greater affection. They will have been shaped with your own hands.

During its first year of growth, the fruit plant is a single shoot and is called a maiden. At the end of its first year it has a fairly uniform character. Throughout its length it bears numerous buds which are a little thicker at the top than at the base. Each of the buds is capable of producing a new shoot which will resemble the main stem. If the growing conditions have been very favourable during the first year, some of the buds in the centre of the stem may produce shoots and grow just a little. Such one-year-old trees are called *feathered maidens*. If the tree is left to itself it will, during succeeding years, develop gradually into its natural form.

Trees have several natural forms, the two most common amongst fruit trees being the upright and self-arching forms. Pear trees are often upright in form; it is one of slow growth and, consequently, thick branches which do not bend are produced. The self-arching form is produced by quick growth and this gives long supple branches which bend under the weight of the fruit or even the foliage. From the apex of the arching branches vigorous and upright shoots commence to grow and these will themselves bear fruit and bend over. The self-arching form is common to the citrus and frequently amongst the apples. It is generally impracticable to train citrus trees, which should be helped towards their natural form. By helping trees in this way, fruiting will often be hastened.

When trees are trained to artificial forms they are termed either 'flat' or 'round'. 'Flat' forms are the cordon, espalier and fan. They are, more or

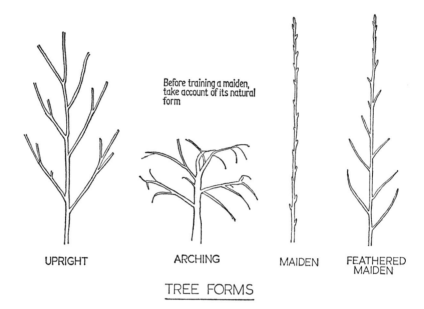

Before training a maiden, take account of its natural form

UPRIGHT   ARCHING   MAIDEN   FEATHERED MAIDEN

TREE FORMS

less, two dimensional, having only height and width, and are usually trained against a wall or fence. The 'round' are more natural in appearance and, fundamentally, they are either pyramid or bush trees. Pyramid trees are sometimes described as being of fuseau or dwarf pyramid form; with these the trunk predominates as a central vertical axis with framework branches growing out from it through its entire length. Bush trees—sometimes described as open bush, vase, or goblet—have no predominant trunk. In this form, the trunk terminates where the first branches grow out and these have all formed, approximately, at the same point.

Some forms are better suited to pot cultivation than others, and to different fruit. The forms described here are those normally used in fruit cultivation in general, though some are not usual for pot cultivation. Knowledge of them may be helpful in adapting a form to meet a special requirement.

'ROUND' FORMS

THE DWARF PYRAMID

A maiden, preferably without feathers, should be potted in the autumn. In the following spring, that is, in its *second year of growth*, it must be cut back to a bud about 30in above the level of the soil, and then allowed to develop into a strong shoot and grow up vertically as an extension of the

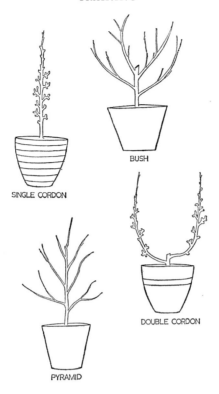

SINGLE CORDON

BUSH

DOUBLE CORDON

PYRAMID

TREE FORMS

original stem. In the winter this extension should be cut back to about half its length, the cut being made at a bud on the opposite side of the one where the stem was cut in the spring. The reason for cutting at a bud on the opposite side is to keep the stem growing as straight as possible. For the same reason when the stem is cut in following years it should be cut at opposite buds each year.

During the *third year of growth* four or five lateral shoots should be growing out in a spiral fashion from around the stem. If it is necessary to stimulate the young tree into producing the four or five lateral shoots, this can be done by nicking the bark just above the buds which have been selected to produce branches spirally around the stem. In the winter these laterals which have been produced should be cut back to a bud on the underside and about 5 or 6in from the stem. These laterals will now form side branches.

In the summer of the *fourth year of growth* any strong lateral shoots growing from the side branches produced in the preceding year are

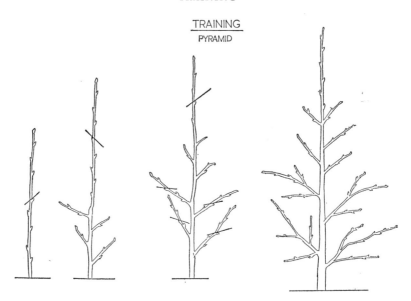

shortened by cutting back to a leaf 5 or 6in from the branch. In the winter the extension of the central stem or leader is again cut back by about one half and the side branches are also cut back to about 5 or 6in from the stem.

The following summer a second set of side branches will grow out spirally from the stem and these should be treated in the same way as the first set. Future pruning should then follow the lines described under the separate fruit headings. *Provided it makes quick growth, a dwarf pyramid tree can be made to produce fruit in a comparatively short period of time.*

BUSH OPEN CENTRE (Vase or Goblet)
A well-developed maiden is potted in the autumn and cut back in the winter to a bud about 18in above soil level. During the *second year of growth* several strong shoots will grow out spirally just below the stem's terminal bud. In the following winter three or four of these are selected to make a symmetrical goblet or vase shape, the remainder being cut out completely. The branches which have been selected are then cut back hard to about 6in from the stem and to buds which point either outwards or downwards, according to whether the tree is arching or upright in its natural form.

During the next winter, that is, in the tree's *third year of growth*, the young branches are again cut back to about 6in from their base, and any shoots growing from them are pruned according to the kind of fruit (see

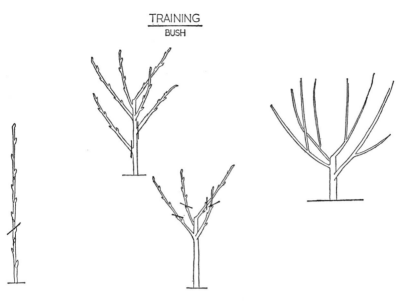

TRAINING
BUSH

individual chapters). *This form is fairly easy to produce and is suitable for most of the fruit in this book.*

HALF-STANDARD BUSH

'Standard' forms are basically the same as the one just described, except that the head of the tree is formed well above ground level. Normally the head of the half-standard is about 4ft 6in above ground level, but it can be formed at any convenient height.

The young tree is allowed to grow unchecked until the required height has been reached; then, in the winter, the stem is cut back to the point at which it has been decided to form the head and all unwanted laterals are removed. Training then continues as described for the bush. *This is a form of tree which is often convenient for gooseberries and red and white currants.*

DELAYED OPEN-CENTRE BUSH

This is a combination of the pyramid and bush. During the first year the stem, with selected shoots growing evenly around it, is allowed to grow, much like a pyramid. When it is decided that no further extension of the centre stem is needed, the young terminal shoots at the top are directed outwards away from the centre, as in the ordinary open-centre bush. In order to prevent the centre from becoming too crowded the two buds immediately below the two at the top should be removed. The main point

25

TRAINING
STANDARD

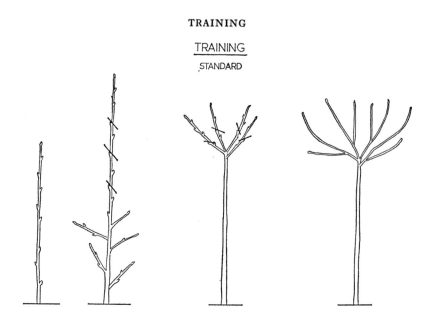

when training this form is to see that the shoots are spaced evenly around the centre stem and that they will grow in the required direction. The tree comes into bearing comparatively early because, in the beginning, there is very little pruning.

TRAINING
DELAYED OPEN-CENTRE BUSH

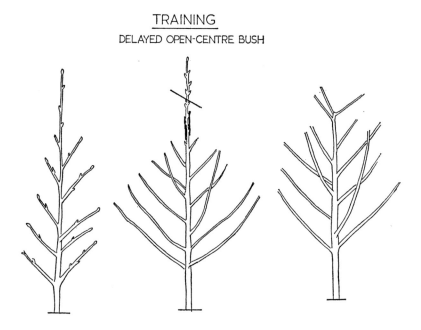

'FLAT' FORMS

For pot cultivation these should only be considered for special positions. A wall, especially a sunny one, should be taken advantage of, because not only will the tree be protected from cold and strong winds but the fruit will ripen better. With these 'flat' forms it is necessary that the vertical and oblique branches are tied to canes to keep them in the right position and to prevent them rubbing against the wall. The branches should be tied with raffia or soft string and not tied direct to wires fixed on the wall or fence. If they are tied to wires and rub against the wall, causing chafing, this may result in canker in apples and pears, or gumming in the stone fruits. Difficulties may also arise when the trees need to be repotted.

SINGLE CORDON

No actual shaping is required for this form; it consists of a single-stemmed tree trained to grow vertically. A maiden tree is potted and the stem allowed to grow unchecked, but the laterals, during the summer, are pruned back to a leaf 5 or 6in from the stem. When the stem has reached the required height, it is cut back; the tree will then turn its energies to bearing fruit instead of extending its growth. Meanwhile, each summer,

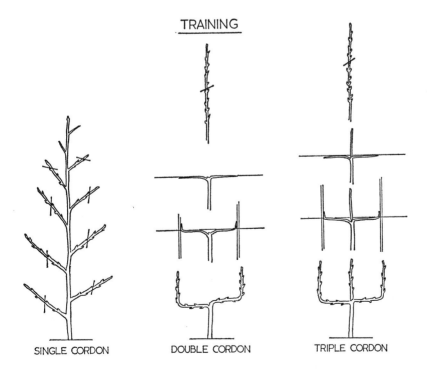

TRAINING

SINGLE CORDON   DOUBLE CORDON   TRIPLE CORDON

27

the laterals will continue to be pruned back to 5 or 6in from the stem, as they were during the tree's early years. *This is a form suitable for apples, pears, gooseberries, red and white currants.*

DOUBLE CORDON

In this form, two upright vertical stems are used instead of one. A maiden is cut back at about 12in from the soil and at a point where two buds face in the opposite direction. In the summer, after the stem has been cut back, the shoots which have grown from the two buds are trained to grow horizontally by tying them to canes fixed to a wire set at the required height. When the shoots are about 6–8in long, they are gently bent upwards and tied to vertical canes. If one of the stems is growing more vigorously than the other, it can be tied slightly outwards and downwards, in order to check its growth and allow the other to catch up. During the winter, the two stems are cut back to an extent depending on the vigour of their growth. Side shoots are cut back in November to two buds and these form fruiting spurs.

TRIPLE CORDON

This has three vertical stems. The maiden is cut back at about 12in from the soil, but at a bud which is pointing upwards. When this bud and the two immediately below it, one on the left and the other on the right, have each grown about 6in, the central shoot is trained to grow vertically by tying it to an upright cane, while the other two are at first trained horizontally (as in the Double Cordon). If the central stem grows more vigorously than the other two, its tip can be pinched out when it is about 2ft long. In the autumn the two side shoots are untied from their canes and trained to grow vertically, each at an equal distance from the central stem. In the winter each of the three stems is cut back by about one-third of its length.

ESPALIER

This is a form popular in Europe for growing pears and apples in garden borders. It can be utilised for pot cultivation when it is desired to make use of a low wall or fence. It is a form suitable also for gooseberries, red and white currants.

An unfeathered maiden is cut back to about 15in from the soil at a point where there are two buds close together, one on either side of the stem and just below the terminal bud. The shoot from the terminal bud is trained to grow vertically, while the two shoots below it are trained one to the left

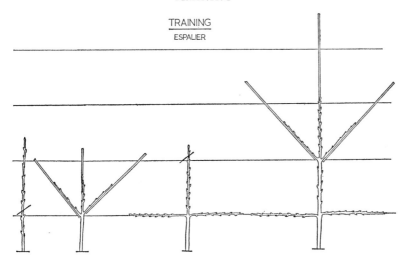

TRAINING

ESPALIER

and the other to the right. To encourage more rapid growth, the side shoots should first be fastened at an angle of 45° for the first year, but after this trained to grow horizontally at about 12in from the top of the pot. At the end of the first year of training the central stem is cut back to about 2ft and a second tier of side branches is then formed in the same way as the first. If required, a new tier can be formed each year.

It is fairly easy to form this kind of tree. When the first tier of side branches has been produced, all the shoots on these should be cut back in the summer to about 5in, as this will encourage the formation of fruiting spurs instead of new wood. Each winter the side branches should be shortened by up to half the current season's growth.

FAN
This form is used mainly for the stone fruits, when grown against walls. It takes three years to make the framework, and patience as well as some skill are required. The method of producing the fan is included for those who would like to try their hand at it and make use of the form in the potted orchard.

The top few inches of a maiden are cut away in the autumn and then, in the following spring, the buds, as they begin to 'break', are removed— with the exception of the two strongest at about 12in from the 'union' (ie where the scion or maiden was grafted to the rootstock). When the shoots from these two buds have grown to about 18in the main stem above them is completely removed. The two shoots are then tied to canes, which should be fixed at an angle of 45°. In the following winter the shoots—or side

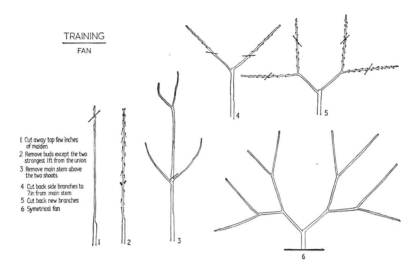

TRAINING

FAN

1. Cut away top few inches of maiden
2. Remove buds except the two strongest 1ft from the union
3. Remove main stem above the two shoots
4. Cut back side branches to 7in from main stem
5. Cut back new branches
6. Symetrical fan

branches, as they now are—should be cut back to a bud about 7in from the main stem. During the summer, four shoots—to later form branches—are allowed to grow from the two existing side branches. In the following winter the new branches are cut back to about 2ft of well-ripened wood.

FERRUGATI CORDON

The arching of main branches of some kinds of fruit is often practised to encourage cropping. In Italy, for example, small vertical cordons are grown and the central stems are cut back each year, the length varying with the variety. The laterals, instead of being cut back to within a few inches of the central stem, are left unshortened and, as they grow, are arched over on to wire supports. By this method the tree produces heavy crops, but soon becomes exhausted. It is not a form to be used for pot cultivation but may be tried if trees are grown in the ground.

THE SPINDLE BUSH

This form is intermediate between the vertical cordon and the pyramid, differing from the former in that its lower branches are allowed to grow to a greater length than those above, and from the latter in that its main branches are never as stout or well developed as the pyramid. The branches are intermediate between fruit-bearing shoots and framework branches.

The form can be developed from well-feathered maidens or two-year-old pyramids. After planting, the central stem of a maiden should be cut back to the required height and at a point a few inches above the topmost

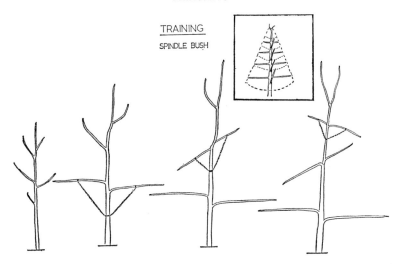

TRAINING

SPINDLE BUSH

feather it is intended to use as a branch. When a two-year-old pyramid is chosen, the lateral shoots are all pruned back to a bud pointing downwards, and those shoots at the bottom are left longer than those above. During the first season of growth the laterals are trained into a horizontal position, although in the case of a feathered maiden this is usually not necessary until the second year. To train the laterals to a horizontal position, string or raffia is attached to the middle of each and then tied at the same place on the stem, giving the tree an umbrella-like appearance. They should be tied down in August because, if this is done before growth has ceased, the ends of the shoots will begin to grow upwards again; if they are tied down too late, the whole purpose of the tying down will be missed and they will not become fixed in the required position. The ties can be removed after leaf fall or left until the following summer. The laterals should be tied so that they are straight, not arched, otherwise strong vertical shoots will grow from the top of the arch; this is why the tie should be made in the middle of the lateral.

The aim of the training should be to build up a tree with a vertical central stem and with horizontal branches radiating from it, so that it takes an over-all cone-like or pyramid form. To maintain this pyramid form it is necessary for the lower branches to retain their preponderant length; this is done by pruning them more lightly than those above.

FURTHER PRACTICES

In training trees it is often possible to obtain the required effect without waiting for a shoot to grow and then cutting it out. Three ways of doing this are by disbudding, pinching and summer pruning.

Disbudding means the suppression of unwanted buds before they have started any real development in the spring. Buds can be removed completely, thus preventing the growth of shoots where they are not required. A main bud may be flanked by two others and, if this main bud is removed, it is possible to obtain two weaker shoots instead of the strong one.

Pinching consists of pinching out the tips of young green shoots when in full growth. To be effective this needs to be repeated several times.

Summer pruning is the same as pinching but is performed at a later stage when the shoots have ripened or matured, and secateurs must be used. It is done when repeated pinching does not sufficiently check a strong growing shoot.

Remember always: summer pruning checks growth, winter pruning stimulates it.

3

THE ORCHARD HOUSE

The extent to which an orchard house can be an asset—and the *kind* of house to be used—will depend on climatic conditions. If, for example, the trees only need protecting when they are in blossom against the danger of night frost, all that is required is a shed or a barn to which they can be moved. In a colder climate, however, if fruit like peaches and nectarines are to be grown, a glass house must certainly be considered, and, in the case of citrus fruit, artificial heat. The varieties of fruit grown in much of the temperate zone, which are the concern of this book, do not—with the exception of citrus—need a glass house.

The trees must, though, be protected from consistently cold winds and also have plenty of light. If trees are to remain in the orchard house for a long time, as against a short stay during a gale or frost emergency, the maximum of light is essential. Although an all-glass house will admit maximum light, it will lose heat more quickly than one which is partly constructed of timber or bricks and, when artificial heating is provided, cost more to heat.

Glass on its own may not give sufficient protection during really low temperatures at blossom time; at such times, sacking or other material can be put over the glass, or newspapers put to the inside. Artificial heating, when required on a temporary basis, is best provided by paraffin heaters, which are mobile.

The purpose of the orchard house is not so much to enable us to control the climate inside as to protect plants from the climate outside. Increased warmth during the ripening period, though, will mean that many fruits can be harvested to greater perfection than when ripened outdoors. So, when a moderate supply of fruit only is required, the trees should be in the open for part of the year and brought into the orchard house in succession, as and when they require protection or warmth. Because the trees will not

c

be remaining in the house permanently, wide doors are essential to enable them to be moved in and out. Where sliding doors can be fitted, these are admirable.

The house will not serve its proper purpose if it is sited in an unsuitable place. In a garden it is often not possible to have the ideal position, but it should not be put in the shadow of tall trees or buildings. On the other hand, although it needs to be in full sun for most of the day, it must not be exposed to the prevailing cold winds of the winter. A cold wind will lower the temperature of the house much more than equally cold but still air. A hedge or fence across the direction of prevailing winds will reduce their velocity and give considerable protection.

Temperature and ventilation are married to each other—they cannot be divorced—and irrespective of whether there is artificial heating both must be considered together. With some glass houses, ridge ventilators only are provided and these are assumed to be sufficient; however, although these allow the rising warm air to escape, side ventilators are also desirable in hot weather, as they let in plenty of fresh air at the lower levels without causing too much draught. Success in growing fruit under glass depends very much upon adequate ventilation. Ventilation controls the humidity in the house. When the temperature is high and ventilation inadequate, the humidity may be so great—the atmosphere being laden with moisture—that the trees or plants cannot lose their own waste moisture.

High humidity may result in the destruction of the leaves and shoots of some plants, especially grape vines. This occurs when growth has already become soft and weak through having to contend with successive spells of moisture-saturated atmosphere. When the ventilators of a house are closed for the night, the plants continue to transpire, thus increasing humidity. Then, when the sun appears, the temperature of the atmosphere in the house rises very quickly whereas that of the plants rises more slowly. If the ventilators remain closed, condensation will occur on cooler growth which in turn may result in browning and rotting of leaves and shoots.

On the other hand, hot, dry conditions encourage red spider mite; also the trees, being in pots, will lose their moisture too quickly. In hot weather, therefore, the trees may be sprayed overhead and the ground round about dampened. This, though, must not be overdone because the trees are not lovers of a damp, humid atmosphere. In the autumn, winter and spring, watering should be done in the morning so that the foliage and atmosphere will have time to become dry before the ventilators are closed down; in summer it can be done in the evening.

34

It should not normally be necessary to provide shading in the summer. A plant that has been heavily shaded during the summer will not stand up to the winter as well as one that has not been shaded. With proper ventilation, a plant which does not suffer from scorching by the sun outside will not do so under glass. When the weather is exceptionally hot, a very light shading can be provided by smearing a light covering of whiting or window cleaning liquid over the glass; this should be wiped off when the heat-wave has passed. In climates where summers are really hot and winters cold, blinds can be fitted so that they can be let down during hot spells and also used as protection against spring frosts.

Cleanliness is important. All rubbish, such as dead leaves, paper, old string, etc, should be removed, as these harbour pests and diseases. The glass should be kept clean of green algae, because this robs the plants of essential light. Fungus spores and insects get into cracks and crevices so, if possible, the house should be completely emptied periodically and thoroughly cleaned and fumigated. Many pests that attack fruit trees outdoors can become established in an orchard house, giving rise to a great deal of trouble. Keep a constant lookout for the first signs of attack so that immediate measures can be taken.

Diseases are comparatively rare but, if ventilation is inadequate, the two most likely to occur are botrytis and powdery mildew. Two troublesome pests are red spider mite and whitefly. The latter, because it has many host plants, is sometimes difficult to eradicate and as soon as it is cleared from the house a fresh migration from host plants, including weeds growing outside the house, may occur. However, most pests and diseases can be effectively controlled by insecticides or fungicides.

Because the trees in an orchard house are to a very large extent isolated from insects and wind—the two principal pollinating agents—some assistance in pollination may be needed, although potted trees will normally, because of the amount of fruit they are allowed to bear, have sufficient flowers pollinated. Assistance can be given by giving each tree a sharp tap with a stick when they are in blossom. Some fruits—the pear, for instance—have a sticky pollen and, when necessary, assistance in pollination needs to be given with a camel hair brush.

Depending on local climatic conditions and the kind of fruit being grown, a timetable for the admission of trees to the orchard house can be followed. Apricots, figs, nectarines and peaches can be brought inside at the beginning of February and, as soon as they are cleared of fruit, returned to their positions outdoors. Apples, pears and plums can be admitted for a short stay to protect their blossom from spring frost and then

35

given a favourable position outdoors from the beginning of June. If choice plums are required, the trees can be brought into the house in succession for their fruit to ripen. Currants, cherries, gooseberries and mulberries may be left in the house until their fruit has been gathered.

4

OUTDOOR PROTECTION

Although it is not essential, and perhaps not possible or convenient, to have an orchard house we should be prepared, when the occasion arises, to give the trees some protection. If we have only a few trees, it is obviously impracticable to incur expense by making special or elaborate provisions. Various ways of giving protection from wind, frost, excessive rain, sun, birds, etc, will be self-evident; garden positions can be utilised to the best advantage and improvised shelter made from whatever is to hand.

WIND

If the site of the potted orchard is on top of a hill or near a wind-prone coast it may be troubled with gales. Exposure to warm but strong winds can do damage because of their persistent battering. Prolonged winds can have a very severe effect both on tree growth and fruit yield. If cold winds occur early in the season, even at the pre-blossom stage, the skin quality of apples and pears may be affected and russeting occur. If the wind occurs late in the season, abrasions of the skin may be caused by the fruit banging together or rubbing against the branches. A wall, fence, hedge or a belt of trees can be an asset at such times.

The extent of the area benefiting from the shelter of walls, etc, is governed mainly by the height of the 'break' and its density. An area behind a moderately permeable 'break' may extend to about thirty times the height of the 'break', although the effect beyond twenty times its height is slight. In fact, the maximum reduction of wind speed normally takes place at three to six times its height. When moving air meets a solid obstruction it pushes up over the top and, if it is a strong wind, will produce a vicious eddy on the other side which may be worse than the constantly strong wind itself. So, although a stone wall or solid fence cuts down the wind abruptly, this has effect for a short distance only—about ten times the height of the wall—and beyond this there is considerable turbulence. For this reason, the width of a walled garden should not exceed approximately ten times the height of the surrounding wall. As a temporary measure, artificial windbreaks can be made of plastic netting which will lessen the violence of the wind.

FROST

Windbreaks, however, have to be considered along with the problem of frost. Both the flower and fruit buds of all deciduous fruit trees have a dormancy or rest period and, during this time, they seem to require an adequate exposure to a chilling temperature to enable them to open naturally and satisfactorily in the spring. Although the length and intensity of this chilling varies according to the species, apples, pears, plums and cherries require from two to three months with temperature averaging 48° F (8·8° C) or lower.

However, this does not mean that potted trees can be left to stand exposed to sub-arctic conditions. Where a severe winter is expected the trees should be moved to sheltered positions or otherwise buried into the earth up to the rim of the pots. It is in the spring when we must be on guard against frost, not only during the actual time when the trees are in blossom but also just before and immediately after that period. Damage to apple blossom, for example, occurs at the following temperatures:

Buds still closed but showing pink	27° F (−2·8° C)
Full bloom	28° F (−2·2° C)
Small green fruitlets	29° F (−1·7° C)

On a still night with a clear sky, the ground and all objects on it rapidly lose their heat by radiation until their temperature falls below that of the surrounding air. A layer of cold, heavy air is then formed near the ground and, because hot air rises and cold air sinks, this means that the cold air will drain or roll away to the lowest level. If there is any obstruction in its path, such as a fence, the cold air will be stopped; it will build up behind the fence and perhaps engulf small fruit trees as a result. But if there is a hole or opening, such as a gate, in the fence this will allow the cold air to flow through it. On a sloping hillside it is possible for cold air to drain away to lower areas of the surrounding country, but on low-level land or in valley bottoms this cannot happen.

Wind will have the effect of mixing the layers of cold and warm air so that the temperature may be kept above freezing point. Although in the

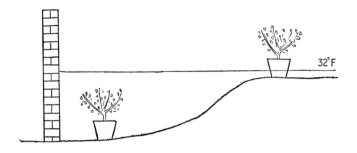

AIR DRAINAGE STOPPED BY WALL

COLD AIR FLOWS THROUGH OPENING IN WALL

usual conditions of a spring frost—that is, on a clear, still night—damage to fruit crops is more severe in valleys and on low ground than on high ground, this is not so when a freezing wind is blowing. When a strong wind is blowing from cold regions, causing persistent freezing, fruit crops on high ground, being more exposed to the wind, will suffer more than those on low ground. The advantage of potted trees is that they can be moved away from the flow and saturation of cold air. If, for some reason, this cannot be done, the simplest way to protect them from spring night frost is to tie or fix newspaper around them. Sacks, hessian screens or wattle fencing panels can also be used to protect the trees and then removed in the day time.

RAIN AND HEAT

Excesses of rain can be minimised by putting the trees behind a sheltering wall, while deficiencies can be made good by increased watering. Under

39

no circumstances should the soil of potted trees be allowed to become bone dry in summer. In cold climates a south-facing brick wall will act as a good storage of warmth, but in a period of excessive heat it may be desirable to give some shade to the trees.

BIRDS

In some areas birds are a menace when they peck holes in hard fruits. If the hole heals quickly, not much harm is done apart from blemishing the fruit. But, if it does not heal, the hole may be invaded by wasps or brown rot fungus. To ensure perfect fruit, the only real way is to cage the trees or bushes completely, or cover them individually with netting, or to protect the individual fruits. Peaches, apples, pears, etc, can be enclosed in muslin, or paper bags kept in place with elastic bands. Even better are small plastic bags, which will withstand rain, but these must have a few air holes in them. For pears, another method is to use postcards cut in halves. A hole is made in the centre of the card and a slit cut from one edge to the hole. The card is then slid over the stalk end of the pear and held in position by the stalk. This may appear to offer a platform for birds, but in fact even tits find the perch unstable and it is soon avoided.

5

HEALTH AND WELFARE

As our relationship with fruit trees will be closer than it would be if they were planted out in the open orchard, a deeper understanding of their health and well-being will be appreciated.

Life is an eternal struggle. The insects which settle upon fruit trees, feeding upon them, weakening them, are all part of that struggle. So also are the beneficial insects, such as the bees that fly from flower to flower pollinating them and assisting the procreation of the species. Diseases, mites, insects, plants are all in correlation to form the food or fuel of unending life. If humus is the vehicle of life, then organisms are the fuel. Pest control should, therefore, whenever possible, be natural control. Yet very often, by supplementing natural processes with chemicals, man tends to upset the balance of nature. It is commonsense to use chemicals only when really necessary, but this means asking ourselves whether the extent or likely extent of the pest damage is so small that it can be tolerated. We must be alert to the first symptoms and, in order to assess the potential damage, identification of the pest or disease is essential. This is not always easy and the insect seen on the tree may not be the cause of the trouble. The real enemy may be feeding at night or it may have completed the feeding stage of its life cycle and migrated elsewhere.

DISEASES

Diseases are even more difficult to diagnose and expert advice may be required. Apart from being parasitical—that is, caused by organisms such as fungi, bacteria and viruses—diseases can also be physiological and caused by a deficiency in nourishment or by some environmental factor.

PARASITIC FUNGI

Fungus diseases are brought about through the attack of various parasitic fungi. Some fungi obtain their food by living on dead or decaying organic matter, while others obtain it from living host plants, debilitating or even killing them in the process. The harmless fungi are usually large and easily seen, but the parasitic fungi are microscopic, although their presence can often be detected because of a grey or fur-like growth. There are a large number of parasitic fungi and they attack practically every known plant. They reproduce themselves by releasing enormous numbers of spores, or seed-like bodies. These can be carried a considerable distance in moving air, also by water and other means, such as insects.

The majority of parasitic fungi live within the plant tissue, others on the surface of the plant. Infection is usually the result of two processes: (1) penetration of the spore into the plant tissue, which can be likened to a seedling's root penetration, (2) establishment of the fungus growth in or on the host. The first process can only occur when the spore is able to remain in contact with the tissue of the plant and when conditions for germination (ie moisture and warmth) are satisfactory. Fungi damage plants by taking food from the cells and weakening or killing the infected area. Ancillary damage can occur, such as the production of poisons which penetrate into the plant and kill it.

BACTERIA

Another form of primitive microscopic plants—bacteria—also cause disease. These multiply by simple fission, which means that they split into two producing cells identical to the parent so that the same hereditary characteristics are passed on to the offspring. The multiplication occurs fairly rapidly—two or three times per hour—so that, in favourable conditions of food and warmth, etc, a very slight infection quickly develops into a severe one. Like the fungi they are parasitical and require other organisms for food. Bacterial infection of plants may occur through the pores of the leaves, lenticals, flowers or wounds. However, the bacteria which attack living plants are of a selective type and only infect closely related species. They do not, as far as is known, produce resting spores, which remain in the soil or other places so maintaining an infection. They only persist in plant tissue so that the disease is only in, say, a piece of diseased root left in the soil and not in the soil itself. This is in contrast to parasitical fungi, which may produce resting spores remaining in the soil for years. Infection usually causes recognisable symptoms, the two main kinds being: (1) Wilts. These are caused by the bacteria penetrating into the sap of the plant where it multiplies so rapidly that a blockage occurs causing the plant to quickly wilt; (2) Soft rots. In this kind of infection the soft tissues of the plant are attacked and rapidly broken down causing a soft putrid mass with or without an offensive smell. However, in crown gall disease *(Phytomonis tumefaciens)*, unlike most other known bacterial diseases, the host cells are not broken down and destroyed, but are stimulated into uncontrolled and irregular cell divisions, causing tumours.

VIRUS INFECTION

Diseases are also caused by virus infection. Viruses may live anywhere within the sap of a plant and in many of their characteristics, such as their power of multiplication (fission), they resemble living organisms, but some have been identified as nucleo-proteins which shows a link between the organic molecule and the living organism. Virus diseases may be transmitted when taking cuttings from infected plants; by using infected buds and scions, or by sucking insects, such as leaf hopper and aphids, which pierce the tissue of a diseased plant to suck out the sap and then go on to a healthy plant taking the disease with them. Once a plant has become infected it continues to carry the virus, so any part of it used for propagation will be affected. Virus diseases, however, are seldom transmitted in the seed or soil. Virus infection may be suspected when symptoms are observed such as small or distorted fruit, reduction in cropping, or a general stunting of growth.

PHYSIOLOGICAL DISORDERS

Physiological disorders are diseases caused by nutritional or environmental deficiencies, such as poor light, unsuitable temperature, incorrect watering or deficiency in feeding. The cause or causes of such diseases are sometimes very difficult to diagnose. Stunted growth can be a symptom not only of virus infection but also of nutritional deficiency. The most common of the element deficiency symptoms are as follows:

Nitrogen deficiency Usually to be seen in the leaves, which are slow to develop, become small and are of a pale greenish colour with tints of orange, red or purple. Shoots are spindly, blossom is reduced and the bark shows a reddish tinge. Defoliation is often premature.

Potassium deficiency Stunted growth, dieback of shoots and branches. Leaves, bluish green in colour, turn brown and become crinkled at the edges. Although this 'scorching' of the leaves is a fairly distinctive symptom, there may also be interveinal Chlorosis (whiteness), especially in the case of the stone fruits. Apples, gooseberries, currants and raspberries all have high potassium requirements.

Phosphorus deficiency   Symptoms sometimes resemble those occurring when there is a deficiency of nitrogen. Growth is slender and weak; leaves are small and fall prematurely. Leaf and flower bud opening is retarded. However, foliage colour is a distinctive feature, being a dull bluish green, with either a purplish or bronzing tint. Usually it is the leaf colour in the growing tree which shows the deficiency.

Magnesium deficiency   Symptoms are most marked in the foliage and, because magnesium is a constituent of chlorophyll, leaves may be of a chlorotic character. Sometimes, though, brilliant colours may develop. Too heavy applications of potassium can cause a deficiency of magnesium. A good way to correct magnesium deficiency is to apply a solution of magnesium sulphate (Epsom salts) by spraying the foliage. This can be made by dissolving $\frac{1}{2}$lb of Epsom salts in $2\frac{1}{2}$ gal of water.

Iron deficiency   Symptoms are usually chlorotic-tipped foliage, which in some instances may be severe, associated with a marginal scorching of the leaves and shoot tips. It is possible to reduce this condition with Sequestrene, a compound containing iron and manganese. On an alkaline soil, the elements iron and manganese are involved in chemical actions and become inactive, or inaccessible to the plants which need them to manufacture chlorophyll. It is no use, therefore, adding ferrous compounds to the soil, but Sequestrene is a chelating agent which clings to the elements and prevents them becoming involved in chemical action with the calcium present in the soil.

Manganese deficiency   Symptoms are varied, but interveinal chlorosis of the foliage is the most common.

Although the general recommendation is to give balanced liquid fertilisers, the term 'balanced fertiliser' sometimes has little real meaning because of the differing nature of soils being used plus the requirements of the trees themselves. Observation and a little experimentation, therefore, need not go amiss. Physiological disorders are non-infectious but can severely affect the productiveness of a tree, as well as lowering its resistance to infection by parasitical disease, which in turn endangers other trees in the orchard. A plant's capability of resistance is in fact the best defence against disease and the aim must be to assist in building up this resistance.

When there is known to be a danger of disease—because of the time of year or climatic conditions—the tree can be covered with a protective chemical film which will kill the fungus or prevent its spores from germ-

inating. Various chemicals, called fungicides, are available to combat all
the known parasitical diseases. They can be applied as a dust or spray;
while, in the orchard house, fumigant smokes can be used.

INSECTS

Of the world's teeming horde of insects, only a fraction are known to most
of us; a comparatively small number are injurious, while some are beneficial. Among the beneficial insects are bees, flies and moths which assist
in pollination; others are parasites or predators feeding upon the harmful
insects, while others feed upon dead matter, both vegetative and animal,
resulting in the formation of humus and chemical compounds which give
nourishment to soil, bacteria and plant growth.

Millipedes and centipedes are allied to insects but differ from them in
many characteristics, the most obvious being the presence of legs on
practically all the main body segments. Millipedes are a dirty white or grey
colour and possess a greater number of legs than centipedes. Centipedes
are a yellow orange colour and move much faster than millipedes. As far
as fruit growing is concerned, the millipede is somewhat injurious; it will
feed upon the strawberry, for example. The centipede is beneficial as it is
carnivorous and feeds mainly on insects, small slugs and worms.

Mite pests include the byrobia mites and the fruit tree red spider mite
(Panonychus ulmi), all of which suck the sap from the foliage. Oribatid or
'beetle' mites are blood red; because they are found in clusters on twigs,
where they are feeding upon algae, they are sometimes thought to be red
spider mite eggs. Their movement will, however, show their true identity.
Gall mites are carrot shaped and have their legs set near the head, but are
microscopic. On the black currant they cause swollen buds (black currant
gall mite). Mites have natural enemies which feed upon them and so keep
them under control. Amongst these predators are several species of capsid
bugs which, generally, are beneficial although some species are plant
feeders. Other predators are the anthocarid bug and black ladybird. Mites
can be controlled by chemicals, known as acaricides or miticides, but these
also take a heavy toll of many predators.

Insects which obtain their food from plants can be roughly divided between those which chew the plant tissues (eg caterpillars) and those which
pierce the outer surface of the plant tissues in order to suck out the cell
contents (eg aphids, scale insects). Sucking insects extract chlorophyll, so
reducing the food-making efficiency of the plant, as well as covering the
foliage with sticky exudates which provide a medium for soot-like fungi.
This kind of plant-feeding insect may also carry viruses. Because some

45

aphids produce their young without being fertilised by a male, and a female aphid may produce up to 100 other females, which mature in about six to seven days, it is apparent how rapidly an infestation can occur. Aphid production is rapid in 60–70° F (16–21° C) temperatures and, even if these occur for only a few hours a day, in a few weeks their numbers will increase tremendously. Fortunately, parasites and predators which attack the aphids appear in greater numbers as temperatures rise and the aphid invasion is held in check.

Some insect species are reproduced by means of eggs which hatch into legless larvae (eg grubs or maggots); these turn into chrysalids or pupae to become flies, beetles or moths. The eggs of other species hatch into larvae with legs (eg caterpillars) and eventually become moths. The damage done by these insects depends on the stage of their development when they are feeding. Moths, for example, do not feed upon plants, but their larvae do. Flies are generally harmless, but their grubs burrow into roots, leaves or stems. On the other hand, plant-feeding beetles, both at the adult and larvae stage, will eat the vegetation.

In a natural environment all plant-feeding insects are under more or less constant attack by some form of virus, bacteria, fungi or insect and this is perhaps the most important agent of natural control. The principal predators are members of the order Hymenoptera (bees, ants, wasps), the most abundant being tiny wasps which attack and develop within or on the bodies of caterpillars, scale insects, etc. The lacewing, relative of the dragon fly, feeds on a number of insects, including aphids and mites. Sucking bugs (Hemiptera) feed upon aphids, thrips and mites by piercing the body of their victim to draw out the fluid. Many beetles are highly beneficial predators and feed upon caterpillars, aphids, thrips and scale insects. Some beetles feed by night and hide by day, while others feed by day and hide by night. The best known of these beetles are the ladybirds which are predaceous at both the adult and larvae stage.

CONTROL OF PESTS AND DISEASES

It is apparent, from such a close interrelation between the varied forms of life that a sustained and indiscriminate use of chemicals can shift the natural balance. A natural means of maintaining the balance is through the evolvement of resistant varieties or species of plants. Some plants, through being continually exposed to infection, have through the process of natural selection by evolution become resistant. On the other hand, species which have existed in isolation from certain forms of infection may suffer severely when the parasite is introduced into the area.

Man is continually experimenting with and devising new methods of protecting his plants and today a vast and ever-increasing amount of chemicals is arrayed before the amateur to enable him to control pests and diseases. From the great range of proprietary brands of chemical substances, it is not always possible to know which is the best to use. Sometimes the trade names conceal the identity of the chemicals. Very often the combining of two or more compatible chemicals makes it possible to obtain control of more than one kind of pest at the same time. For example, one insecticide may control both sucking and biting insects: an insecticide and an aracide, or miticide, may be combined, or an insecticide and fungicide. Whenever there is any doubt as to what to use, the advice of an expert should be obtained; horticultural and agricultural advisory officers are always helpful.

6

APPLES

The most favourable areas for apple cultivation are between latitudes 30°
to 60° north and south of the equator. Nearer than 30° to the equator, the
apple can only be grown successfully at high altitudes and, because it
requires a period of dormancy amounting to about fifty days with temperatures under 45° F (7° C), a definite winter is essential. At the other
limit, latitudes above 60° give a too low winter temperature and the
growing season is too short. Temperatures of −40° F (−40° C) will kill or
at least seriously injure trees of most varieties, although in the USSR a
rootstock *(Kitajka Barhatnaja)* has carried varieties which have withstood
temperatures at −41° C for twenty-four hours. To enable the hardiest
early maturing varieties to satisfactorily develop a crop, a period of
approximately 100 days free from any severe frost is required. Even so, the
apple is one of the hardiest of the deciduous fruits and as a result its
northern range and high altitude limit is beyond that of most other fruits.

Although the apple can be grown under conditions of moderately high
rainfall and low sunshine, these are not ideal conditions. High quality
dessert apples are grown in areas with a rainfall of 20–25in a year and
with a fairly good amount of sunshine; under such conditions there is a
natural check to excessive growth while at the same time a good skin
colour and texture of fruit is produced. Relatively low night temperatures
and a high light intensity by day during the final ripening period will give
better colour to the fruit. Cloudy days during the summer months cause
poor colouration. In areas where there is more than 40in of rain, dessert
apples are difficult to grow, although cooking apples can be successfully
grown in a much wetter climate.

As with many fruits, a climatic problem is late frost which damages the
blossom. In Britain, in most years, the apple blossoms during the first
three weeks of May but, apart from central England, central northern

Scotland and frost pockets, a late frost after 21 May will usually only occur one year in five.

Most apple trees are raised by grafting a bud or scion of the variety required upon a young plant of a closely related species, which is known as the rootstock. Trees can be obtained which, because they are grown on special rootstock, will behave in a predictable manner, especially in regard to tree size and earliness of maturity.

A number of rootstocks selected at the East Malling Research Station, in Kent, have been given the identifying prefix Malling (M for short). A further group, raised jointly by the East Malling Research Station and the John Innes Institute at Merton, have the prefix Malling Merton (MM for short). Rootstocks can, very simply, be divided into four groups as follows:

Very dwarf	M9
Semi-dwarf	M7, M26, MM106
Semi-vigorous	M1, M2, M11, MM111
Vigorous	M16, M25, M26, MM104, MM109

D

A rootstock very widely used in continental Europe and one which it is usual to choose for pot trees is M9. It is a rootstock particularly suitable for dessert varieties and, although it produces a small tree, the fruits are of a good size and colour, with the trees cropping early in life (at about three years). There is also a tendency for its fruit to be ready for picking somewhat earlier than the same varieties on different rootstock. Its disadvantages are that its roots are brittle and the branches of some varieties grafted on to it tend to be weak and weeping (pendulous). It is resistant to potassium deficiency but susceptible to magnesium deficiency. As trees on dwarfing rootstock tend to expend their resources at a quicker rate than others, it is essential that, especially with pot cultivation, they have a balanced diet. When using a dwarfing rootstock, care should be taken to see that the scion it carries does not come into contact with the soil, otherwise this might itself take root and a very vigorous tree may be the result. Trees must be potted in the compost at the same level at which they were growing in the nursery.

For apples, a rich heavy loam is required which contains both humus and nutrition. Either at the time the trees are repotted or in December, the addition or application of a little fish manure, which contains a high percentage of nitrogen, potassium and phosphorus, is therefore highly beneficial. Normally, dessert varieties should be given less nitrogen than culinary varieties. It is potassium and not nitrogen which will add to the non-green colour of an apple. Cooking apples and those dessert varieties of an all-green colour (eg Granny Smith) will have a better green colour with additional nitrogen, while the scarlet and orange of dessert varieties will have richer colouring when given liberal supplies of potassium. All varieties which are known to have a low resistance to scab disease should be given less nitrogen because excessive growth encourages this disease.

If trees are not making good growth, an application of sulphate of ammonia may be given in the spring, when growth commences. A deficiency of potassium, phosphorus and magnesium will not become apparent until the tree comes into bearing, although a lack of potassium may be suspected if the foliage turns brown and becomes crinkled at the edges. A deficiency of nitrogen will show itself by the fruit being small and hard but usually developing bright colours and possessing good keeping qualities. When there is a deficiency of potassium, the fruit will be small, of poor colour, tend to be sub acid, of a woody texture, and will not keep well. Phosphorus deficiency will cause apples to develop a green base colour although they may be distinctively flushed, have an acid flavour, soft flesh and poor keeping quality.

Either the pyramid or bush form can be chosen for potted trees, but care must be taken in choosing the varieties, avoiding what are known as 'tip bearers'. For example, the well-known Worcester Pearmain and Bramley Seedling carry their fruit buds, especially in their early years, at the ends of twiggy laterals. If these laterals are cut back in winter to within a few inches of their base, then obviously the fruit buds will also be cut away and very little fruit will be borne. Varieties such as Cox's Orange Pippin, Golden Delicious, Orleans, Reinette, etc, carry a large proportion of their fruit buds on either fruit spurs which have formed naturally or on spurs which have formed as a result of pruning back the lateral shoots. They can also be kept neat and small without reducing cropping, provided the leaders are not pruned too hard when the trees are coming into bearing. During the first season's growth the laterals should be pruned back to 3–5in from the base, according to their strength. The stronger the lateral, the more lightly should it be pruned. In the following season, wood buds

FRUIT SPURS

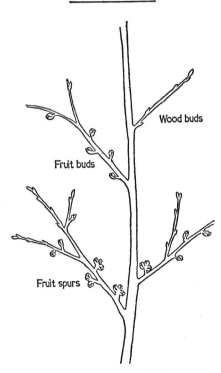

APPLE AND PEAR

51

on the laterals may send out shoots of varying length, while perhaps a bud or two near the base will swell and give the appearance that they are fruit buds. However, it is advisable not to cut the laterals back in the winter to these plumper buds, but to cut back the newly formed laterals to within ½in to 2in of their base, according to their vigour. Better results are obtained if fruit buds are allowed to form naturally on the spurs rather than stimulating them into growth by cutting back to them in the first year.

Fruit buds on the apple tree are easily seen. They are large, somewhat downy, and greyish brown in colour. They are found on the short spurs and along two-year and older shoots. Wood, or growth, buds are quite distinctive from the fruit buds; they are small, pointed, and most easily seen on one-year-old shoots. Careful pruning will encourage the formation of fruit buds in suitable positions, but hard pruning will not make an unfruitful tree fruitful. Winter pruning, which is performed when the tree is dormant, stimulates the growth of strong shoots from well-developed wood buds the following spring. Summer pruning is performed when the tree is in full growth and the removal of green shoots and leaves results in a check in growth.

Pollination also requires consideration in apple cultivation. When pollen is transferred to the stigma of the same flower from which it originated, or to other flowers of the tree or flowers of other trees of the same variety, then *self-pollination* has occurred. When pollen is transferred to flowers of other varieties then *cross-pollination* has occurred. Unless a variety is a good self-pollinator, it is necessary to grow another variety which will pollinate it. Varieties may be what are known as diploids or triploids. With diploids the pollen germinates readily, while with triploids the germination is poor. Triploids being poor pollinators should not be grown to cross-pollinate other varieties. If a triploid is grown it is desirable —unless a good self-pollinating variety is also available—to grow two other varieties so that one of them can pollinate the triploid and they can pollinate each other. Fortunately, even if not self-pollinating, most varieties of apple are diploids. When choosing two varieties these must flower at the same time so that cross-pollination can be assured. The majority of varieties flower mid-season and, if choosing an early or late flowering variety, an early or late flowering variety should be available to match it. If there is a good mixture of varieties, pollination should not be a problem, especially when bees are active.

When the fruit has formed, the centre fruit of each cluster is removed because it usually develops into a mis-shapen fruit which does not keep well. The best way to thin apples is to take the stalk between the first and second fingers of the right hand and push the apple gently but firmly off its stalk with the thumb of the right hand.

Early ripening varieties need to be picked over more than once and they cannot be kept for more than a few weeks unless cold storage is available. Late varieties which keep well should be allowed to remain on the trees as long as possible. To ascertain whether an apple is ready for picking, lift it gently on its stalk; if it comes away easily it can be considered of sufficient ripeness to continue to mature in storage. Apples for storing should be picked when thoroughly dry.

DISEASES

SCAB (BLACK SPOT) *(Ventura inaequalis)*

Small, dull, olive-green patches appear on the young leaves in spring. As the spread of the fungus becomes general, dark sooty spots develop and leaves fall prematurely when infection is severe. Blister-like swellings may be produced on the spurs and young shoots. Scab on the fruit may be only superficial or large patches may develop. Mis-shapen and cracked fruit may result when a severe attack commenced early.

This is a fungus disease common throughout the apple-growing regions of the world, with the exception of warm, dry areas. It is severe in the north-eastern United States and the adjoining regions in Canada.

The disease is conveyed year to year by two distinct kinds of spore. One kind is existent on the leaves and develops on the dead leaves after they fall. The spores mature on the dead leaves on the ground and then, during rainy weather in early spring, are disseminated into the air. From the opening of the buds until the leaves are fully extended is the most critical period. The other kind of spore lives within the bark of young shoots which have been infected the previous year. These spores become active in the spring and summer, bursting through to the outer surface and forming blisters where further spores are formed.

Fallen leaves should, of course, be gathered up. When scab is troublesome, spraying with a fungicide from the time of bud burst and during the critical period, will give good control. Wood which shows sign of scab infection can be cut out at the end of the growing season.

CANKER *(Nectria galligena)*

This is usually a sunken area of bark around a bud, leaf scar, base of a small dead side shoot, or a wound. The area increases in size and, as it does so, the bark in the central area flakes off, leaving the tissues around this part swollen and producing a typical canker. The wood immediately beneath the canker and often for some distance beyond it has a brown discolouration. Smaller branches are often completely encircled by the canker and when this happens the part above it quickly dies. Primarily this is a disease of the bark but fruit may also be attacked. Fruit so attacked has a flattened, dark-brown, rotted area usually centred round the eye.

The disease is caused by a fungus which has two kinds of spores. One kind appears on the cankered bark, mainly in spring, summer and autumn in whitish pustules in roughly parallel lines. These spores are short lived, but are easily spread by wind-blown rain. The second kind exists in clusters of bright red, pear-shaped bodies which develop on cankered branches during autumn and winter. These spores are disseminated into the air during wet weather at any time of the year, but especially during the late winter months. Infection can only take place by entry where there is a break in the bark caused by injury or pruning, or via the leaf scars following leaf fall. (A leaf scar is liable to infection for approximately twenty-four hours.)

Infected wood should be cut out, or infected bark can be pared away until healthy tissue is reached. The bared tissues should be treated with Stockholm Tar, or pruning paint.

APPLE POWDERY MILDEW *(Podosphaera leucotricha)*
First seen on trees soon after bud burst. The young leaves and flower buds are covered with a white mildew which causes the leaf and flower parts to wither and drop. The fungus spreads to other leaves during the growing season and stems may become affected, giving a whitened appearance.

The fungus sends its feeding roots down into the surface tissues of the affected parts and produces spores at the surface. As they mature, the spores are carried away in the air and, under suitable conditions, cause fresh infection elsewhere. The fungus develops best in the growing tips of the twigs, but the mycelium which it forms on the wood dies when tree growth ceases in late summer. It survives the winter only in the buds.

During the pink bud stage, affected blossom and leaf rosettes should be cut out or picked off, but it is advisable not to do this on a warm day as disturbance of the foliage may set free a large number of spores (the spores germinate at temperatures ranging from 50 to 68° F (10–20° C)). In the winter and when shoot-tip and terminal-bud infection is apparent, all one-year-old wood should have the top few buds removed. All infected areas of shoots should be removed as far back to at least three buds behind the limit of infection.

BITTER ROT *(Glomerella cinqulata)*
Circular depressed areas of decay appear on the fruit, and the flesh imme-diately beneath is brown and corky. The fungus may also attack twigs and branches where it may persist for several years with cankers on spurs and shoots. Fruit begins to be affected from June onwards. Remove all can-kered spurs and shoots in February. Spray with a suitable fungicide.

BROWN ROT *(Sclerotinia fructigena; S. laxa)*
Soft brown spots appear on the fruit until the whole apple is affected. Buff coloured pustules develop in concentric circles on the surface of the fruit. The apple eventually becomes dry and withered. In early stages the fruit hangs loosely and is easily detached, but when in contact with a branch the pustules adhere to it and may 'fix' the apple to the branch.

The pustules, which are the reproductive parts of the fungus, are readily dispersed to other apples. The fungus growth is very rapid and within a week or ten days the fruit is destroyed. The spores germinate on skin ruptures caused by wasps, earwigs, bird pecks, hailstones, frost and such like. Insects crawling over the fruit may carry the spores from one apple to another and it is also easily dispersed by the wind. Diseased apples remaining on the tree become mummified and, although these are not a source of infection during the winter, they will in the next season produce fresh spores which will cause infection to young fruit. Mummi-fied plums can cause infection to apples and vice versa. All diseased fruit should be removed and either burnt or deeply buried.

Care should be taken not to injure or bruise fruit when it is being har-vested. Apples should always be picked with their stalks still attached otherwise a point of entry for the fungus is available. Control should be exercised over caterpillars and earwigs.

INSECT PESTS

CODLIN MOTH *(Cydonia pomonella)*
This is one of the best-known pests of the apple and occurs in almost every region where apples are grown.

The moth is about ⅜in long and has greyish brown forewings with a copper-coloured patch near the tip. They are, however, seldom seen as they are mainly active at dusk. They emerge in late spring and lay their eggs singly on the fruitlets, twigs or leaves. The eggs are translucent, flat and round about ½in in diameter. The caterpillar burrows into the fruit and feeds principally on the core and flesh surrounding it. Then, after about a month, it tunnels its way back, feeding all the time, to the outer surface, when it leaves the apple. It then finds a sheltered place, such as under a crack in the bark, where it spins a cocoon. Normally there is only one generation each year, although sometimes in the warmer climates, including southern England, a second generation may be produced.

The codlin moth has several natural enemies, such as insect predators and parasites, as well as birds which consume large numbers of the hibernating caterpillars.

As soon as they are seen, maggoty apples should be picked off and burned or deeply dug into the ground. All rubbish in which the caterpillars might spin their cocoons should be cleared away. Chemical control (insecticides) can, if necessary, be used.

APPLE SAWFLY *(Hoplocampa testudinea)*

This pest damages apples in a similar way to the codlin moth. The adult sawfly is black with reddish-yellow legs and underside. These insects appear in late spring—their greatest number being when the trees are in full bloom—and are active on warm sunny days. Eggs are laid on the underside of the petals just below the base of the sepals. When these hatch, the white, black-headed maggots begin to burrow into the fruitlet and feed on the flesh. Very often, ribbon-like scars are produced on the skin of the fruit. After about a month the maggot falls to the ground and pupates. In contrast to the codlin moth, it is the flesh rather than the core which is damaged, and the apple tends to have an unpleasant smell.

Infested fruit should be picked off and destroyed. The trees should be inspected early in the summer when the maggots are still feeding on their first fruit, as they normally attack at least two fruitlets and perhaps a third. If necessary chemical control can be used.

APPLE CAPSID BUG *(Plesiocoris rugicollis)*

Several species of capsid bug occur on fruit, but most of them are beneficial because they prey on pests, such as spider mites, apple suckers and leaf hoppers. The apple capsid bug is, however, a pest of fruit trees.

The bugs are small, green or reddish, and active. When disturbed they may take to flight or run quickly over a leaf to hide on the other side. They appear in spring and may continue their attack until early autumn. Leaves, young stems and flowers are punctured and sap sucked from them; as a result, the tree parts become distorted and fail to grow properly. Leaves and buds develop rust-coloured spots. In extreme cases a badly shaped or stunted tree may result. Fruits are also attacked, corky areas or pimples developing.

Control by means of chemicals.

APPLE BLOSSOM WEEVIL *(Anthonomous pomorum)*

This is a major pest of the apple. The adult is small and dark in colour with a long rostrum or snout and on its back is a yellowish V marking. The weevils emerge in the spring, usually at the time of the expanding blossom buds, and feed at night on the young leaves which will sometimes be left skeletonised. Eggs are deposited in the unopened flower buds. The maggots quickly hatch from the eggs and eat away the base of the flower which, because it is so badly damaged, never opens. The white maggot can be found underneath the brown flower petals.

The weevil has natural enemies, including insect parasites like the grub of the ichneumon *(Ephiattes pomorum)*, and is readily eaten by birds, especially tits. All infested blossom should be picked off. A band of sacking can be tied around the stem of the tree in early summer and, from this, hibernating weevils can be collected in the winter. Control can be by chemicals.

JAPANESE BEETLE *(Popillia japonica)*

Though common in East Asia and now established in a large area of North America, this beetle has not yet gained any hold in western Asia or Europe. However, a large part of continental Europe, where there are warm and not unduly dry summers, lies in the zone where heavy infestation could occur once the beetle is introduced. Some of the most commonly attacked fruits are: strawberry, raspberry, apple, cherry and plum.

The adult beetle is fairly broad and deep, bluntly ovoid in shape and about $\frac{1}{2}$in long. The head, thorax and legs are a metallic green and the wing cases a dull coppery brown. The body is green, with a row of twelve tufts of white hair on the sides and hind end. It is similar in appearance to the garden chafer *(Phyllopertha horicola)*, but this lacks the white tufts on the body, and its legs, which are brown instead of green, are thinner.

The beetles emerge from the soil in summer and fly about actively in search of suitable food. They avoid deep shade and choose foliage exposed to the sun. The damage to leaves consists of holes eaten out between the veins; leaves badly affected turn brown and fall off, with the result that trees may become completely defoliated. The beetles burrow a few inches into the soil to lay their eggs and, although they prefer to do this in pasture, some are laid in open soil.

57

WOOLLY APPLE APHID *(Erisoma lanigerum)*

This pest now occurs in all areas where apples are grown.

The brown or greyish purple aphids attack stems, branches and twigs, but in some countries root infestation may occur. Their glands secrete a white wool-like mass of waxy strands as a protective covering. The part of the tree infested becomes swollen and may crack, allowing fungus spores to enter. The principal injury, though, is the weakening of the tree's vigour, while the heavy secretion provides a medium for a smut fungus to grow.

The activity of the aphids commences in spring when 'wool' begins to be secreted and in about six weeks breeding colonies are established. During early summer colonies are found mainly on the spurs and branches, but later the infestation spreads to the new, succulent growth. They breed very quickly; it is estimated that every adult female can produce as many as ten young every day.

Among their natural enemies are the ladybirds, hover flies and lacewings. In warm dry countries a parasitic wasp *(Aphelinus mali)* plays a considerable part in the control of the aphid and this has been introduced with some success into south-east England. Control, however, is usually by chemical means.

APPLE APHIDS

In Britain, eight species of aphid have been found attacking the apple and, leaving aside the woolly aphid, four of these are capable of causing serious injury.

The life history of the numerous species varies, but in most instances they spend all or a large part of their life in the tree, feeding on foliage, twig and fruit. They overwinter in the egg stage on the apple or related trees. In the spring the newly hatched aphids crawl up the twigs and collect on the opening buds which they probe for sap. At this time the aphids are extremely vulnerable to insecticides, but as the buds begin to open they move down into the crevices where they become protected. These aphids are all females and when maturity is reached they begin to produce living young. Successive generations do likewise until the last one, which is the only time in the life cycle when males as well as females appear. After mating, the females lay the overwintering eggs.

They have the same natural enemies as the woolly apple aphid. Chemical control can be used.

APPLE SUCKER *(Psylla mali)*
This is a small insect related to the aphids and not unlike them. At first creamy white and wingless, later it is green with a pair of transparent wings.

Its eggs are oval, pale straw coloured, barely visible to the naked eye but easily seen with a hand lens. Usually the eggs are laid around the fruit spurs and, after they hatch in spring, the young suckers attack the bud or blossom, frequently killing it. The petals of the flower become brown and withered so that the blossom looks as though it has been damaged by frost.

A natural enemy is the anthocorid bug *(Anthocoris memorum)*.

MUSSEL SCALE *(Lepidosaphes ulmi)*
Scale insects are small louse-like insects which attach themselves to the stem, bark or leaf of a tree and suck sap from the living tissues, so causing debility. They are related to aphids, whiteflies and mealy bugs. As they mature they cover themselves with a hard shell which becomes a protection for their eggs and young. The mussel scale and the San Jose scale are typical examples.

The adult female mussel scale is a soft white insect, covered with a light to dark brown mussel-shaped shell up to 3mm long. The adult stage is reached by about the middle of summer when it produces up to eighty minute white eggs and then dies—its dead body or shell protecting the eggs and later the newly hatched young.

Larvae of very small wasp-like insects, mites, fungus diseases and small birds are all natural control agents. Small infestations of scale can be removed with a knife. Artificial control is with chemicals.

SAN JOSE SCALE *(Quadraspidictus perniciosus)*
This is a pest common to USA where it damages apple, pear, peach and cherry. The insects overwinter as partly grown nymphs or 'crawlers' that cling to the bark of the tree. As soon as the sap begins to flow in early spring they start to feed and become fully grown by the time the tree is in full blossom. Females give birth to as many as 500 young in six weeks. Migration occurs during the 'crawler' stage when they are blown by the wind or carried by man or animal.

Heavy infestation causes the foliage to turn yellow and the tree to become seriously weakened, while infested fruit becomes spotted.

FRUIT-TREE RED SPIDER MITE *(Panonychus ulmi)*
Several kinds of mite pests (red spider mites, byrobia mites) affect the fruit tree; the fruit-tree red spider mite is a typical example.

The adult mite is very small, about 0·4mm long; it can only just be seen by the unaided eye, but is easily visible with the aid of a hand lens. The female is oval, dark red and with a convex back from which arises a number of long bristles. Bright red eggs are laid, from late summer till about leaf fall, mainly on the undersides of the spurs and smaller branches: when infestation is heavy, the bark appears to be red. The eggs hatch in the following spring and early summer; the young mites vary in colour from bright red to pale yellowish-green. Immediately after hatching the young mites move to the undersides of leaves where they live and feed. They remain active, however, and soon spread from leaf to leaf. When populations are high some mites will migrate by spinning a silk strand on which they are carried away by air currents to other trees.

Injury is caused by the feeding of large numbers of both young and adult mites. They suck sap from the leaves, in which the first symptom is a minute speckling. With the continuing infestation the foliage turns dull green and finally assumes a brownish green or bronze colour. Severe attacks, especially in early summer, reduce the yield of fruit and may lead to a reduction in fruit-bud formation, so affecting the following season's crop.

When no chemical control is practised the population of the fruit-tree red spider mite seldom becomes high, because it is under constant attack by various predators, principally typhodromid mites, anthocorid bugs, capsid bugs, and black ladybird. The use of chemicals takes a very heavy toll of these beneficial insects; in addition, strains of mites emerge which are resistant to the acaricides (miticides) previously effective in controlling them.

SHOT-HOLE BORER (*Scolytus rugulosa*)

This and the other two beetles described below are more common to the USA.

The shot-hole borer is a small brown beetle which tunnels into the inner bark of fruit trees. Leading from these main tunnels are branch or grub tunnels in which the female beetle lays her eggs. When fully grown the grub pupates at the end of the tunnel and then bores straight out through the bark, making the 'shot-holes'.

Leaves of an infected branch turn yellow and fall; small trees may even be killed. However, beetles very seldom attack healthy trees, so the best protection is to keep them in good health. Infested wood should be cut out and burned. Further control can be with chemicals.

FLAT-HEADED APPLE-TREE BORER *(Chryso bothris fermarata)*
The grubs of this pest burrow into apple, pear and other fruit trees. The adult beetles, about ½in long, emerge in early summer and commence to feed on leaves or twigs, but do little damage. Young grubs usually work near the soil line where they have hatched, but the older grubs feed higher and bore deeper. Two or even three winters may be spent in the grub stage. When severely infested, a young tree can be completely girdled and killed. Attacks are usually against young or weakened trees.

The grubs can be dug from their burrows with a knife or wire probe or insecticides used on the burrows.

ROUND-HEADED APPLE-TREE BORER *(Saparda candida)*
The grubs of this pest burrow through the inner bark and sap wood. They work mainly on the sunny side of the tree but are especially damaging to young trees. During the winter they hibernate in their burrows which are filled with excrement and sawdust. Like the grubs, the adult beetles are also active on the sunny side of the tree. It is possible to protect young trees by wrapping their stems with paper or cloth.

VARIETIES OF APPLE

There is great variation here: some trees are vigorous, for example, while some are more resistant to disease and pest attack. But it is the fruit by which people differentiate between one apple variety and another.

The following varieties are listed in order of flowering so that a selection can be made to provide pollination. Although some varieties (eg Spartan) are included under only one heading, they may be under cultivation in other parts of the world.

BRITAIN AND NORTH-WEST EUROPE
Egremont Russet Dessert. Medium to medium small. Greenish yellow becoming golden yellow, covered with light brown russet. Flesh firm, rather dry, a rich nutty flavour. Ready October–November. Tree fairly vigorous, spurs freely, moderate cropper.

St Edmund's Pippin Dessert. Medium to small. Greenish yellow becoming golden with occasional orange flush; the whole covered with light brown russet. Juicy, fairly firm, slightly acid, good flavour. Ready end of September to early October. Tree fairly vigorous, upright and spreading, spurs freely.

Lord Lambourne   Dessert. Medium. Rich red flushed over with yellow. Skin greasy. Juicy, sweet, firm. Does not store. Tree very fertile.

George Cave   Dessert. Small to medium. Red striped green. Firm, sweet, juicy. Ready mid-July. Does not store. Moderate growth. Regular and heavy cropper.

James Grieve   Dessert. Medium. Greenish yellow, striped and tinged with red. Juicy, acidic but sweet. Ready September–October. Stores for two or three weeks. Partially self-fertile. Good cropper but susceptible to canker and brown rot.

Merton Worcester   Dessert. Medium. Yellow flushed scarlet and russet. Similar in appearance to Cox's Orange Pippin. Crisp, firm, aromatic. Ready mid-September. Very good cropper.

Holstein   Dessert. Large. Greenish yellow becoming golden russet, flushed orange-red and with red stripes. Sweet, slightly acid, aromatic flavour similar to Cox's Orange Pippin. Ready late September, stores till January. Vigorous, spreading. Spurs freely. Triploid.

Early Victoria   Cooking. Medium. Yellowish green. One of the earliest cooking apples. A very good cooker but it does not store. Very fertile. Spurs freely.

Boskoop   Dessert. Large. Golden yellow skin with russet. Firm, juicy, sweet, sub-acid, good flavour when properly matured in mid-winter. Pick in October or late as possible. Vigorous, good regular cropper. Susceptible to canker and scab.

Lady Sudely   Dessert. Medium. Golden yellow with red stripes. Tender, yellowish flesh, juicy, crisp. Ready August–September, does not keep. Partially self-fertile. Prolific cropper.

Rev W. Wilks   Cooking. Large. Pale yellow and bright red. Juicy, acidic. Ready October–November, does not keep. A hardy, dwarf tree. Self-fertile, good cropper. Susceptible to scab and brown rot.

Ribston Pippin   Dessert. Fairly large. Greenish yellow and brownish red. Firm, crisp, somewhat dry but aromatic, good flavour. Picked as late as possible will store until January. Triploid. Fairly susceptible to canker and scab.

Grenadier Cooking. Medium to large. Yellowish green with white dots. A richly flavoured cooker. Ready August–September. Tree compact, very fertile.

Blenheim Orange Dessert or cooking. Large. Pale yellow with orange-red flush and stripes. Dry but slightly crisp and pleasant. Excellent cooker. Picked as late as possible will store until January. Tree vigorous. Triploid.

Discovery Dessert. Pale greenish yellow flushed bright red. Crisp, juicy, good flavour. Ready August–September, will store a few weeks. A good early apple. Vigorous, upright.

Cox's Orange Pippin Dessert. Medium. Golden, orange and russet skin. Aromatic, juicy, crisp, flesh has a nice balance of sweetness and acidity. Stores well until January. Moderate vigour, good cropper but self-sterile and needs pollinating. Does best in sheltered position.

Laxton's Fortune Dessert. Medium. Rosy red. Juicy and sweet. Will keep until November. Fairly vigorous.

Lane's Prince Albert Cooking. Medium. Pale green, pale red stripes. An excellent cooker. Will keep until April but bruises easily. Compact, fertile, regular cropper. Susceptible to apple mildew.

Oranje de Sonnaville Dessert. Large. Golden flushed red. Similar to Cox's Orange Pippin in taste. Will store until New Year.

Orleans Reinette Dessert. Medium. Golden russet flushed deep red. Sweet, fairly juicy, crisp. One of the best flavoured of all apples. Will keep until February, but shrivels if picked too early. Moderate cropper. Susceptible to canker, especially in cold areas.

Calville Blanche d'Hiver Dessert. Medium. Pale yellow to golden. Sweet, juicy, aromatic. Considered by some to be the most delicious of apples. Widely grown in France, but in England does best in a cool glass house.

Merton Charm Dessert. Medium size. Greenish yellow flushed orange. Tender, juicy, sweet. Keeps until early November. Moderate vigour, heavy cropper.

Landsberger Reinette Dessert. Fairly large. Pale yellow, flushed salmon pink. Firm, juicy, sweet, pleasantly sub-acid, delicate aroma. Keeps well until December. Moderate vigour, good cropper. Susceptible to scab and mildew.

King's Acre Pippin Dessert. Medium. Dull yellowish orange, flushed red and russeted. Needs warm sunny position to colour well. Firm, juicy, excellent flavour. Stores well until March. Moderate cropper, partially self-fertile.

Ellison's Orange Dessert. Medium. Skin greasy, orange-yellow with distinct red stripes and flush. Tender, juicy, distinctive aniseed flavour. Ready September–October, keeps only a few weeks. Strong growth. Prone to biennial bearing.

Acme Dessert. Medium. Yellow flushed and striped bright crimson. Firm, juicy, very similar flavour to Cox's Orange Pippin. Pick mid-November to keep through the winter. Moderate growth.

Merton Prolific Dessert. Medium. Green turning to pale yellow with carmine stripes and flush while in store. Firm, juicy, good flavour. Picked as late as possible, will keep until late February. Moderate growth, semi-upright.

Merton Beauty Dessert. Medium to small. Pale golden yellow, scarlet flush and stripes. Juicy, fairly crisp aniseed flavour. Ready early September, will keep about five weeks. Upright, moderate vigour.

Merton Joy Dessert. Medium. Golden-yellow flushed and spotted with orange-red. Crisp, juicy, aromatic, excellent flavour. Ready September–October. Crops heavily. Resistant to scab and mildew.

Red Charles Ross Dessert. Large. Greenish yellow with broad, distinct orange-red stripes and broken, bright red stripes. Juicy, moderate flavour, coarse texture. Keeps until December. Moderate cropper, spurs freely, compact growth.

Michaelmas Red Dessert. Medium. Greenish yellow, flushed crimson and with bright red stripes. Crisp, juicy, sweet, scented flavour. Ready beginning of October. Should be grown by those who like a Worcester Pearmain; the two are almost identical, except that Michaelmas Red is not tip bearing and ripens a little later. Moderate growth.

King of the Pippins Dessert. Medium. Orange-yellow, flushed and streaked with salmon red. Firm, fairly juicy, sweet, sub-acid, aromatic. Ready end of September, but keeps well and at its best in November. Medium vigour, heavy cropper. Susceptible to canker and scab.

Peasgood Nonsuch Cooking. Very large. Pale yellow mottled and striped light red. Crisp, acidic, excellent cooker. Keeps till November. Vigorous. Susceptible to canker.

Ashmeads Kernel Dessert. Medium. Pale greenish yellow with grey-brown russet and occasional orange flush. Juicy, rich, aromatic, slightly 'nutty'. Keeps till January. Moderately vigorous, spurs freely.

Edward VII Cooking. Medium. Pale green occasionally with brownish flush. A good cooker, excellent flavour. Keeps till April. Upright, spurs freely.

Crawley Beauty Cooking. Medium. Pale yellow with a few salmon-red stripes. Very white flesh. Cooks well. Keeps till March. Moderate growth, spurs freely.

NORTH AMERICA
Unless otherwise stated, these are suitable for cold areas:

Quinte Canadian. Dessert. Bright red. Firm, good flavour. Ready July.

Paulared Dessert. Medium. Bright yellow with red flush. Colours early, but if picked too soon will lack full fruit quality. Slightly sub-acid, excellent flavour. Ready beginning September; keeps till February. Bears on both spurs and tips. Good resistance to scab, only moderately susceptible to fire blight.

Julyred Dessert. Large. Red. Firm, good flavour. Ready July.

Macoun Dessert. Medium. Dark red blush over green. Firm, aromatic, juicy. Bruises easily. Ready September. Upright, vigorous, spurs freely.

Beverley Hills Suitable for southern California. Dessert. Small to medium. Light yellow, striped and stippled red. Tender, sub-acid. One of the few apples suitable for the warmer climates of the south.

Macspur Medium to large. Dessert. Bright red. Very white flesh, tender, sub-acid. Ripens October. Upright, compact, spurs freely. Exceptionally cold-resistant.

Spartan Canadian. Dessert. Golden yellow covered with light brown russet, sometimes with brownish-orange flush. Firm, crisp, rich nutty flavour. Keeps till November. Moderately vigorous, spurs freely.

E

Melba Canadian. Dessert. Large. Pinkish red. Juicy. Ready August.

Beacon Dessert. Large. Bright red. Good flavour. Ripens mid-August. Susceptible to fire blight.

Gravenstein Famous in California's north coast apple districts. Dessert or cooking. Deep yellow striped brilliant red. Crisp, aromatic, good flavour. Also a good cooker. Ripens September, does not keep well.

Red Astrakan Suitable for interior valleys of California. Dessert and cooking. Medium. Juicy, rather acid. Ripens July.

Yellow Transparent Suitable for interior valleys of California. Cooking. Medium to large. Green to whitish yellow, often with slight flush. Tender, acidic. Excellent cooker. Ready mid-June to mid-July.

Winter Banana Suitable for southern California. Dessert. Pale yellow, blushed light pink, shiny. Tender, mildly sub-acid, distinctive aroma, good quality. Ripens October.

McIntosh Dessert. Medium to large. Bright red. Very white flesh, crisp, juicy, sweet, refreshing. Ripens October, does not keep well. Compact growth. Subject to disease.

Puritan Dessert. McIntosh type but slightly larger. Slightly acid, good for dessert or cooking.

Idared Dessert. Medium to large. Bright cherry red. Moderately juicy, sweet, sub-acid, good flavour. Keeps till April. Moderate vigour, spurs freely. Susceptible to mildew and fire blight.

Rhode Island Greening Dessert. Medium. Light green to yellow. Firm, crisp, juicy. Vigorous, spreading. Susceptible to fire blight.

Cortland Dessert. Medium size. Pale yellow striped and flushed with bright red. Crisp, juicy, tender, aromatic, sweet. A good apple. Keeps till January. Fairly vigorous.

Jonathan Dessert. Small. Red. Firm, crisp, moderately juicy, sweet, sub-acid, aromatic. Keeps till January. Vigorous. Susceptible to disease.

Ontario Cooking. Large. Greenish yellow, brown flush. Crisp, cooks fairly well. Keeps till April. Compact growth, spurs freely. Fairly resistant to scab and canker.

Delicious Dessert. Large. Striped red; some types solid red (eg Red Prince, Red Queen). Juicy, aromatic, sweet. Keeps fairly well. Vigorous.

Golden Delicious Suitable for coastal regions, interior valleys of California, as well as the colder regions. Dessert. Medium. Golden yellow with occasional pale orange flush. Crisp, juicy, sweet, pleasant flavour. Keeps well if picked late. Moderately vigorous, rather spreading. Susceptible to scab.

Starking Delicious Dessert. Medium to large. Carmine red, stippled yellow. Tender, juicy, sweet, slightly sub-acid, aromatic. Keeps fairly well. Moderate vigour, fairly good cropper. Susceptible to scab and canker.

Stayman Winesap Dessert. Medium to large. Dull red with grey and russet dots. Tender, juicy, sub-acid. Ripens late summer, keeps until December. (Double Red Stayman is a greatly improved and brilliantly coloured strain of this variety; good flavour and quality, keeps well.)

Wagener Dessert. Medium to large. Greenish yellow with brownish flush. Crisp, fair quality, keeps till May. Compact, moderate growth. Fairly resistant to scab and canker.

White Pearmain Dessert. Medium to large. Pale green, with red flush. Tender, juicy, mildly sub-acid, excellent flavour. Keeps till January. Moderately vigorous.

Yellow Newton Widely grown in coastal districts of colder regions. Dessert or cooking. Medium to large. Greenish yellow with slight russet. Firm, sweet. Keeps till March. Vigorous growth.

Grimes Golden Suitable for coastal regions. Dessert and cooking. Medium. Yellow. Firm, sweet, mildly sub-acid, aromatic. Keeps well.

Summared Dessert. Medium. Pale yellowish green, flushed and striped bright red. Firm, juicy, pleasant flavour. Keeps till December. Moderately vigorous, spurs freely.

Wealthy Dessert. Large. Pale yellow flushed and streaked with carmine. Crisp, tender, very juicy, sweet, mildly sub-acid, refreshing, aromatic. Keeps well. Weak growth. Good resistance to pests and diseases.

Red Rome Dessert or cooking. Large. Yellowish, red flush. Firm, crisp, fair quality. Useful for baking. Keeps till February.

Gallia Beauty Dessert. Large. Brilliant red. One of the best late keeping apples. Tree hardy and productive.

Spuree Rome Dessert. Fruit similar to Gallia Beauty. Compact, spurs freely.

OTHER FAMOUS VARIETIES

Democrat Australian. Dessert. Large. Yellow flushed red. Crisp, sweet. Keeps well. Moderate vigour, crops heavily but tends to be biennial.

Granny Smith Australian. Dessert. Medium to large. Green to yellowish green. Very crisp, not much flavour, sweet, sub-acid. Keeps well. Vigorous, spurs well.

Kidd's Orange Red New Zealand. Dessert. Medium. Lemon-yellow flushed bright deep orange-scarlet. Firm, crisp, juicy, aromatic. Keeps well. Vigorous, spurs freely, good cropper.

Dunn Seedling Australian. Dessert. Medium. Green to yellowish green. Crisp, juicy, acidic. Keeps well. Vigorous, spur and tip bearing.

Tasman's Pride Australian. Dessert. Medium to large. Red. Juicy, sweet. Keeps well. Fairly vigorous. Needs summer pruning to ensure good coloured fruit.

Geeveston Fanny Australian. Dessert. Small to medium. Pale lemon yellow, bright red flush. Crisp, sweet. Vigorous.

Legana Australian. Dessert. Medium to large. Greenish yellow. Crisp, juicy, aromatic. Moderate vigour.

7

APRICOTS

The apricot tree prefers a moisture-retentive soil which, at the same time, is friable and well drained. Because it also has need of a soil tending to alkalinity, a calcareous loam is ideal. Stiff clays and heavy loams should be avoided. When a compost for apricot trees is being prepared, a little chalk rubble or lime can be added if the soil is deficient in this. A good compost would consist of three parts turfy loam, one part well-rotted manure, one part old mortar rubble.

The tree's natural habit is to spread. There are no dwarfing rootstocks similar to those used for apples, and named varieties are budded on to several different rootstocks, some of which may be apricot seedlings. Very often it is a case of having whatever is available, although Brompton and Common mussel plum rootstock are frequently used. St Julian A rootstock produces a fairly small tree and this, when obtainable, should be chosen. In the USA, seedlings from the Western Sand Cherry are sometimes used and these produce semi-dwarf trees.

The pyramid form is the best. The young tree should be placed in a 10in pot which has good drainage. Any strong root shoots should be shortened, so that the tree can be placed in the pot with its roots 1in from the side and its top roots 1½in below the rim. After potting, it should be thoroughly watered, making sure that the compost in the pot has been made moist throughout. It can then be stood either outside in a bed of ashes or in a cool glass house.

The apricot, like its relation the peach, requires a period of winter chilling. In fact, if because of a mild winter its winter chilling requirements have not been met, delayed foliation may occur in the spring. Flowers and flower buds are not more susceptible to frost damage than the peach or plum, but because the apricot blossoms early—several days before the peach—frost-free sites must be chosen if it is to stand outside in one place all the time. Windy, exposed positions which may prevent satisfactory pollination, must also be avoided. In general, it likes a warm day and cool night.

When kept continuously indoors under glass, no attempt must be made to force the apricot, as it is very sensitive to heat. The requirement is a cool house with plenty of ventilation—a close atmosphere or too high temperature causes the blossom to drop. If the trees are kept outdoors during the winter, they can be brought into the house just before new growth commences in the early spring. Once this has commenced, and until the fruits have formed their stones, a temperature of 45° F (7° C) should be the maximum. After this, the temperature can be allowed to increase up to about 50° F (10° C).

From May onwards the apricot must have plenty of water and a mulch of manure or compost will help to retain moisture. The trees should be frequently syringed before and after flowering. Syringing when the fruit is changing colour is also beneficial, as this helps to combat red spider, but when ripening commences the syringing should be discontinued. In dry weather the floor of the house can be dampened. As the fruits develop, an occasional watering of liquid manure is helpful. After the fruits have been gathered, the heat should gradually be reduced and a steady increase of air allowed into the house. Later, the trees may be taken outdoors again.

The apricot, like the plum, fruits on shoots at least two years old, as well as on short spurs produced on older branches. To keep the tree supplied with plenty of new fruiting wood, some of the laterals should be cut back to a few buds each year, or even removed entirely. Old and crossing branches can be cut out as convenient, and vertical shoots growing from the lower horizontal laterals can be tipped so that they replace the drooping ends of the horizontals.

Because of the danger of disease in old trees, all pruning cuts should be kept as small as possible. When large cuts are unavoidable they should be sealed with grafting paint or wax. As far as possible, tree growth should be controlled by summer pinching and stopping. Pruning can be done as soon as the fruit has been harvested, avoiding the autumn and winter. With young trees, however, because the cuts are relatively small and the trees are growing vigorously, it is better to prune during the dormant period in order to obtain good growth from the buds in the spring.

Thinning of the fruit should be progressive, a partial thinning being carried out when the fruits are about the size of large peas and final thinning delayed until the fruit commences to swell again. Most of the varieties obtain a good colour before they are ripe, but they should be left

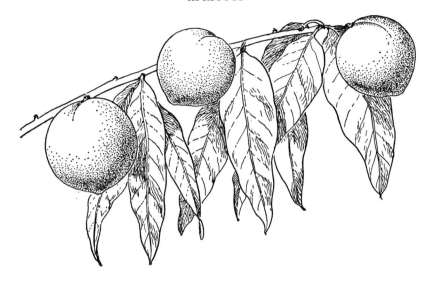

until fully ripe, making sure that wasps do not damage them. They may be picked, left in the sun for a few hours and then kept indoors for a day as this brings out the full flavour.

DISEASES

DIE-BACK, BLOSSOM WILT, WITHER TIP, SPUR BLIGHT, BROWN ROT (*Sclerotinia laxa*)

This disease is found in nearly all countries where the stone fruits are grown, but is of most importance in regions of high rainfall during the ripening period of the fruit. Brown rot of fruit is sometimes serious in the eastern United States when conditions are favourable for the development of the fungus, but in the western states is of importance only in those places where moist conditions prevail, such as in the region of San Francisco Bay. The fungus may also cause serious damage to fruit in some seasons in New Zealand, Australia, Japan and South Africa. In England, die-back and spur blight are the most serious stages of the disease.

Symptoms are usually first seen on the fruit giving the characteristic brown rot. In fact, brown rot of fruit is caused by either of two closely related fungi: *Sclerotinia fructigena* and *S. laxa*; the first produces buff-coloured pustules, while those of the latter are grey. *S. laxa* attacks not only the fruit but flowers, spurs and shoots. Spurs become infected through the flowers, twigs through the leaves, causing the typical die-back symptoms with much gumming of the main branches. Fruit is attacked when approaching maturity, entry of the fungus occurring as a result of the skin having split or wounds being caused by wasps, birds etc. Grey pustules appear and, from these, spores are disseminated to infect other fruits. The fruit itself is rapidly destroyed and finally becomes hard and wrinkled or 'mummified'. When this dry 'mummy' stage is reached, the pustules cease forming spores and remain dormant until the following spring. During the spring the newly disseminated spores are likely to come into contact with the opening flowers and, if they germinate on the stigmas, the mycelium may grow down into the flower stalks and spurs. Such an attack will become apparent about a fortnight after the trees have come into blossom. Flowers wither and die, followed by wilting and death of the surrounding leaves, so that the whole truss is seen to be drooping and withered. The fungus may then spread into the young shoots, where it produces cankers which can girdle the shoots and kill them. Young leaves may also be infected by the fungus, particularly if these have been injured by greenfly etc. When the leaves become infected, the fungus passes down the leaf stalks into the shoots. Cankers may again girdle the twigs, killing them. The fungus then proceeds from twigs to branches.

There is little effective control by chemicals although some control of blossom wilt has been obtained with tar oil preparations applied during winter. Strict attention to other control measures are necessary. All fruit showing sign of brown rot should be removed. On no account should 'mummified' fruit be left to overwinter on the trees, and they should be either burned or deeply buried. All infected trusses, shoots, spurs and dead branches should be cut out, this being done in spring and summer when diseased parts can be recognised.

SILVER LEAF *(Stereum purpureum)*

Common in most countries of continental Europe, especially England, it is fairly general in New Zealand, and occurs in South Africa and USA.

The first symptom is a silvery appearance of the foliage, usually first seen on a single branch. The leaves appear to have a faint silver sheen compared with other leaves elsewhere on the tree. Ultimately the whole of the foliage will appear 'silvered'. The fungus, however, is not living in the leaves but in the wood. The mycelium of the fungus spreads in all directions and produces a toxic substance that is carried by the ascending sap up into the leaves. There the toxic substance causes the skin cells to separate from those immediately below them and it is the presence of air beneath the skin of a leaf which gives it a silvery appearance. If an infected branch is cut across, a dark purplish-brown discolouration is nearly always evident, the area of which is unevenly to one side of the branch and ought not therefore to be mistaken for normal, dark heart wood. When a branch is infected, it gradually dies and, as this is followed by other branches, a large part if not the whole of the tree may ultimately die. Sometimes the tree may recover without treatment, but it will not be immune from subsequent attack. A tree may be only slightly affected and continue to bear a good crop year after year.

When a branch has died but remains on the tree, fructification of the fungus appears on the dead bark. Spores are discharged from these fructifications whenever they become moist and, under alternating dry and wet weather, the discharge can proceed for a very long time. Fructifications may also occur on other dead or dying trees as well as on old stumps and logs. Spores are distributed by the wind but can only cause infection through wounds or injuries, such as pruning cuts, cracked branches etc. Infection is most likely to occur within a week after a wound has been made but seldom after a month. It more readily occurs during autumn, winter and spring. In the summer it can do so only with great difficulty because the tree is subject to rapid gumming which forms a natural barrier to entry by the fungus. It is for this reason that apricot trees should be pruned during summer.

There is at present no known cure for the disease. Strict attention must therefore be paid to hygiene and this is far easier with potted trees than with an open orchard. On no account should diseased wood be allowed to bear fructifications. Cut out the affected part completely; cut well back into living wood so that no sign of the characteristic brown stain-like marking remains. The cuts should always be finished smoothly and made flush with a larger branch or the main stem. Wounds should be coated with soft grafting wax, bitumen emulsion or white lead paint. Diseased wood should be burnt. Wood rubbish should never be allowed to accumulate in an orchard as this is liable to become a dissemination centre for fungi.

PEACH LEAF CURL *(Taphrina deformans)* see under Peaches.

BACTERIAL CANKER *(Pseudomonas mors-prunoram)* see under Cherries.

PESTS
The apricot is less liable to attack by insects than most other fruit trees.

FRUIT-TREE RED SPIDER MITE *(Panonychus ulmi)*
Leaves severely infested by this mite develop a marked silvery appearance during the summer and might be confused with silver leaf disease. Close observation will, however, show the presence of white skin casts on the undersides of the leaves (see further under Apples).

SCALE INSECTS see under Apples.

VARIETIES
The apricot is self-fertile and no cross-pollination between varieties is necessary.

NORTH-WEST EUROPE AND USA

Farmingdale Very early. Medium. Good flavour, moderately juicy. Vigorous growth. Fairly resistant to disease.

Alfred Similar to Farmingdale.

Hemskirk Early. Medium to large. Deep orange, often flushed red. Hardy and fruitful. Stocky growth. Recommended for pot culture.

Royal Early mid-season. Medium to large, oval fruit; pale yellow and spotted purple. Rich flavour, sweet and juicy, texture firm even when fully ripe. Hardy. Good cropper.

Blenheim Early mid-season. Medium, oval to roundish. Orange with red spots. Very juicy. Hardy. Good cropper. Recommended for pot culture.

Moorpark Very late; early September in England. Large, round. Orange-yellow flushed red. Sweet, rich, excellent quality. Strong, vigorous. Good bearer. Recommended for pot culture.

NORTH-WEST EUROPE

Luizet Very early; end of July in England. Large, oval fruit. Deep, rich yellow. Good flavour. Good cropper.

New Large Early Early. Large, oval. Orange, yellow and red. Good flavour. Hardy, prolific.

Breda Mid-season. Small to medium, round. Orange-yellow, flushed red. Good flavour. Stocky, readily forms spurs.

Early Orange   Mid-season. Medium, roundish to oval. Rich orange with red flush. Rich, sweet, juicy. Hardy.

Kaisher   Mid-season. Medium, roundish to oval. Pale yellow and red. Excellent flavour. Hardy, prolific. Recommended for pot culture.

USA

Goldcot   Very early. Medium to large, roundish. Orange. Very fine texture. Hardy, strong.

Phelps   Early. Large, roundish. Orange-yellow. Fine flavour. Early maturing variety for the north-west.

Perfection   Fairly early. Large, oval. Yellow-orange. Good quality.

Tilton   Mid-season. Medium to large, oval. Yellow-orange. Less subject to brown rot than Blenheim but not such good quality.

Franciscan   Mid-season. Similar to Tilton but has deeper coloured flesh.

Wenatchee   Mid-season. Large, oval. Orange-yellow flesh and skin. Suitable for north-west.

8

BLACK CURRANTS

The black currant can survive the most severe winters of the northern limits of the United States but does not prosper in hot, dry climates. Although it can withstand cold, it flowers very early in the year. The flowers appear before there is much leaf to protect them and so are very susceptible to damage by frost.

Although currants will grow in almost any soil and bear fruit, they do best in soil that is cool, moist, is a good medium loam, has plenty of humus and high nitrogen content. A limiting factor in the area of its cultivation is that currants and gooseberries are host plants for blister rust, the black currant being the favourite host. The disease is very destructive for the five-needle, white-pine trees, especially in North America. Because of the timber value of the white pine, the cultivation of the currant and gooseberry is prohibited in many places in the United States. Blister rust is a parasitic fungus which requires two separate species of host plants to complete its life cycle. Spores of the fungus may be carried hundreds of miles by the wind from infected pine trees to the currants, where they settle and germinate on the leaves causing the characteristic blister rust. Then, in late summer, spores released from the under surfaces of the infected leaves are carried again to infect further pine trees. Spores from an infected currant rarely travel more than a few hundred yards, so that provided the bushes are at least 300 yards from the pine trees, they will not be a danger to them.

Some varieties of black currant are resistant to blister rust. For example, two varieties from Canada (Crusader and Coronet) are hybrids between a resistant currant species from Siberia and the black currant. A Norwegian species *(R. petraeum)* is highly resistant and from this an immune variety (Viking) has originated. Growers in the USA wanting to try this fruit should therefore seek local advice.

PROPAGATION

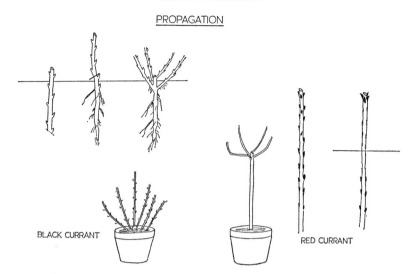

BLACK CURRANT

RED CURRANT

The propagation of black currant can be from hard-wood cuttings taken in the autumn or soft-wood cuttings taken in July. When taking hard-wood cuttings—and this is the most usual method—they should be from the lower part of shoots which are one year old, and should be only from bushes known to be free from reversion virus and the black currant gall mite (Big Bud). The cuttings should be 8–10in long and cut cleanly at the bud at each end. Better rooting is obtained if they are inserted immediately after cutting, so that the cut end does not dry out. They should be set 8in apart and pressed firmly in the soil, so that they are not inserted into an air pocket. To encourage shoot growth and prevent too much leg in the cutting when it has rooted, it should be put into the soil to a depth of about 6in and with two buds only showing above. If the cuttings are taken in early October then usually a high percentage will be found to root.

Artificial forms are unsuitable because fruit buds are formed along the whole length of young shoots; so the main aim must be to obtain a supply of strong new shoots each year. Such shoots will grow best from the base of the bush and even from buds below the surface of the ground, so the best form for the black currant is a stool or bush rising straight out of the soil with no leg or as short a leg as possible. Therefore, as soon as a young yearling or even a two-year-old bush is potted, all the shoots should be cut down to one bud above the soil, in order to get a good strong growth the first year and which will bear fruit the following year. At the end of the following season, all weak shoots should be cut down again to encourage further branching below soil level and the remainder left to crop. It may be necessary to cut down all the shoots, as in the first year, if growth is generally weak. Subsequent pruning will depend on the amount of growth made during the summer. Vigorous bushes may need no pruning at all, but others should have all weak shoots cut back and also one or two of the stronger ones to encourage greater vigour. After this the only pruning necessary may, for two or three years, be nothing more than the removal of trailing branches which tend to interfere with repotting. If the bush shows any tendency towards lessening vigour, some of the oldest wood must be cut right back to its base. As the bush becomes older it will be necessary to remove old wood, but this should be to no more than one-third of the bush. As long as vigour can be maintained with a fertile soil, there is no point in excessive pruning. To obtain heavy cropping, feeding should be the primary consideration and pruning the second.

Nitrogen is the chief manurial requirement but this should not be overdone to the point where too much woody growth is produced. The amount given needs to be judged by the condition of the individual plant. Fish manure, hoof and horn, meat and bone meal can be added to the

compost when repotting. (While repotting, care should be taken to avoid injuring the fibrous roots.) Dried blood or an inorganic nitrogen fertiliser can be watered into the pots in early spring.

During the blossoming period shelter from cold winds is important because, although the wind is not injurious to the flowers, it may prevent adequate pollination and insects will only be active in sheltered positions. Small flies and wild bees are more helpful at this time; the wild bee is active at lower temperatures than the honey bee. Sometimes the top two or three berries set and swell, but the remaining flowers on the strig fail to develop and drop off. This is usually due to inadequate pollination, although it may have been caused by frost killing the lower flowers but not the more developed ones at the top of the strig. Although the flowers are readily killed by frost, the small green berries are a little more resistant.

The season of fruiting can be lengthened by a choice of varieties and growing some in a cool, shady position. Berries for preserving should be picked when firm, but those for dessert can be left on the bush to increase in sweetness. Pigeons will soon strip the bushes, so unless they can be taken into the orchard house during this period they should be netted.

DISEASES

REVERSION

This is the most serious disease of black currants and occurs throughout Europe.

It can be recognised by leaf characteristics or by symptoms at the flower bud stage. Symptoms can be observed just before the flowers open; on reverted bushes the buds are almost hairless and appear brightly coloured, while those on healthy bushes are hairy and so have a grey, downy appearance. At this time it is possible to detect individual reverted branches or even single trusses. Leaf symptoms are more difficult to recognise. Reverted leaves, usually found in the middle regions of the new growth, have fewer sub-main veins and marginal serrations than normal leaves, which have five or more sub-main veins. These differences between diseased and healthy leaves are pronounced by midsummer. The symptoms of reversion do not appear until the year after infection, when they are restricted to individual flower trusses and leaves on a few shoots. After two years the symptoms are more widespread and by the third the whole bush is likely to be reverted. The effect on cropping varies; while some bushes may become barren in three years, others may continue cropping indefinitely but with a reduced yield.

79

LEAF SPOT (ANTHRACNOSE) *(Pseudopeziza ribis)*
This serious disease of gooseberries and currants has been reported from most areas of cultivation. It can become epidemic in black currant crops, resulting in early defoliation of the bushes with a consequent reduction in yield the following year.

Small, scattered, dark brown to black, angular spots appear on either or both sides of the leaves in spring—the basal leaves of the bushes being infected from spores released from fallen, overwintered leaves. Summer spores are produced on the spots on the newly infected leaves and these spores are spread, usually by rain, to affect other leaves. The spots become larger and merge with one another, so that parts of the leaf have a blackish brown or scorched appearance. In wet weather the disease quickly reaches epidemic proportions and premature defoliation results.

Since the fungus overwinters on fallen leaves, these must be raked up and burnt before the spring, so helping to break the cycle. Control can also be with chemical sprays.

CURRANT RUST, ORANGE RUST, WHITE PINE BLISTER RUST *(Cronartium ribicola)*
This rust disease occurs in all countries of the north temperate zone. Because the fungus cannot survive without an intermediary host (white pine species), the disease is not present in those regions free of susceptible pines nor where the distance between the pines and currants is more than a quarter of a mile.

The symptoms are readily recognised by the yellow to bright orange spots which appear on the undersides of the leaves in spring. Usually the spots are widely spaced, but may be so numerous as to occupy most of the surface. Later in the season some defoliation may result. Towards the end of summer the orange colour of the pustules turns to dark brown and spores are produced on threadlike or horny growths. The third stage in the life cycle of the fungus occurs on the five-needle group of pine trees. The Weymouth pine *(Pinus strobus)* in Europe is most commonly associated with the disease.

No control measures are necessary for currants, except to grow them at a distance from susceptible pine trees.

AMERICAN POWDERY MILDEW   see under Gooseberries

EUROPEAN GOOSEBERRY MILDEW   see under Gooseberries.

CANE BLIGHT   see under Red Currants.

PESTS

BLACK CURRANT GALL MITE (BIG BUD) *(Eriophyes ribis)*

Infestation by these mites is most noticeable during the dormant period when the bushes are leafless. Newly infested buds gradually change shape during summer; by the time the leaves fall, they are easily recognisable as galls or big buds, being rounded, much less pointed than normal buds and usually swollen. In early spring the buds swell still further until they may be several times the normal size. If cut open and examined under a powerful lens thousands of white mites—each no more than a hundredth of an inch in length—will be seen. Although the infested buds begin to break, they fail to open normally and do not produce flowers or leaves, but gradually dry up and persist for many months as dead galls.

At blossom time the mites leave the buds and live for a very short time on flowers and leaves. Many migrate to other bushes by jumping, by wind, or by clinging on to larger insects, such as aphids and capsid bugs. Most of the migration occurs between the time of the first opening flowers and early fruit swell. Egg laying begins in the new bud in June and reaches a peak in September. There is a pause in early winter, but a second period of breeding begins in January, reaching a second peak in the spring when the mites are beginning to disperse from the buds. Their reproduction is prolific.

The mite is an agent for the transmission of reversion virus; conversely bushes infected with reversion are more prone to heavy infestation by gall mite. All badly infected bushes should be destroyed. Infected shoots can be pruned and buds picked off during winter where infestation is light. Shoots for cuttings should not be taken from infested or diseased bushes. None of the chemicals at present available kills the mites within the galled buds, so that complete protection from the gall mite is almost impossible, though some may be obtained by spraying with lime sulphur.

CURRANT AND GOOSEBERRY APHIDS

Several species of aphids infest the foliage and young shoots of currants and gooseberries. Some species cause crumpling of the leaves and stunting of young shoots during spring and early summer. When severe infestation occurs, this may result in premature leaf fall and small fruit, while the honeydew excreted by the aphids causes the fruit to become sticky and dirty. Some species are known to be vectors of virus disease.

The aphids are attacked by numerous predators, and their winter eggs are eaten by tits and other small birds. Effective control can be obtained with chemical sprays.

CAPSID BUGS *(Lygus sp.)*

These bugs puncture the young leaves causing small brown spots to appear; when closely examined, the leaves will seem to have been pierced with a pin many times. Leaves so attacked become torn and distorted, while the shoots are often stunted or even killed. The growing points may be so badly injured that new wood is not formed and excessive side branching results.

The bug is easily seen as it is about $\frac{1}{4}$in long, flies slowly but runs quickly. It lays its eggs beneath the rind of shoots and it is the young bugs hatching from the eggs in April and May which cause the damage. When half fed, the young bugs usually leave the currant bush and crawl on to herbaceous plants to complete their development. In any case, when mature in July, they migrate to herbaceous plants and produce the next generation. When this second generation is mature it returns to the currant, or other suitable woody host, where it lays its winter eggs. Control is with chemicals.

BLACK CURRANT LEAF CURLING MIDGE *(Dasyneur tetensi)*

Leaves are puckered as though nipped, and crushed on one side; the growing point may be attacked so that extension growth stops. Splitting of the shoot may then occur.

The cause of this trouble is a midge which appears in June and lays its eggs on the leaves. After about two weeks the eggs hatch into little white maggots which feed on the leaves. This pest causes a certain amount of trouble because of its erratic hatching period—several broods appearing during the season. On occasions the damage can be severe. Control is with chemicals.

RED SPIDER *(Tetranychus urticae)*

Although the fruit tree spider does not seriously attack black currants, the species usually occurring in glass houses does.

First symptoms of attack are small areas of whitish spots visible on the upper leaf surface. These indicate the position of the colonies living on the undersides of the leaves and sucking the sap. As the infestation increases, the leaves become more speckled and later develop a bronze hue. Examination of the leaves will show the spiders and their summer eggs, just visible to the eye. With severe attack there is premature leaf fall and the vigour of the bush will be reduced. Uncontrolled red spider attacks will cause not only severe lack of growth (essential to the black currant) but a consequential loss of crop in both the present season and the following one.

Under normal conditions predatory insects destroy large numbers of mites, but extensive use of insecticides may sometimes have reduced this natural control. Local advice should be obtained when controlling with acaracides.

CURRANT SAWFLY *(Nematus olfaciens)*
Damage caused by the caterpillar is first seen in the form of small holes, each about ¼in in diameter in the leaves, usually in the centre of the bush. The caterpillars, which are green with black markings, eat the whole of the leaves except the main veins and stalks.

The adult sawfly has transparent wings with a body black in front and yellow-orange behind. It appears in May and is active in sunny weather, flying around and running over the leaves. Its eggs are laid singly or in small numbers along the veins on the undersides of the leaves. The black currant sawfly has two or more generations during the summer, with the first adults emerging in May and June and the second between July and September. The generations overlap and all stages may be found together towards the end of the season. It overwinters in its cocoon, usually within a few inches of the surface of the soil.

In a potted orchard, with only a few bushes, it is possible to pick off the caterpillars by hand. When an attack is noticed at an early stage, the leaves on which the eggs have been laid should be picked and destroyed. Otherwise derris dust can be puffed or shaken over the bushes.

CURRANT CLEARWING *(Conopia tipuliformis)* see under Red Currants.

MAGPIE MOTH *(Abraxas grossulariata)* see under Gooseberries.

VARIETIES

Differences between varieties are often in the growth and foliage rather than in the fruit. Most varieties flower at about the same time. In Britain, the principal area for black currants, the following are the most popular; all are good for jam.

Laxton's Giant Very early. Very large berries, sweet, juicy. Heavy cropper. Bush of spreading habit. Medium vigour. Disease resistant.

Boskoop Giant Early. Large, sweet, thin skinned. Long strig. Very heavy cropper. Large, spreading, vigorous bush. Requires shelter from cold winds.

Tor Cross Early. Large, juicy. Exceptionally heavy cropper. Bush of medium vigour, cup shaped.

Wellington XXX Early. Good berries with fine flavour. Very heavy cropper. Straggling bush, very strong vigour.

Goliath (Victoria) Mid-season. Medium-sized berries on short, horizontal, exposed twigs. Exceptionally sweet, very good flavour. Moderate cropper, sometimes heavy. Fairly vigorous. Straight, unbranched shoots. Very lime-sulphur shy.

Raven Mid-season. Large berries, large strigs. Good cropper. Very vigorous, spreading.

Seabrooks Mid-season. Medium-sized berries. Good colour and flavour, thick skin. Good cropper. Compact, vigorous. Fairly resistant to black currant mite.

Baldwin (Hilltop) Late. Thick skinned, especially rich in vitamin C. Heavy cropper. Compact bush, medium vigour.

Malvern Cross Late. Good berries. Heavy cropper. Upright bush, strong vigour.

Amos Black Very late. Large berries. Good cropper. Upright bush, medium size, very little branching. Moderate vigour.

9

BLUEBERRIES

There are many Vaccinium species, known as blueberries, which are native to several areas in North America. Some species produce berries of low quality whereas others are harvested commercially. Notable among species which have been improved by breeding are the highbush blueberries *(Vaccinium corymbosum* and *V. australes)* and rabbiteye blueberries *(V. ashei)*. The rabbiteye blueberry, native along the large streams in northern Florida, south-eastern Georgia and south-eastern Alabama, is now being grown on a limited scale in the south-east states.

Blueberries require certain specific soil conditions which *must* be supplied for successful cultivation. They will only thrive in an acid soil, in which a root fungus or mycorrhiza is able to exist. The most suitable pH ranges from 4·0 to 5·0; when the pH is 5·5 and higher, they produce chlorotic leaves, become stunted and may, in fact, fail to survive. The best growth usually occurs when acidity ranges from pH 4·3 to 4·8. The blueberry is a shallow rooted plant and the nature of the fibrous root system makes an open porous soil desirable. The fine roots of the highbush blueberry find difficulty in penetrating compacted, heavy soil. Light, well-drained, sandy loam, with a large amount of organic matter, makes the best blueberry soil. Although blueberries require moisture, they cannot tolerate poor drainage and, if kept in soil continuously saturated with water, their roots may be killed.

With potted blueberries, the right kind of soil can be provided. The use of liberal amounts of peat moss or similar organic matter will improve the physical structure and water-holding capacity of many soils. The incorporation of organic matter, such as woodland soil, pine needles etc, will introduce essential root fungus (mycorrhiza). Soil can be made acid—again by adding pine needles, well-rotted leaves, peat moss, sawdust etc. Wood-ash should not be added, as this will have the opposite effect because of the minerals contained in the ash. Powdered sulphur or ammonium

sulphate can also be used to improve acidity. When sulphur is to be used, the compost should be prepared as long as possible in advance. A local soil may be considered good for blueberries if azaleas, laurel or heather are seen to be growing very well in the area; but for pot work a suitable compost can be made up of 4 parts sandy soil, 2 parts peat moss, 1 part sawdust. Before using any compost, its acidity should be tested to make sure that its pH is in the range already mentioned.

Varieties of blueberry may be propagated from suckers or cuttings. Suckers which grow around plants may be dug up and replanted. By this method large plants are produced in a relatively short time, but the plants must be pruned back severely to compensate for the loss of the root system when it was severed from the parent. Plants can be propagated from hard-wood or soft-wood cuttings. Hard-wood cuttings are the best method for highbush blueberries and soft-wood cuttings for rabbiteye blueberries.

Young plants should be potted during November or early spring. Two-year-old plants may have flower buds; these are located on the terminal part of the shoots and are much larger than leaf buds. Any flowers produced the first year should be rubbed off to allow the plants to make good growth. Removal of flower buds in the year following planting results in better growth and heavier yield in subsequent years. Plants will, in fact, produce a partial crop the second year after planting. They will need very little pruning until they begin to bear, but weak stems or branches may be cut out, and completely removed from the crown of the plant. Most varieties of blueberries, provided they are properly pollinated, tend to crop too heavily, so that one purpose of pruning, once the plant commences bearing, is to remove some of the flower buds. The largest berries are borne on the thickest, more vigorous wood, so the thin, twiggy stems should be removed, as well as any which are diseased and injured.

During the growing period the blueberry requires ample moisture; water should be given little but often. A mulch of sawdust, pine needles or similar material is beneficial during hot weather; this not only helps to retain soil moisture but adds organic matter. The blueberry requires the same nutrient elements as other fruits, so a general liquid fertiliser can be used. Where a compost with a marginally high pH has had to be used, it is desirable to supply nitrogen in the form of ammonium sulphate, which the blueberry can utilise more effectively than it can in the nitrate forms.

Both highbush and rabbiteye blueberries benefit from cross-pollination by other varieties. When this occurs, it results in a greater set of fruit and larger and earlier ripening berries. Therefore at least two varieties should be grown. All varieties within a species overlap enough in their flowering to be effective pollinators for any other variety. Pollination, however, largely depends on visits by insects, especially bees. During a cold spring, the pots should be moved to sheltered positions where bees are more likely to work.

DISEASES

LEAF RUST *(Pucciniastrum myrtilli)*
This disease occurs in most species of Vaccinium. It ranges from Nova Scotia to Wisconsin, south to Florida and Arkansas, and in the west from Alaska to New Mexico. It occurs also in South America, Europe and Asia. In these places, where blueberries are grown near hemlock *(Tsuga canadensis)*, which acts as an alternate host for the disease, serious defoliation may occur in some years. Sometimes there may also be defoliation in the

southern Atlantic states, although there is no alternate host; this is because the winter is mild and it continues its life cycle in the blueberry and so starts an early infection. Generally, because of its sporadic appearance, the disease is not of great economic importance.

The symptoms are discoloured spots appearing on the lower surface of the leaf. Yellow pustules begin to appear on the spots during the summer months. Defoliation usually occurs late in the season, but may start as early as July.

BLOSSOM BLIGHT, TWIG BLIGHT *(Botrytis cinerea)*

This well-known fungus disease has a very extensive host range, causing fruit rot as well as blighting twigs and blossom. As a disease of the blueberry it occurs throughout North America and Europe.

Severe infection can occur in the spring when the flower clusters and shoots are most susceptible. From the infected blossoms the fungus grows down into the shoots to start twig blight. Leaves are infected when they come into contact with the blighted twigs or flower clusters. Twigs and blossom soon become covered with a grey mass of fungus and further infection may occur during rainy or misty weather. The fungus persists in the blighted twigs throughout the year.

Greater infection occurs when a peat mulch rather than one of sawdust is used. Nitrogen applied in early spring tends to increase infection more than when it is given during the full bloom period. Chemical sprays will control this disease.

POWDERY MILDEW *(Microsphaera alni)*

This is the commonest and most widespread disease of blueberries. Although not destructive, it can when climatic conditions are favourable cause serious defoliation. Dusting with sulphur gives control.

CANE CANKER *(Physalospora corticus)*

This is most common in highbush blueberries in North Carolina and in rabbiteye varieties in Alabama, Florida and Mississippi.

Symptoms first appear in late summer as reddish conical swellings on the shoots of the current year. During the second year the lesions enlarge and become fissured. By the end of the second year the older parts of the canker are black, rough and deeply fissured; the final effect is the girdling of the stems and their death. The disease reduces the cropping of the bush, which is best destroyed.

88

HIGHBUSH VARIETIES
('Scar' refers to the point of separation of the berry from the stem.)

Wyemouth   Earliest of all blueberries, ripening about first week in June. Medium, soft, dark colour, poor flavour, large scar. Medium-sized bush.

Earliblue   Large berries, firm, light blue, sweet, low acid content. Vigorous, medium cropper. Loose fruit clusters.

June   Medium, light blue, good quality. Erect bush.

Cabot   Large berries, good quality. Very heavy cropper. Susceptible to cane canker.

Rancocas   Very small berries, good colour, fair flavour, large scar. Erect, very productive. Sometimes crops so heavily that special care must be taken to prune the bush to ensure a good crop the following year. Ripens about the same time as Collins and five days after Earliblue.

Collins   Large berries, good quality, light blue. Vigorous.

Pioneer   Large berries, light blue, sweet. Vigorous bush, tending to spread in width rather than height. Susceptible to cane canker.

Stanley   Small berries, poor colour, large scar. Flavour very good, very aromatic. Bush erect.

Blueray   Very large berries, light blue, very good flavour, aromatic. Very vigorous and productive.

Bluecrop   Large berries, excellent colour, small scar, good flavour. Sparse foliage, good cropper.

Concord   Large berries, good colour, very good flavour. Vigorous, upright.

Berkely   Very large berries, light blue, fair flavour, sweet. Vigorous and productive.

Coville   Very large berries, firm, excellent colour, strong aromatic flavour, acid.

Dixie   Large berries, medium blue, fair flavour, large scar, aromatic. Good cropper, long picking season.

Atlantic Large berries, light blue, good quality. Bush open and productive.

Pemberton Large berries, firm, good quality. Hardy, exceptionally vigorous.

Rubel Ripens early July. Medium-sized berries, medium blue, good flavour, rather acid. Upright, very vigorous, hardy, productive.

Jersey Medium to large, light blue, medium scar, fair flavour. Vigorous, productive.

Herbert Very large, dark blue, tending to be soft, tender skin, good aromatic flavour. Vigorous, spreading, good cropper.

Burlington Small, medium blue, very small scar, slightly aromatic. Sturdy, upright, moderate vigour, good cropper.

RABBITEYE VARIETIES

Tifblue Medium to large, light blue, heavy waxy bloom, attractive, very small scar, good flavour. Very tart until fully ripe. Upright, vigorous, very productive.

Woodward Medium to large, very light blue, medium scar, good flavour, aromatic. Very tart until fully ripe. Medium vigour, productive.

Menditoo Medium to large, dark blue, soft, very small scar, fair flavour. Vigorous, fair cropper, long picking season.

Callaway Medium, dark blue, good flavour, medium scar. Upright, spreading, moderately vigorous.

Coastal Medium, dark blue, good flavour, small but deep scar. Berries subject to cracking under rainy conditions. Vigorous, spreading.

Garden Blue Small, medium blue, good flavour, medium scar. Berries subject to cracking after rains. Vigorous, large.

Homebell Medium, dark blue, sweet, slight acidity, small scar. Vigorous, medium production.

Southland Medium, heavy bloom giving light blue colour, good flavour, small scar. Very tart until fully ripe. Vigorous, good producer.

Briteblue   Large, light blue—heavy bloom, good flavour, small scar. Very tart until fully ripe. Should not be picked until red colour around stem has disappeared. Moderately vigorous, spreading.

Delite   Medium to large. Despite heavy bloom, the red under-colour shows through when ripe. The only rabbiteye variety whose berries are not tart before reaching maturity. Very good flavour. Fairly vigorous and productive.

10

CHERRIES

There are two main groups of cherries: dessert (sweet) and culinary (acid or sour). A third and lesser group—Duke cherries—are similar to sweet cherries in habit and growth, but are more like acid cherries in their fruit.

Cherries, in general, are grown in temperate areas where winter temperatures are not too severe yet cold enough to cause a period of dormancy. Sweet cherries can withstand winter temperatures down to about −15° F (−26° C) while for acid cherries they can go as low as −25° F (−31° C). Neither kind grows well in hot or humid climates.

The cherry crops well in areas of moderate rainfall and where the soil is a light to medium loam, deep, but well drained. It does not like either heavy, wet soil or very light sandy and gravelly loams which soon lose their moisture. Blossom time is before the apple and just after the peach, consequently at this time cherries need shelter from cold winds and protection from spring frosts.

SWEET AND DUKE CHERRIES

Under natural conditions the sweet cherry grows into a fairly large tree. Also, because cross-pollination necessitates growing more than one tree, it is not suitable for a small garden. It is, however, adaptable to pot culture.

There are, at present, no real dwarfing rootstocks available for the amateur. Suckers from wild cherries—which are called Mazzards or Geans—are frequently used. However, a Malling rootstock (F 12/1) is becoming more widely used and this is fairly resistant to bacterial canker. Others may be available; in Switzerland, for example, the rootstocks W4845 and W3187 have proved as good as the English F12/1.

The choice of rootstock will therefore have to be limited to whatever is available. Potting is best done in October. Potted cherry trees will thrive in a compost consisting of two-thirds loam and one-third old mortar rubble, wood-ash, bone meal and charcoal. They require fairly high nitrogen feeding as well as potassium, and are liable to suffer from magnesium deficiency.

Although sweet cherries are happiest when allowed to grow to their own natural shape, they can, because they crop on fruit spurs, be grown in any restricted form in a similar manner to apples and pears. Crops are normally obtained after three years. Dwarf pyramids make excellent pot trees and the bush form is a reasonable one to use. The danger of training to a rigid form is the severe pruning which is necessary and the susceptibility of the cherry to bacterial canker.

FRUIT BUDS

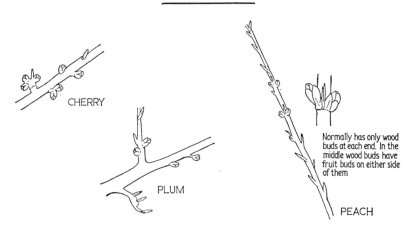

CHERRY

PLUM

Normally has only wood buds at each end. In the middle wood buds have fruit buds on either side of them

PEACH

Fruiting spurs and young shoots can be pinched back to five or six leaves and the laterals shortened again in October to three or four buds to encourage spur formation. Once the tree has sufficient fruiting spurs to ensure a good but not exhaustive crop, it should be pruned as little as possible. Annual pruning of mature trees entails the removal of dead, injured or crowding branches and shortening others as required. All cuts should be made flush to the stems to avoid snags. This pruning can be done in the late winter and spring or after harvesting; although there is some danger from silver leaf disease, this is less than with apricots or plums.

If the cherry trees are brought into the orchard house, only slight heat, and this gradually, need be provided. Until the flowers break, the temperature should be no lower than 40° F (4° C) by night and no higher than 55° F (13° C) by day. When the flowers open, they should be dusted daily to ensure good pollination. Afterwards, when fruit is setting, the trees need to be syringed daily. Temperatures should now be allowed to rise to 50° F (10° C) by night and 60° F (16° C) by day. While sudden rises and falls in temperature must be avoided, as much air as possible should be admitted to the house. Once the fruit has set, the trees should be given nourishment in the form of liquid manure. A danger with potted trees is that moisture will be inadequate and the resulting fruit small and hard; adequate watering is therefore necessary.

As the fruits ripen, the trees should be gone over regularly and fruit taken only when it is really ready. To avoid damage to the spurs, the stalks of the fruit should be cut with scissors.

ACID CHERRIES

These are less susceptible to frost and, flowering a few days later than sweet cherries, can be grown in more exposed sites. They will, in fact, normally crop well against north and east walls and in shaded positions. Their range of soils is also wider, but for preference they like a rich, retentive loam with plenty of nitrogen.

PRUNING

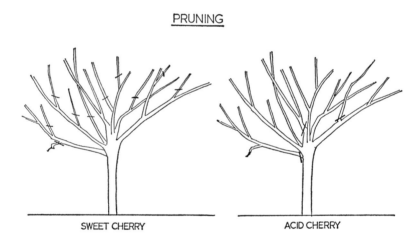

SWEET CHERRY   ACID CHERRY

They fruit on wood formed the previous year and on spurs which form, less frequently, on old wood. Because they flower differently to sweet cherries, they need to be pruned differently— the aim being to promote new shoot growth every year. They start fruiting when two or three years old, make small trees and can be grown conveniently as bushes. Once a tree commences cropping, the aims must be to keep plenty of young wood throughout the tree, and to avoid too much old and bare wood in the centre, which is a natural tendency with the acid cherry. After the cherries have been picked, old and crowded shoots can be cut out and side shoots lightly cut back. Pruning can be in a manner similar to that for black

94

currants. In order to promote new growth they should be given a liberal supply of nitrogen fertiliser. Acid cherries are prone to blossom wilt, the fungus causing a number of twigs to be killed; these must always be cut out and burnt.

DISEASES OF SWEET AND ACID CHERRIES

BACTERIAL CANKER *(Pseudomonas mors-prunorum)*
This bacterial disease is known in Japan, Australia, Brazil, New Zealand, USSR, China, Europe and North America.

A very serious disease, it is responsible for the premature death of cherry, plum, apricot, peach and apple trees. Its development in young stone fruit trees is rapid, but in apple and mature trees it is chronic. Acid cherries are particularly susceptible, as are the following sweet cherry varieties: Napoleon, Bigarreau de Schrecken, Florence, Bradbourne, Black Ohio and Early Rivers.

Symptoms will usually be observed during spring and summer when leaves will be seen to have turned yellow and often to have become rolled and wilting. Small circular spots, at first pale yellow and later turning brown, are produced and eventually these fall away from the leaves giving them a 'shot-hole' effect. Leaf spotting is more common on plums and cherries in England than in California where dry conditions prevail during spring and summer when the leaf infection occurs. The same bacteria which causes these spots also produces cankers on the branches.

Cankered areas, possibly with copious, cloudy yellow gumming, will be observed on the branches. The bark, particularly in the crotch of branches, will be killed and the branches themselves may die. If the canker occurs in the trunk and spreads far enough to girdle it, then the whole tree may be killed. It is more usual for the branches to be killed than the tree. Provided the branch or trunk is not girdled, a natural recovery will usually occur when the bacteria dies.

The most likely means of infection is through wounds in October, November and December; because of this it is preferable to prune between May and August. Control is by chemicals during late summer and early autumn.

LEAF SCORCH *(Gnomonia erythrostoma)*
The characteristic symptom of this disease will be observed in the autumn when it is seen that the leaves fail to drop. Although dead, they hang on the tree even during the winter. When the new leaves appear in the spring

95

these in turn are infected by spores emanating from the fungus on the dead leaves. Yellowish patches, which later turn brown, appear on the leaves. Gradually the fungus passes down the leaf stalk causing an adherence which prevents the leaf from falling. The disease can be severe in some seasons, but with potted trees effective control can be exercised by stripping the tree of its leaves during the winter and burning them.

BLOSSOM WILT *(Sclerotinia laxa)*

This is one of the most serious diseases of acid cherries and some varieties of sweet cherry (notably Governor Wood) are susceptible to it. Spores of the fungus infect the flowers and the infection then goes down into the young shoot of the acid cherry or fruit spur of the sweet cherry. Shoots and spurs are killed and, as a result, withered brown leaves and flower trusses contrast with the green foliage of the tree.

With acid cherries it is possible to cut out and burn all the dead shoots and twigs during the summer, but with sweet cherries the most effective control is with chemicals (see also under Apricots).

LEAF SPOT *(Coccomyces niemalis)*

This disease is common to USA and Canada and particularly destructive where humid conditions are prevalent. It occurs but is less known in Europe, Australia and Japan.

When the attack begins in late spring and early summer the first symptoms appear as small spots of dying tissue on the leaves which enlarge slightly but become very numerous with a heavy infection. Later the area in the centre of the spot may die and fall out giving a 'shot-hole' effect. On the undersides of the leaves, a white mildew-like growth may be seen. Severe defoliation often results, reducing the vigour of the tree. The disease also attacks the fruit and its stem.

The extent of the build-up of the leaf spotting is dependent on rainfall or wind-blown mists. If, after primary infection, only light rains occur there may be little evidence of the disease until fairly late in the season. Normally the period of maximum infection and the beginning of defoliation is about half-way between blossom time and harvest time. Defoliation prior to the ripening period reduces the size and quality of the fruit as well as exposing it to sun scorch.

Some control is possible with chemicals and the orchard house can provide protection during inclement weather when the disease is known to be prevalent.

VIRUS DISEASES

Stone fruits are affected by numerous virus diseases about which there is still much to be learned. The diseases are often spread by insects, but they are easily transmitted by grafting and budding. Many of the viruses are a complex of several forms and strains, but the symptoms are of various types, the most common amongst cherries and plums being 'ring spot', 'mottle' and 'mosaic'. Although 'ring spot' is widely distributed throughout the USA, Canada, Europe and Asia, it is not of such great economic importance as the others.

These are two representative virus diseases:

YELLOW LEAF (Yellows)
This affects acid cherries and is widely spread throughout the acid cherry growing areas of USA, as well as British Columbia and Ontario in Canada. It is thought that the symptoms may be the result of the combined action of two or more viruses.

Symptoms are yellow and green mottling of the leaves followed by a shedding of the leaves. The yellowing occurs in waves during the season and the first signs appear three or four weeks after petal fall. Diseased trees may live their normal life-span but after several years twig growth becomes willowy with long bare lengths and few fruit-bearing spurs. The much reduced spur system causes a consequential loss in yield. However, the fruit produced is of good quality and larger than those on unaffected trees. The disease is transmitted by budding and grafting. Seeds from diseased Mahaleb cherries (sometimes used as rootstock) carry the virus and can transmit it to the seedling.

CHERRY LEAF ROLL
This is caused by a virus which has some similarities with Arabis Mosaic (see under Strawberries). Its most characteristic symptom is an upward rolling of the leaves often accompanied by a reddening along the leaf margins. Extension growth is also checked and gum exudes through cracks in the bark, so that there may be some confusion with bacterial canker. Certain varieties of sweet cherry (eg Early Rivers, Governor Wood, Napoleon) can become so severely affected that they die within a few years of the first symptoms appearing.

The virus can be transmitted by eelworms (nematodes). Eelworms of the group that transmit viruses move about freely in the soil and can live for two to four years, breeding in spring and early summer. They can withstand months, even years, of starvation, resuming breeding when food becomes available, so that the absence of suitable host plants does not bring about a swift population decline. Little can therefore be done to control them by cultural methods, but chemical control by soil fumigation is practical in the potted orchard.

PESTS

CHERRY FRUIT MOTH *(Argyresthia curvella)*
The adult, brown and white in colour, is a small delicate moth with a wing span of about ½in. It appears in summer and, when flying, seems to do so in a dancing manner. Its eggs are laid in cracks in the bark of the cherry tree, under bud scales and other such places. The eggs are extremely hard to see because being greyish brown they are almost the same colour as the bark of the tree. They are oblong in shape, about 1/20in in length and are firmly attached to the tree. At the end of the summer the eggs hatch into minute caterpillars which, after feeding for a short time on the leaves, spin cocoons in crevices and then hibernate. In the following spring, as soon as the flower buds burst, the small green caterpillars, active again, crawl into the buds and, when the flower petals fall, they bore into the little fruitlet now formed. As the cherry develops, they feed inside, hollowing and destroying it. In late spring the caterpillars drop to the ground and turn into chrysalides about 1/5in in length. These remain in the soil for about a month, after which they emerge as adult moths and the life cycle is completed.
Control is by means of chemicals.

CHERRY BLACKFLY *(Myzus cerasi)*
This aphid is common in cherry growing areas throughout the world. In summer masses of the black lice-like insects may be found feeding on the young shoots and leaves, which often turn a reddish colour until they become black and drop off. Frequently, because of the amount of sap being sucked from them, the shoots die. During the summer, colonies may become established on cherry trees by winged aphids flying across from neighbouring, infested trees. The winter is spent as shiny black eggs on twigs and branches.
The PEACH APHID *(Myzus persicae)* also attacks cherry trees, causing curling and distortion of leaves and shoots in early summer. The attacks of both pests vary in their intensity from year to year but a heavy infestation can be damaging to young trees.

PEAR AND CHERRY SLUGWORM see under Pears.

SAN JOSE SCALE see under Apples.

CHERRY FRUIT FLY *(Rhagoletis cerasi)*
This is a serious pest on the continent of Europe. Apart from cherries, it will also attack pears, plums and other fruit. The females cut slits in the fruit where they lay their eggs. Maggots hatching from these eggs then feed on the flesh of the cherries, causing them to become dwarfed, misshapen or decayed. When fully grown, the maggots drop to the ground where they pupate in loose soil. Late the following spring the adults emerge and commence feeding on the leaves and developing fruit, by scraping the surface and sucking out the juice.
    Control is by chemicals.

POLLINATION OF CHERRIES

The majority of sweet cherries are *self-incompatible* (ie they fail to set a crop of fruit when their flowers are pollinated only by their own pollen). Many varieties of sweet cherries are also *cross-incompatible* (ie they will not set fruit even when trees are pollinated by one another). Because of this, the pollination of sweet cherries is more difficult than is the case with most other fruits. In contrast some of the Duke cherries and most of the acid cherries are *self-compatible* (ie they are capable of setting a full crop without pollen from other varieties).
    Most varieties of cherry produce an abundance of flowers, so the regularity of flowering is not a problem. They flower over a long period, which may be longer in dull seasons but short when the weather is sunny and warm. Sweet cherries may be in bloom in succession over three to five weeks; acid and Duke cherries will prolong the season another two weeks. (Most of the acid and Duke cherries flower later than sweet cherries.)
    In a commercial orchard the choice and arrangement of varieties for pollination are affected by the ripening sequence. Trees grow to a large size and picking is usually done from tall ladders. So an orchard must be planned with required varieties in rows to pollinate their neighbours but also in sequence of ripening to avoid moving ladders long distances. With a potted cherry orchard, this picking problem does not apply; all that is needed is a selection of varieties capable of pollinating one another. Sweet cherries are classified into groups and, with the exception of one universal donor group, these are called incompatibility groups. The varieties in a group will not fertilise each other, but must be pollinated by some variety

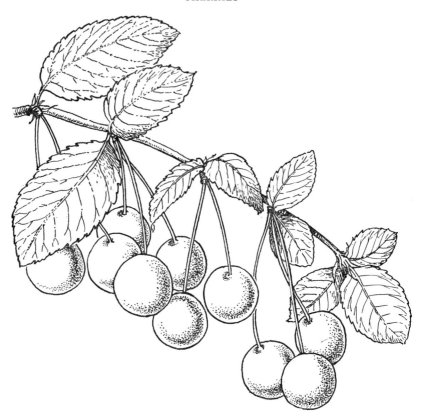

outside the group to set a crop of fruit. When choosing a pollinator for a particular variety, consider its flowering season and its incompatibility group. Any of the varieties in the group called 'universal donors' will successfully pollinate any other variety of cherry provided they flower at the same time.

The varieties of cherries in this book are a selection from various countries, so that, although some guidance is given, no attempt has been made to put them into their incompatibility group. A good nurseryman will always give advice on the most suitable varieties to grow together.

VARIETIES OF SWEET CHERRIES

GENERAL SELECTION

Black Heart Medium to large, heart-shaped. Dark purple to almost black. Sweet, juicy. Ripening early season. Hardy, good cropper. Flowering early. Pollinators: Early Rivers, Elton.

Early Rivers Large, heart-shaped. Glossy black. Rich, melting, juicy. Keeps comparatively well. Ripening early season. Vigorous. Flowering early. Pollinators: Merton Favourite, Governor Wood, Noir de Guben, Turkey Heart.

Noir de Guben Large, roundish. Dark reddish brown. Good flavour. Ripening late mid-season. Heavy cropper. Flowering early. Universal donor group. Pollinators: Early Rivers, Werder's Early Black.

Werder's Early Black Medium, heart-shaped. Black. Ripens early season. Flowering early. Pollinators: Early Rivers, Noir de Guben.

Bedford Prolific Large, heart-shaped. Glossy purplish black. Good flavour. Ripening early mid-season. Flowering semi-early. Pollinators: Merton Glory, Bigarreau de Schrecken, Merton Favourite, Bigarreau de Mezel.

Merton Favourite Large, heart-shaped. Black with dark crimson flesh. Good flavour, juicy, sweet, rich. Ripening early mid-season. Vigorous, good cropper. Flowering semi-early. Pollinators: Black Tartarian, Bedford Prolific, Bigarreau de Mezel, Merton Glory.

Bigarreau de Mezel Very large, white. Sweet, juicy. Ripening mid-season. Flowering semi-early. Pollinators: Merton Glory, Bedford Prolific, Bigarreau de Schrecken, Merton Favourite, Black Tartarian.

Bigarreau Jaboulay Medium, heart-shaped. Light red. Sweet, juicy. Ripening early season. Flowering semi-early. Pollinators: Merton Glory, Black Tartarian, Bigarreau de Schrecken, Merton Favourite, Bigarreau de Mezel.

Belle d'Orleans Medium, heart-shaped. Pale yellow to bright red. Fine flavour, sweet, juicy. Ripening late mid-season. Flowering semi-early. Pollinators: Early Rivers, Frogmore, Waterloo.

Black Eagle Large, roundish. Purplish black. Rich, sweet, juicy. Ripening mid-season. Hardy. Flowering semi-early. Pollinators: Bigarreau de Schrecken, Merton Glory.

Bigarreau de Schrecken Large, roundish. Shiny black. Very good flavour. Ripening early mid-season. Flowering semi-early. Pollinators: Early Rivers, Merton Glory, Bigarreau de Mezel, Bigarreau Jaboulay, Black Tartarian, Bedford Prolific.

Black Tartarian   Very large, heart-shaped. Deep black. Very rich flavour. Ripening early mid-season. Hardy, good cropper. Flowering semi-early. Pollinators: Merton Glory, Bigarreau de Schrecken, Bigarreau de Mezel, Bigarreau Jaboulay.

Waterloo   Large, heart-shaped. Glossy reddish black. Rich, juicy, sweet. Ripening mid-season. Heavy, fairly regular cropper. One of the best flavoured black cherries. Hangs well on tree after ripening. Moderate and compact. Flowering semi-early. Pollinators: Merton Glory, Black Tartarian, Bedford Prolific, Bigarreau de Mezel, Merton Heart.

Merton Heart   Large, heart-shaped. Very dark red. Excellent flavour, juicy. Ripening early mid-season. Vigorous, but spurs well. Resistant to bacterial canker and blossom wilt. Flowering semi-early. Pollinators: Merton Glory, Black Tartarian, Bedford Prolific, Bigarreau de Schrecken, Bigarreau de Mezel.

Merton Glory   Large, heart-shaped. Creamy white colour. Good flavour. Ripening mid-season. Vigorous. Flowering semi-early. This is a universal donor, compatible with all groups.

Frogmore Early Bigarreau   Medium, heart-shaped. Pale yellow, tinged red. Very good flavour, juicy, sweet. Ripening early mid-season. Hardy, good cropper. Flowering mid-period. Pollinators: Roundel, Governor Wood, Peggy Rivers.

Governor Wood   Large, heart-shaped. Bright red over pale yellow. Thin-skinned. Fair flavour, sweet, juicy. Ripening early mid-season. Hardy, prolific. Very susceptible to blossom wilt and cherry leaf scorch, but resistant to bacterial canker. Flowering mid-period. Pollinators: Roundel, Frogmore Early, Peggy Rivers.

Roundel   Very large, heart-shaped. Purplish black. Dark red flesh, very juicy. One of the best flavoured. Ripening mid-season. Hardy, prolific. Flowering mid-period. Pollinators: Frogmore Early, Merton Bigarreau, Governor Wood, Peggy Rivers.

Merton Bigarreau   Medium, heart-shaped. Black. Firm red flesh. Very good flavour. Ripening mid-season. Vigorous. Flowering mid-period. Pollinators: Roundel, Governor Wood, Peggy Rivers.

Peggy Rivers   Large, heart-shaped. Bright red over pale yellow. Sweet, juicy. Ripening early mid-season. Flowering mid-period. Pollinators: Roundel, Frogmore Early, Merton Bigarreau, Governor Wood.

Kentish Bigarreau (Amber Heart) Medium, heart-shaped. Pale yellow, red flush. Good flavour. Ripening late mid-season. Hardy, prolific. Flowering semi-late. Pollinators: Merton Crane, Napoleon Bigarreau, Ohio Beauty.

Napoleon Bigarreau Very large, heart-shaped. Bright red. Rich flavour. Ripening late mid-season. Prolific. Susceptible to bacterial canker and silver leaf disease. Flowering semi-late. Pollinators: Merton Crane, Kent Bigarreau.

Stella (formerly Lambert 2C–27–19) Large to very large, heart-shaped. Dark crimson, mahogany almost black when fully ripe. Good flavour. Small stone. Ripening mid-season. Vigorous, fairly upright. Flowering just after Napoleon. Self-fertile.

Emperor Francis Large, heart-shaped. Dark red. Good flavour, sweet, juicy. Ripening late mid-season. Hardy, good cropper. Resistant to bacterial canker. Flowering semi-late. Pollinators: Merton Crane, Kent Bigarreau.

Merton Crane Medium to large, heart-shaped. Dark mahogany to nearly black, very shiny. Flesh dark purple, rich, sweet. Ripening mid-season. Vigorous, branches inclining to be upright. Flowering semi-late. Pollinators: Emperor Francis, Napoleon Bigarreau, Kent Bigarreau.

Bigarreau Gaucher Large, heart-shaped. Black. Sweet, juicy. Ripening late. Flowering late. Universal donor group.

Florence Large, heart-shaped. Bright red. Good flavour, sweet, juicy. Ripening late. Heavy cropper, very susceptible to bacterial canker. Universal donor group.

Bradbourne Black Large, heart-shaped. Black. Exceptionally good flavour. Ripening late mid-season. Susceptible to bacterial canker. Flowering very late. Pollinators: Florence, Morello.

NORTH AMERICAN SELECTION
Times of ripening are for the north-western states. Cherries ripen about a month earlier in California.

Black Tartarian Very large, heart-shaped. Black. Sweet, rich. Ripening June. Pollinators: Bush Tartarian, Republican. (See also under GENERAL SELECTION.)

Bush Tartarian Large. Good flavour, sweet. Ripening June to July. Very small tree. Pollinators: Black Tartarian, Republican.

Vista Larger than Black Tartarian. Very good quality and flavour. Ripens end June.

Ontario 35033 Large. Similar to preceding.

Emperor Francis Large. Good quality. White. Sweet, rich. Ripens beginning July.

Valera Medium. Dark red. Very good quality, sweet. Ripens beginning July. Vigorous, productive.

Schmidt Large. Black. Firm, excellent flavour. Ripens beginning July. Moderate cropper.

Ulster Large. Dark red. Firm, excellent flavour. Similar to preceding, but more productive and fruit ripens a little later.

Windsor Medium. Almost black. Used for Maraschino cherries. Ripens middle July. Very vigorous, upright, productive.

Hudson Medium to large. Black. Very sweet, good flavour. Ripens end July. Fruit hangs well, keeps in good condition. Vigorous, spreading.

Bing Very large. Excellent flavour, sweet, juicy. Ripening June to July. Pollinators: Black Tartarian, Republican.

Royal Ann (Napoleon) Large, heart-shaped. Red. Ripening early July. Moderately vigorous, very productive.

Van Large, heart-shaped. Mahogany when fully ripe, very shiny. Pleasant flavour, sweet, moderately juicy. Ripening July. Very vigorous. Pollinators: Black Tartarian, Royal Ann, Republican.

Republican (Black Oregon) Medium. Dark red. Rich, juicy. Ripening late. Pollinators: Black Tartarian, Republican.

Lambert Large. Dark red. Rich flavour. Ripening very late. Pollinators: Black Tartarian, Republican.

EUROPEAN (CONTINENTAL) SELECTION

D'Annonay (French) Medium, roundish. Dark red. Sweet, juicy, slightly sub-acid, refreshing. Ripening very early. Moderate vigour. Good, regular cropper. Flowering early. Pollinators: Early Rivers, Noir de Guben.

Ramon Olive (French)   Very large, heart-shaped. Very dark cherry red streaked lighter red. Fair flavour, very juicy, sweet. Ripening mid-early season. Vigorous. Flowering early. Pollinators: Early Rivers, Noir de Guben.

Kernielse (Belgian)   Large, heart-shaped. Purplish black. Sweet, slightly bitter after-taste, good quality and aroma, juicy. Ripening mid-season. Moderate vigour. Flowering early. Pollinators: Noir de Guben, Merton Glory.

Flemish Red (Belgian)   Medium, roundish. Bright cherry red, shiny. Very juicy, sub-acid, agreeably sweet, good flavour, very refreshing. Ripening late. Moderate vigour. Flowering late. Self-compatible. Useful as pollinator for late-flowering sweet cherries.

Bigarreau Napoleon (German)   Large, heart-shaped. Bright red. Aromatic, rich flavour. Prolific cropper. Ripening semi-late. Moderate vigour. Flowering semi-early. Pollinators: Early Rivers, Ramon Oliva.

Abesse De Mouland (Belgian–Dutch)   Medium, heart-shaped. Purplish black. Very sweet but slightly bitter, agreeable flavour, moderately juicy. Ripening late. Commences bearing early in life, crops regularly. Flowering early. Pollinators: Early Rivers, Noir de Guben.

Hedelfinger Reisenkirsche (German)   Large, heart-shaped. Purplish cherry red, almost black. Very juicy, very good flavour and quality, very sweet. Ripening very late. Fairly vigorous. Flowering semi-late. Pollinators: Bigarreau Gaucher, Florence.

VARIETIES OF DUKE CHERRIES

May Duke   Medium, heart-shaped. Deep crimson. Flesh tender, rich. Ripening early mid-season. Valuable for its earliness. Excellent for bottling. Upright, compact, with short shoots. Exceptionally reliable cropper if pollinated. Recommended for pot culture. Flowering mid-period. Partly self-compatible. Pollinator: Morello.

Royal Duke   Large, heart-shaped. Deep crimson. Good flavour. Ripening late mid-season. Poor cropper. Flowering mid-period. Partly self-incompatible. Pollinator: Morello.

Archduke   Large, heart-shaped. Deep red turning to black. Rich, sub-acid. Ripening late. Flowering late. Pollinator: Morello.

Belle de Chatenay Large, heart-shaped. Rich crimson. Flesh yellowish red, juicy, pleasantly sweet-acid. Ripening very late. Vigorous. Flowering late. Self-incompatible. Pollinator: Morello.

Belle de Choisy Large, roundish. Bright crimson with dark spots. Ripening very late. Moderate growth. Flowering late. Pollinator: Morello.

Late Duke Large, heart-shaped. Bright red, juicy. Large stone. Ripening very late. Compact, well spurred. Excellent for pot culture. Flowering very late. Self-compatible.

VARIETIES OF ACID CHERRIES

Kentish Red Medium, roundish. Bright scarlet, with glazed appearance. Flesh pinkish yellow. Firmer than Morello, bottles well, excellent for tarts. Ripening mid-season. Good growth with plenty of young wood if kept well pruned. Flowering semi-late. Self-compatible.

Flemish Red Medium, roundish. Bright cherry red. Very juicy, sharp acid flavour. Ripening late. Very hardy. Reliable cropper. Flowering late. Self-compatible.

Morello Large, roundish. Deep red to black. Very juicy, suitable for dessert when fully ripe. Small stone. Ripening late. Vigorous, makes plenty of new wood. Hardy, prolific cropper. Considered the best acid variety. Flowering late. Self-compatible. Good pollinator for all cherries whose flowering period overlaps.

Coe's Carnation Medium, roundish. Deep red or black. Very juicy, cooks and bottles well. Ripening very late. Useful after Morello has finished. Fruits may hang till October when sited against north-facing wall. Weak growth. Flowering very late. Self-incompatible. Pollinator: Morello.

I I

CITRUS FRUITS

The citrus fruits—lemons, limes, mandarins, oranges, grapefruits—are generally classified as sub-tropical, although commercial cultivation exists also in near-tropical and warm temperate areas. However, except in a warm climate, such as in Florida, Spain, South Africa etc, they will need to be grown under glass for at least part of the year.

The best climate for the orange is one where there are well-defined summer and winter seasons and a moderate rainfall. If temperatures are not high enough, the fruits do not ripen properly and are insipid. But, although warmth is required for the fruit, the orange tree can develop considerable resistance to cold—in fact, more than any other citrus species, with the exception of the mandarin species (which includes tangerines, clementines and satsumas). However, although mandarin trees are slightly more resistant to cold than oranges, they need a higher temperature to perfect their fruit. In contrast, lemon and lime trees are less resistant to cold than orange trees, but their fruit does not need such a high temperature. The citrus tree most resistant to cold is the Seville orange or sour orange; the others—in descending degree of resistance—are mandarin, sweet orange, grapefruit, lemon and lime.

A daily average temperature lower than 60° F (16° C) will stop the growth of the Seville orange and mandarin; colder weather afterwards does not affect their growth to the same extent as in some of the other citrus species. The orange develops a resistance with temperatures just below 50° F (10° C). The lemon does not stop growth at these temperatures so readily; it will only do so when there have been two or three weeks with a night temperature near to freezing point and day temperatures too low to permit growth. If this has not happened and the temperature suddenly falls to 20° F (−7° C), the wood of the lemon tree may suffer severe injury. A period with temperatures 2° or 3° above freezing appears to increase the frost resistance of the lemon, but if it is damaged by frost it does not have the same ability to recover as does the orange tree. Flowers and very young fruits may be killed at a temperature of 29° F (−2° C). A temperature of 26° F (−3° C) may kill the shoot tips.

The lime is even more tender than the lemon, although its resistance to citrus scab makes its culture possible in areas of high rainfall, which are not suitable for the lemon. The citron is the least hardy; not only is it susceptible to damage by freezing temperatures, but the leaves and fruit are more liable to be injured by high temperatures than those of other citrus trees.

Although their cultivation is broadly similar, there are some differences in the size and character of the trees when growing under natural conditions:

Lemon and Lime trees grow more quickly than other citrus species and come into bearing earlier. They form small trees or shrubs 8–12ft tall. Branches spread outwards more than those of other species.

Sweet Orange grows 15–30ft tall. While the tree is young its branches bend downwards under the weight of their own leaves and fruit. Upward-growing shoots or branches develop from those bending downwards, giving the tree an upright appearance. It is slower than the lemon or grapefruit to commence bearing.

Seville Orange is a medium-sized tree and one of the hardiest of the citrus species. Seedlings are frequently used as rootstock for the sweet orange.

Grapefruit Generally smaller than the orange tree but there is variability between varieties. Commences blossoming early.

Mandarins, Tangerines, Clementines, Satsumas Branches of young trees do not bend downwards from the weight of their leaves as do those of the orange tree, but those bearing fruit may be nearly bent to the ground. Branches tend to be brittle and bending may cause them to split. Unlike the orange tree, these do not usually send up long shoots from small branchlets. The mandarin is a thickly branched and bushy tree, while the tangerine is more upright. The satsuma is dwarfish and spreading. The clementine makes a small tree.

Citron is a dwarf-like tree growing to 8–10ft. It has short, stiff branches and thick twigs.

Varieties are usually perpetuated by budding. The rootstock of other citrus species is frequently used to improve vigour and hardiness, as well as to increase resistance to disease. Some species are more satisfactory than others; lemon rootstock, for example, tends to reduce the flavour of sweet-orange fruits. Mandarin rootstock, on the other hand, does not cause any loss of flavour and the trees usually grow well. Sweet-orange seedlings give vigour and do not cause any loss in flavour of the fruit. A related species, *Poncirus trifoliata*, provides a rootstock with increased resistance to frost.

Amateur growers in citrus-growing areas will have a greater choice when buying stock, but even elsewhere some useful varieties on suitable rootstock are available. For pot cultivation, the younger the trees the better. The smallest pot that will take the roots of the tree should be used, but at three years old the tree will probably need an 11in pot and this will normally be adequate during the next two or three years. Citrus trees will grow in a variety of soils, ranging from those which are very sandy to heavy clay loams. For pot work, a good fibrous loam, to which has been added a good sprinkling of bone meal, should be used.

A characteristic of citrus trees is that they grow what are known as water sprouts. These vigorous growths occur on the upper side of spreading branchlets when they are only a year or two old. Water sprouts become much larger than the branches from which they are growing and out of proportion to the tree's symmetry. When they make the tree too tall or get in the way of other branches, they should be cut back to their point of origin. Except for those necessary to form the framework of the tree, any growing in the centre should be cut out, leaving the ones which start well out on the branches. These will develop fruiting wood and help to give the tree a more upright character.

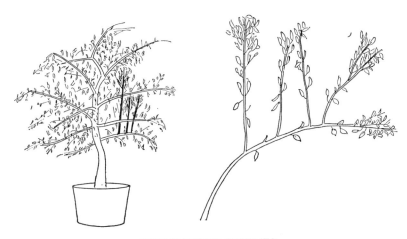

CITRUS WATER SPROUTS

Citrus trees do not require the same amount of pruning as deciduous fruit trees. Being evergreen they do not respond in the same way; consequently young trees cannot easily be trained to the form required. Some pruning of young *orange* trees is necessary in order to develop a good shape. This pruning should commence soon after the scion buds have started to grow. If left, it will not grow as a single stem like a deciduous tree, but will start branching close to the union with the rootstock, so that a very low-headed, bush-like tree is formed. All low shoots should, therefore, be removed as they appear. After the trees have started bearing fruit, there should be no regular pruning. The only pruning necessary is—in summer—the removal of the tips of straggling shoots and—in winter—any branches which may be crowding others, preventing light getting to the tree and fruit. Less pruning is needed for the *grapefruit* than for the *orange* because the tree has a much greater tendency to spread low and to send out fewer water sprouts. But when branches bend low they can be cut away. *Mandarins, tangerines, clementines and satsumas* require very little pruning except for the removal of any excessive growth. The *lemon* needs to be trained a little more than other citrus because its branches are more willowy and straggling, but no attempt should be made to develop a set number of branches. Shoots can be removed at any time during summer, but unwanted large branches, which may be crossing and touching one another—as well as any that have died—should be removed during the winter. Like the other citrus, the less the *lemon* is pruned the better.

There are also differences in the blossoming habits of citrus trees. If, for example, climatic conditions are favourable, lemon and lime trees will be blossoming more or less continuously throughout the year at each new growth flush. Fruit and flowers are borne by the tree at one and the same time. Their greatest amount of blossom will occur in the spring, especially when the winter has been too cold for much growth. The orange, on the other hand, will bear almost all its flowers during the spring. The mandarin, tangerine, clementine and satsuma will, when warm weather is to a large extent continuous, bear flowers at more than one time of the year and with a series of growth flushes, something like the lemon. The grapefruit tends to have most of its blossom at one season of the year, but with a little more out-of-season blossoming than the orange. Pollination does not normally cause a problem because the flowers are self-compatible and, even if fertilisation does not occur, the fruits develop parthenocarpically. Normally the number of flowers borne annually is far too many for a pot-tree to carry, if they all set fruit. When cross-pollination occurs, this may influence the number of seeds in the seedless varieties. Satsumas and clementine varieties are seedless, or nearly so, but when the flowers receive pollen from another variety they tend to produce more seeds.

Temperature is the most important influence in determining the time it takes for the fruit to mature, which may be seven to fourteen months. Water deficiency also affects the rate of growth and, if the tree suffers a continuous shortage of water, the fruit will be smaller than normal. Because the fruit may not be ripening until late in the year, there is a danger that it may be damaged if subjected to a temperature at freezing point. When temperatures are too low, or watering and humidity have been too high, the fruit may be insipid in taste. Oranges have a better flavour when grown at a mean temperature above 65° F (18° C). Satsumas, especially, are spoilt if temperatures are too low during the ripening period; when not properly matured, they are more acidic and have more of the flavour of the orange than the true aromatic mandarin flavour. In fact, low temperatures have greater influence on the flavour of all mandarin types than on that of sweet oranges. When matured in a temperature suitable for them, the segments are tender, soft, juicy, sweet and fragrant. Grapefruit, too, is more influenced by temperature than the orange and adequate warmth to ripen the fruit is required. If temperatures are too low, the fruit may be on the tree for fifteen to seventeen months, which means a second crop will be on the tree at the same time. This places a heavy strain on a pot-tree, and the fruit may in any case drop before it has reached its desired sweetness. Cool weather will not affect lemons and limes to the same extent; they

will develop their required acid flavour in temperatures too cool for the orange.

If the crop is too heavy for the tree, some of the fruit may be very small, but thinning the fruit does not greatly affect the size of the remainder. When citrus fruits are being harvested they should be snipped off with secateurs, care being taken not to bruise them or break the peel with a finger-nail or a spine of the tree, otherwise a mould will form on the fruit when stored. Mandarins, tangerines, clementines and satsumas show when they are mature by their rough and loose rind. With the lemon and lime, the best quality and best keeping fruit is that which makes a good size while still green. Such lemons and limes can be stored at 60° F (16° C) until the rind turns yellow. Citrus fruits can be left on the tree for considerable periods of time without deterioration; whenever possible this is the best method of storage. They are, however, subject to damage by wind and frost, and eventually they become overripe and unpalatable. The longer the fruit remains on the tree after maturity, the shorter the time it can be kept in storage.

The temperature requirements of citrus fruit means that in cool areas they will need to be under glass, at least part of the time. An orchard house, glass house or conservatory, which is suitable for peach cultivation, is ideal for citrus. They require plenty of light as well as ventilation and should be taken outdoors whenever the weather is warm enough. For lemons and limes the temperature in the house should not fall below 40° F (4° C) at night and 45° F (7° C) by day. In general, spring temperatures should not be less than 50° F (10° C), rising to 70° F (21° C) by May. Mid-summer temperatures should not rise above 85° F (29° C). If there is very strong sunlight some shading of the glass may be necessary to prevent scorching. A potted orange tree can be taken into your home for special occasions, but unless it is in a very light room it should not be kept there too long.

NUTRITIONAL DEFICIENCIES

As with all fruit trees, citrus are liable to suffer from and show the effects of nutritional deficiencies. Essential for normal development are the following:

NITROGEN

Deficiency will cause weak growth. There is apt to be dying of branchlets, reduced blossom and dropping of flowers and young fruits. Citrus trees may show these symptoms quite severely when in soil that is able to supply other kinds of fruit trees with sufficient nitrogen. Nitrogen is needed to produce the spring and early summer growth flushes which are essential to give leaf surface and enable the tree to bear the subsequent fruit. Nitrogen should be applied about a month before blossom time.

PHOSPHORUS
Symptoms caused by a deficiency of phosphorus may be a weak spring flush, producing small leaves of a dull green colour. Fruit will have thicker, rougher rinds, a low percentage of juice and a loose, open core.

POTASSIUM
Fruit will be smaller than normal but of good quality. Twisting, curling and puckering of the leaves may occur if the deficiency is acute.

CALCIUM
Symptoms will be small dead spots along the margins of the leaves, with premature shedding of the leaves and dying back of the shoots. There is also weak, stubby root growth. This deficiency will not normally occur with pot cultivation.

MAGNESIUM
In winter the leaves will become a pale colour; much of the leaf may turn yellow and fall early. The fruit crop is small and trees suffering from this deficiency have a tendency towards alternate bearing.

IRON
Pale green and flecks of yellow show between the dark green veins. With an acute deficiency the whole leaf, with the exception of the vein, may be yellow and the tree is weak.

DISEASES

BROWN ROT GUMMOSIS (FOOT ROT) *(Phytophthora citrophthora; P. parasitica)*
This disease occurs in all citrus growing areas. Wet soil and poor drainage favours the growth of the fungus. The commonest symptoms are the bark lesions and exudation of gum. The lesions may extend upwards for several inches, killing the bark and staining the wood a darkish colour. In dry weather the bark shrinks and splits. Under the soil, injury to the roots may be so serious that it kills the tree. Other factors, such as nematodes, may be responsible, but examination of the roots will show whether the disease is present. If healthy feeder roots are found only in the upper part of the root system, and are sparse or absent at lower levels, it is almost certain that

H

Phytophthora species are present. If feeder roots have sloughing bark, or larger roots have spots on them, both *P. citrophthora* and *P. parasitica* can be suspected.

Infection of the crown roots can be treated by removing the soil to expose the crown and roots, allowing them to dry. Dead bark can be cut out and painted with disinfectant. Soil used for intensive citrus cultivation and suspected of being infected should be fumigated. One of the most effective means of protection is to use rootstock, such as Seville orange and *Poncirus*, which is resistant to the disease. Sweet orange is particularly susceptible.

LEAF SCAB *(Elsinoe fawcetti)*
Lemon trees are highly susceptible to this fungus, which is one of the reasons why they are little grown commercially in Florida or other rainy districts. The disease occurs on all citrus species.

Irregular, corky, wart-like lesions appear on both the upper and under surfaces of the leaves. These can be mistaken for symptoms of bacterial canker, but newly formed lesions are not surrounded by a yellowish halo. Young shoots and fruits are also affected. The disease can be effectively reduced with lime-sulphur sprays.

WITHER-TIP *(Gloesporium sp.)*
Wither-tip affects almost all kinds of citrus, causing a loss in productiveness. Trees that are grafted, weak, or exposed to frost are the most susceptible, whereas those grown from seedlings are usually more resistant. Shoots affected by frost become infected and turn brown at the apex. The dead and living portion is clearly defined, as the 'die-back' proceeds along the twig. Older shoots have a silvery-grey appearance.

The incidence of wither-tip can be reduced by removing the affected shoots and spraying with copper fungicides in spring. Building up healthy trees with fertilisers will help to avoid deficiencies of minor elements, frost injury and incompatible rootstocks. All dead wood etc should be removed from the vicinity of the grove.

CANKER *(Xanthomonas citri)*
This is a serious bacterial disease of citrus. The first symptoms appear on young leaves as small, bright yellow spots; these develop into small eruptions which are a whitish, pale yellow in humid temperatures but more brown when conditions are arid. Around the margin of the eruptions the leaf is a paler green than normal, and this develops into a distinctive yellow

halo. The number of spots or eruptions shows the severity of the infection. As the disease progresses, lesions appear on the branches and trunk; on the branches they reach a diameter of 2–2¾in and on the trunk nearly 6in. Fruit from a diseased tree show similar symptoms to those on the leaves, except that the yellow halo around the spot is less marked. On grapefruit and orange the lesions, like small craters or depressions, are about ⅛in in diameter, but on lemon and lime they are much smaller.

Sensitivity varies greatly between the different kinds of citrus, depending on the climatic conditions of the area in which they are grown. In Florida, grapefruit is the most sensitive, followed by the orange, lime and then lemon. In New Zealand, lemon varieties, such as Ponderosa, Eureka and Lisbon, are the most sensitive. Some defence against the disease can therefore be obtained by choosing varieties with the most resistance in your area. Attention should always be given to hygiene, such as removing and burning all dead or diseased fruit, wood and leaves. Control can also be obtained with chemicals.

VIRUS DISEASES

Numerous viruses affect citrus trees, in some districts causing considerable loss. Seeds from virus-infected trees seldom carry the disease, so that a strain free from the virus can be propagated from a nucellar seedling. The most important of the known virus diseases are:

TRISTEZA (QUICK DECLINE)

This virus is spread by *Aphis* vectors, such as *Aphis spiraecola* and *A. gossypii* in North America. Some trees affected by the virus decline and die quickly while others linger on for years. Some citrus rootstocks are more susceptible than others. Seville orange rootstock of infected sweet orange trees, for example, cannot make enough growth to supply water to the top. The trees then show rapid weakening and dying back of the tops. On the other hand, when sweet orange is the rootstock of sweet orange, the virus is practically harmless. In those districts where the disease is prevalent the least susceptible rootstocks should be used.

PSOROSIS

This is a group name for certain virus diseases with somewhat similar symptoms. The most conspicuous symptom is the formation of concavities of various sizes under the bark of the trunk and larger limbs. The bark scales or cracks, and gum exudes. The disease develops slowly but after about five or six years the bark is so injured, as well as the wood of part of the trunk or limbs, that the tree is weakened, becomes unfruitful and eventually dies. There is no known cure.

As far as is known, the virus is not transmitted by vectors but seems to be carried through grafting. Control is by propagating only from trees which do not carry the disease.

XYLOPOROSIS

This again is a virus which appears to be transmitted through grafting from infected trees. The wood becomes pitted, with the bark growing into the pits. Leaves become smaller, growth weaker and the branches slowly die. Mandarin hybrids or mandarin varieties used as rootstock are most susceptible to the disease.

PESTS

NEMATODES

Several species of nematodes or eel worms attack citrus trees in various areas of the world. The citrus nematode *(Tylenchulus semipenetrans)* occurs in all the citrus growing areas, but has a very small host range and is not commonly found except in areas where citrus is present. Infestation of the roots causes what is known as 'slow decline'. The most common rootstocks of citrus are susceptible to this nematode, but the trifoliate orange *(Poncirus trifoliate)* is highly resistant. In Florida both the citrus nematode and the burrowing nematode *(Radophulus semilis)* cause considerable trouble, but the two are very seldom found in the same grove. The burrowing nematode causes 'spreading decline' and is confined to very sandy soils where there is little or no organic matter. The symptoms are typical of decline caused by other root pests, but the decline may start with one or two trees and slowly spread throughout the grove at the rate of one or two trees a year.

These pests should give no trouble in the non-citrus growing areas, but in citrus growing areas soil for pot compost should not be taken from places where citrus have been grown. If such soil has to be used, it should be fumigated. In the USA, nursery stock can be purchased which is certified free of certain nematode pests.

CITRUS RED MITE *(Panonychus citri)*

This mite, called purple mite in Florida, is one of the most important pests of citrus. It is especially serious in California. The leaves of infected trees become speckled, turn brown and fall. The fruit also becomes discoloured. Control is with chemicals.

CITRUS RUST MITE *(Phyllocoptruta oleivora)*
This mite causes similar damage but is more serious in Florida, where it damages mainly oranges, but also attacks grapefruit, lemons and limes. Control is with chemicals.

CITRUS BUD MITE *(Aceria shelooni)*
Occurring mainly in California, it feeds on the blossom and buds of lemon, less frequently on other citrus. Fruit, leaves and twigs become deformed.

CITRUS WHITEFLY *(Dialeurodes citri)*
This pest occurs in most citrus growing areas. The main trouble is caused by the honey dew it secretes, on which 'sooty mould' fungus thrives. The fungus is entirely superficial but, due to the thickness of its growth, the photosynthesis of the tree is impaired; its life is shortened, while the fruits become unsightly. If the whitefly population becomes heavy, chemical control will be necessary.

SCALE INSECTS
A considerable number of scale insects give trouble, particularly the California red scale *(Aonidiella aurantii)*, which is one of the most serious enemies of citrus trees in the south-western United States. It attacks leaves, wood and fruit. Individual scales can be scraped off.

CITRUS THRIP *(Slirtothrip citri)*
This is a serious pest in California, but does not occur in Florida. The insects feed on buds, new growth and young fruit by scraping away the outer tissues and sucking up the juices. Infested trees grow slowly and the fruit shows a distinctive ring-like scar. Thrips winter in the egg stage on the leaves and stem. Control is with chemicals.

VARIETIES OF ORANGES

NAVELS

Washington Navel   Large, with a rather thick rind. The pulp is as rich in flavour as any other sweet orange, but not one of the juiciest. It is usually seedless. In California, in some of the warmest parts, it ripens in time for Christmas.

Several mutants of Washington Navel have produced new varieties, some of which are listed below:

Little Bahia (Bahianinha)   Fruit is smaller than Washington with a less pronounced navel.

Thompson Navel   Smooth rind; ripens earlier than Washington, but lacks a good flavour.

Texas Navel   Appears to set better crops than Washington in south Texas but not in California.

Navelina (Dalman) (Smith's Early Navel)   Ripens early, about the same time as Thompson. The orange-red rind is very attractive.

Atwood Navel (Atwood Early)   Similar to Washington, but ripens very early.

Gillette Navel   Similar to Washington, but ripens a little earlier.

Skaggs Bonanza Navel   Exceptionally early variety.

Tulegold Navel   Early ripening variety. Tree produces early in life.

Frost Washington   Ripens a little later than Washington.

COMMON ORANGES

Late Valencia   This variety, with Washington Navel, constitutes the majority of sweet oranges throughout the world. Varieties may in fact be Valencia, but are grown under different names in the Mediterranean basin and other parts of the world. It is a variety very important in Florida and its economic value is in its late ripening. It also has an abundance of richly flavoured juice and few seeds.

Pineapple   The product of a Florida seedling. Excellent flavour but rather seedy. The tree is very productive.

Homassa   Another Florida seedling. Very rich flavour, but again rather seedy.

Jaffa   A very richly flavoured variety, which has fewer seeds than the previous two.

Shamouti   Very high quality and almost seedless.

Parson Brown   Early variety. Important in Florida, where it possesses a good flavour by autumn.

Marrs Early Very popular in Texas. Fairly sweet, moderately juicy, moderately seedy.

Casa Grande (Oasis) Popular in Texas.

BLOOD ORANGES
Blood oranges are those that have red pigment in the pulp. Grown more in the Mediterranean basin than the United States, they have a sweet, pleasant flavour. Some of the best are: Ruby, Maltaise and Egyptian.

MANDARINS
These include satsumas, tangerines and clementines. The range of fruit and tree characteristics is wide. In Japan, satsumas are divided into two groups: Wase, whose fruits ripen early, have large juice sacs and more tender pulp; Common, with later fruits, and a little coarser. The clones of the two groups give a continuous supply of these aromatic seedless fruits from the beginning of October till December.

Owari This is grown extensively along the coast of the Gulf of Mexico from Louisiana to North Florida. It ripens from October to Christmas or later, depending on the climate, but soon becomes overripe if left too long on the tree. Medium to large, juicy, practically seedless. In a warm climate, such as in the Gulf states, it is sweet and pleasant; where temperatures are cooler, it is too acid.

Dancy (Dancy Tangerine) Medium-sized fruit. Rind deep orange-red, almost scarlet. Flesh deep orange, of excellent quality, sweeter than Owari, but has numerous seeds. Tree large and vigorous for a mandarin. In California, it is at its best in the interior, but is cold resistant and can be grown under varying conditions.

Clementine (Algerian Tangerine) Medium size, excellent quality and flavour, few seeds. It can be left on the tree longer than most mandarin varieties. Unless grown with another variety for pollination, it will usually bear light crops. It will develop a good flavour in districts too cool in summer for most other mandarins to do so. The tree is medium in size.

King Large fruit with a rather thick, rough rind. It ripens later than most other mandarins. The flavour is very pleasant when grown in fairly high temperatures, but where these are low it is too acid. The tree is strong growing, but tends to over-bear and then alternate in its cropping.

Kara A cross between a satsuma and King. Large fruit for a mandarin but fewer seeds than King. Juicy, very aromatic, generally pleasant. Vigorous, spreading, fairly large tree.

Kinnow A cross between King and Willow Leaf (a small, tight-skinned, sweet, spicy fruit). Medium, yellowish-orange fruit. Rich and less acid flavour than Kara, but rather seedy. Vigorous, upright.

Carvalhal Very early variety, but can be left on the tree till January. Fruits very seedy.

Ortanique Very large with distinctive flavour. Rind rather adherent to the flesh. Fairly seedy.

Murcott (Meune Shui Shang) Very important variety in Florida. Very early. Smooth rind, rather adherent to the flesh. Good flavour, but numerous seeds.

Malvasio and *Anana* Two similar varieties. Very early. Medium. Rind rather adherent to the flesh. Very juicy, highly aromatic. Moderately seedy.

Fairchild A cross between a clementine and a tangelo. Ripens very early. Good quality, but numerous seeds. Suitable for southern California and Arizona.

TANGELOS
Tangelos are the result of crossing mandarins and grapefruit. They are highly flavoured, and have characteristics of both parents.

Minneola A cross between Duncan grapefruit and Dancy mandarin. Large fruit. Rind smooth, orange-red, peels well. Rich tart flavour, few seeds.

Orlando Similar cross to preceding. Medium to large. Slightly rough, orange rind, rather adherent to the flesh. Mild, sweet flavour, many seeds.

Pearl A cross between Imperial grapefruit and Willow Leaf mandarin. Medium. Nearly smooth rind, yellow, rather adherent to the flesh. Mild sweet flavour, many seeds.

TANGORS
Tangors are a cross between the mandarin tangerine and the sweet orange.

Temple Large. Slightly rough rind, highly coloured red-orange, peels fairly well. Tart to sweet flavour, many seeds. High temperature needed to bring fruit to perfection.

GRAPEFRUIT

Marsh Large, averaging 4in diameter. Thin rind. Grapefruit grown in cool areas is of poor quality and this variety is no exception. In temperatures, such as those of the warm interior areas of California, the pulp of Marsh is sweet and pleasant. It is seedless or nearly so. The fruit may be allowed to remain on the tree for four months after it reaches maturity. Vigorous, bears heavily.

Duncan Very similar to Marsh but seedier.

Ruby Rosy red flesh. Red blush on the rind. Otherwise similar to Marsh.

Webb Similar to Ruby, but with more seeds.

LEMONS

Eureka Usually bears fruit all the year round, where temperatures are right for it. Medium. Rind smooth. Almost seedless. High quality. Tree small, almost thornless, highly productive.

Lisbon Similar to Eureka, but matures most of its fruit in the autumn, although some will be borne throughout the year. Vigorous, thorny, more resistant to cold than Eureka.

Meyer This lemon carries fruit through most of the year. Similar to the ordinary varieties, except that it is almost orange in colour. Very juicy, a little less acid than other varieties, pleasant aroma. Dwarfish, sturdy, very productive, more resistant to cold than other lemon trees. Known to carry the Tristeza virus, so needs care.

Admopoulos An 'ever-bearer' with very juicy, very acid fruit.

LIMES

Bearss A very popular lime. Bears some fruit during most of the year. Medium to large, up to 2in diameter. Excellent quality, rich lime flavour, very juicy, very acid, practically seedless. Medium, upright, vigorous, practically thornless.

Mexican Several varieties are included under this name. Small, about 1in diameter. Rind thin. Pulp greenish yellow, highly acid, juicy, strong rich lime flavour. Dwarfish, almost bush-like, with fine twigs, small leaves, many small thorns. Susceptible to frost.

CITRUS VARIETIES IN BRITAIN

Embiguo (Navel Orange)   Large, good quality. Pulp pale orange.

St Michael's (Common Orange)   Thin skin, very good flavour.

Jaffa (Common Orange)   Very large, few seeds.

Valencia Late (Common Orange)   Large. Thin skin, good flavour. Vigorous, productive.

Malta (Blood Orange)   Medium. Pulp stained deep crimson. Thin skin, delicious flavour.

Satsuma (Mandarin)   Very hardy, good cropper.

Paradisei (Grapefruit)   Large, oval. Very good cropper.

Foster (Grapefruit)   Large. Pink pulp.

Imperial (Lemon)   Large. Very good aroma. Vigorous.

Bigaradia (Seville Orange)   Used for marmalade.

12

FIGS

A warm dry climate is the most favourable for the fig, but it will do quite
well in cooler and wetter areas and is, in fact, often cultivated where fairly
low temperatures are experienced. It can be grown in southern Victoria,
Australia; in the open as a standard tree in the south of England, and in
the USA, with winter protection, as far north as New York City. In cool
districts, however, it must be sited where it will obtain maximum sunshine
and warmth.

Although the fig can withstand a temperature as low as $10°$ F ($-12°$ C)
during its period of dormancy and as a mature tree, it is highly susceptible
to frost when it is young and can be injured even when dormant. The new
young shoots on a tree can be damaged if the temperature falls below
$30°$ F ($-1°$ C). Consequently young trees and others just breaking into
new growth should not be left in positions exposed to freezing temperatures.

The fig will tolerate a wide range of soils, but the size and quality of the
fruit will generally be better on well-drained loams. Acid soils are unsuitable. Wood growth needs to ripen or become mature otherwise it will not
bear fruit. In cool climates, therefore, the tree must be thoroughly
exposed to the sun throughout the day and there must be a good circulation
of air to help the branches to ripen. In climates where the wood does not
ripen easily, it can be helped to do so by restricting its roots; an effective
means of doing this is to grow the tree in a pot. In a rich soil and left to
itself the tree grows quickly, becomes lanky and has excessive unripened
wood. In an alkaline soil it remains smaller, the fruit develops well and
has a high sugar content; too much alkalinity, though, may cause the
leaves to fall. The tree can be kept small by restricting its roots in a
9–12in pot.

Pot cultivation of the fig can be practised indoors or out and there can be a combination of both. A young bush tree may at first need a 6–8in pot, but the smallest size needed to take its roots should be used. Good drainage is essential. A suitable pot compost would be seven parts good loam, three parts sharp sand, three parts peat; to each bushel can be added $4\frac{1}{2}$oz hoof and horn meal, $2\frac{1}{2}$oz sulphate of potash. The tree should be potted in the autumn and repotted each following autumn. Some of the old compost should be shaken from its roots before repotting into new. Placed outdoors on a patio or roof garden, it fulfils a decorative function as well as bearing fruit.

Fig trees are propagated from cuttings which root quite readily. The cuttings should be short, jointed shoots of the previous year's growth, about 8–12in long and with 1in of older wood at the base. They need to be cut in October or November and inserted 6in deep in a warm, sheltered position. To protect them from frost, they should be covered with peat, straw or leaves. When all danger from frost has passed, uncover them but leave them until the following autumn when they can be lifted and potted. It is also possible to propagate the fig by layering of the branches of a tree and this should be done in the summer. Bend a branch down to the ground, covering it with a few inches of soil and securing it firmly with a peg. By the autumn it should have rooted and can then be detached from its parent. It can, of course, be bent down directly into a pot, but the soil should be kept moist. Propagation can also be from suckers of mature trees, but this is not the best way because they very often inherit a tendency to sucker freely.

To build up a tree with a good framework, harder pruning is at first required, but later pruning should be kept to a minimum in order to encourage fruiting. When a maiden tree is potted, it should be headed back to about 18in from soil level. The aim should be to develop it into an open bush, with a strong framework being built up in the first three or four years. Subsequent pruning should aim at maintaining a compact, well-shaped head which is not too dense, but in hot climates it should not be so open that the branches are exposed to hot summer sun. Although the main pruning can be done in March, any buds or young shoots likely to cause overcrowding should subsequently be removed. Any lateral shoots that are growing too long can be pinched or snipped off at the sixth leaf. The fig tree extends it growth from the terminal buds and its old wood becomes bare. Consequently another aim must be to maintain as many one- and two-year-old shoots as possible—by cutting back some of the branches to suitably placed joints; this should be done in the autumn as soon as the leaves have fallen. The fig breaks into new growth very easily from invisible, dormant buds, so that, if a branch is cut back to a suitably placed stub, new shoots will come from it the following spring.

In warm climates and under glass the tree will produce two crops of fruit, or even three. The first crop comes on wood of the previous season's growth and the second or main crop on wood of the current season's growth. When cultivating under these conditions, the aim of pruning should be towards developing plenty of new growth to ensure maximum yields from the second crop; to achieve this it may be necessary to prune a little more heavily in the winter. Strong growth should be headed back, and weak and crossing laterals removed. This winter pruning will drastically reduce the first crop of fruit, but greatly increase the second or main crop.

In cool climates and when the trees remain outdoors, only one crop must be expected. During summer the thick, rather fleshy, young shoots will bear embryo figs and growth buds. Some of the small figs may not start growing until late in the season and will not have matured before the onset of cold weather. At the commencement of winter the tree will be left with these small partly developed figs but also, mainly on the tips of the one-year-old shoots, there will be dormant embryo figs and growth buds. If these embryo figs are protected by a wall or by some other suitable means, and provided the winter is not too severe, they will develop into fruit the following year (they will then be borne on two-year-old wood). As these fruits develop, new growth will continue above them. With these

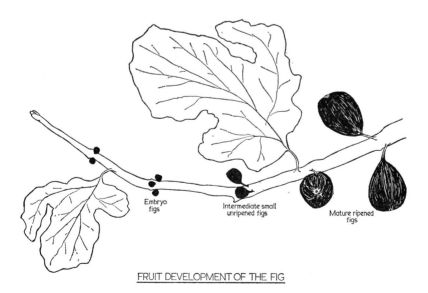

Embryo figs

Intermediate small unripened figs

Mature ripened figs

FRUIT DEVELOPMENT OF THE FIG

growth and fruiting conditions under a cool climate, the aim of pruning must be to reduce any wasting caused by late formed fruit which fails to ripen before the cold weather and, at the same time, to encourage the embryo figs to develop next year on two-year-old wood.

Embryo figs are more likely to survive the winter if they are borne at the base and not the top of the one-year-old shoots. Embryo figs can be stimulated to grow nearer the base of the shoots if those occurring in the axils of the leaves, and which can be seen from mid-summer onwards, are rubbed off. Some growers pinch the shoots back at five leaves about the end of August or beginning of September; this induces the formation of embryo figs which will ripen the following season. However, if the shoots are pinched back too soon, this will cause a too early development of figs which will not stand the winter. The fruits which are to ripen the next season must be not much larger than a pea at the commencement of the winter. All others should be removed as this will encourage further figs to be produced which will stand the winter and develop the following year.

In warm countries or when a heated orchard house is available, the aim is usually to obtain two crops—the first in June or July and the second by the end of September. If the tree commences its new growth in February, it should fruit in June. If, however, it is started into growth in December in a temperature of 65° F (18° C), rising to 80° F (26° C) in later months, a first crop is obtained in March, a second in July and a third in October. It must be given the maximum light possible, during the dark winter months and, should growth stand still, it can be encouraged with a light dressing of nitrogenous fertiliser.

Pruning for three crops of fruit is much simpler if the following is remembered: the first crop develops from the small embryo figs which remain dormant during the winter and until new growth commences; the second comes on the young shoots which grow during the spring, while the first crop is maturing; the third comes on young shoots which grow while the second crop is maturing. While the third crop is maturing, embryo figs will again be forming at the tips of shoots and, because these will provide the fruits for the next first or spring crop, care must be taken not to cut the tips unnecessarily.

As soon as it is possible to decide which of the third-crop fruit will ripen and which are so small that they will not bud but will remain dormant during the winter, all those in between these two stages should be removed. Then, having decided which shoots to leave to give a satisfactory crop, the remainder may be removed by disbudding and the others stopped beyond the fruit. When a tree is producing three crops of fruit a year, care should be taken not to exhaust it by over-production or there will be poor fruiting in following years.

Whether indoors or out the tree should get enough water during the summer months to ensure that growth continues without any check. Under cool conditions, until a tree breaks into growth in the spring, it will require little moisture but, when growing, water must never be lacking. In a warm house where three crops a year are being produced, it should never at any time be short of moisture or the fruit will shrivel and drop. During periods when fruit is ripening, the supply of water must be reduced otherwise the fruit may split. If splitting does occur the house should be given more ventilation and the floor dampened instead of syringing the foliage. At other times when the weather is warm the foliage should be syringed daily and under very hot conditions it will help if wet sacking is tied around the pots.

Figs will grow well with very little fertiliser. Although soil fertility should be kept at average levels, an excessive application should be avoided. A good humus level should be maintained with mulches and included in the compost when repotting, but too much nitrogen will cause excessive growth and delay ripening of the fruit, which will also become susceptible to splitting.

When about the size of a pea, the fruits may be thinned so that, on average, not more than three are left to a shoot. When mature, the fruit is soft to the touch and, when really ripe, a drop of nectar appears at the 'eye' or small opening at the base of the fruit and the sides show signs of splitting. Fruit should be as near to dead ripe as handling will permit and, if a fig has not ripened on the tree, it will not be suitable for eating. It can be harvested by twisting it at the neck or by cutting. In Turkey and California the best *dried* figs are those which are allowed to become practically dried on the tree but this can only be done in warm climates. Some of the fruit will fall and these must be picked up at once, spread out on trays and allowed to dry in the sun. Generally, fallen figs are inferior to those that have dried on the tree.

DISEASES

Figs are comparatively free of disease.

CANKER *(Phomopsis cinerescens)*
This may cause the death of an affected branch, the bark of which is roughened at the area of the canker and often resembles the markings of an oyster shell. The disease, which starts at pruning wounds and snags,

may girdle whole branches. In damp weather the spores of the fungus are released from whitish tendrils scattered over the surface of the canker. Diseased branches should be cut out below the canker and no snags left. All cuts and wounds should be painted. All tools, such as saw and knife, should be sterilised with disinfectant before being used again. All diseased wood must be burned.

GREY MOULD *(Botyritis cinerea)*
This fungus will sometimes infect young shoots and fruit. The young shoots wilt and the fruits rot and fall, although sometimes remaining on the tree during the winter to produce spores the following spring. This is a common fungus easily recognised by its greyish, felt-like appearance. All dead shoots and fruit should be removed.

PESTS

These are not a serious menace, but in some years it may be necessary to apply insecticides to control thrips, mites and dried fruit beetle. White fly, which may cause the foliage to wilt and curl, and red spider, which cause silvery leaves and premature defoliation, can give trouble in the orchard house.

VARIETIES

Fig varieties are classified into four groups:

SMYRNA VARIETIES

These produce the best quality fruits, but contain female flowers which must be pollinated. When fecundity is achieved, the seeds develop and the fruit swells. Much of the characteristic and superior flavour of these varieties is caused by the oil in the seeds. Because the Smyrna figs need to be pollinated by the minute fig wasp *(Blastophaga grossorum)* which lives only in warm climates, these kinds are not suitable for cooler areas. It is, however, possible to cause an artificial setting of the fruit by using a hormone spray which is marketed in USA. The spray is applied at the normal time of pollination, which corresponds to the time when shoot growth has ceased and the leaves are fully expanded. Fruit set by this means are comparable in size, colour and sugar content to pollinated figs, but are seedless.

ADRIATIC (COMMON FIG) VARIETIES

These develop without needing female flowers to be pollinated and can, consequently, be cultivated in those areas where it is too cool for the fig wasp to live. The fruits have no seeds, but hollow shells without the inner kernel and embryo.

SAN PEDRO VARIETIES

These have the pollinating characteristics of both the Smyrna and Adriatic kinds. The first crop at the beginning of the season occurs without pollination, but for the second crop the flowers must be pollinated.

CAPRI FIGS (WILD FIGS)

These are primitive kinds from which the others have developed. They produce both male and female flowers, but the fruit is practically inedible.

Except for the Smyrna and San Pedro varieties, the first crop is best for fresh use as the fruits are larger and juicier. If, because of pruning, the first crop is lost, the second crop may be as good as the first in size and quality.

SELECTED VARIETIES

White Adriatic Medium to large, round to pear shape, usually green, sometimes developing purplish tinge. Flesh varies from light pink to deep red. Good flavour.

I

White Marseilles Medium. Pale greenish white; white flesh. Sweet, rich. Very useful for cool houses. Fairly hardy.

White Ischia Small. Purplish black; red flesh. Sweet, juicy, good flavour. Hardy.

Brown Turkey (known as Magnolia in Texas) Medium to large. Purplish brown with pink to brown flesh. Rich, sweet. Vigorous.

Brunswick Medium. Reddish brown; flesh amber. Good, sweet. Good cropper.

Cape White Small. Yellowish green; flesh creamy white. Attractive yellow colour makes it popular for jam. Compact, vigorous.

White Genoa Large. Amber yellow; flesh amber tinged with pink. Sweet. Useful for cooler districts.

Negro Largo (or San Pedro Black etc) Large. Purple to black; flesh and juice red. Sweet, juicy. Good for a warm house.

Mission Medium to large. Black; red flesh. Excellent quality. Popular in central California fresh or dried, or for jam.

Calymyrna Large. Lemon yellow; flesh amber. Excellent for all uses, but first crop insipid. Good cropper. *Must be cross-pollinated with the Capri fig.*

13

GOOSEBERRIES

Gooseberries excel in cool areas and are fairly tolerant of light shade. They can be placed under trees as they dislike intense sunshine but need shelter from cold winds. For extra late ripening they can be put against north and east walls, provided they are not exposed to cold winds, and for early ripening they can be placed in a partially sunny position or the orchard house. Although good shelter is an asset, it should be remembered that hedgerows and trees also encourage troublesome birds, such as the bull-finch.

Gooseberries—the first of the soft fruits—flower very early in the spring; in some years the blossom starts to open by the middle of March. Both the flowers and the young fruit are easily damaged. It is important not to put them in frosty places during the flowering period. In all but the lightest frost young berries are destroyed. Typical damage seen after a late, light frost is a brown mark on the berries, as though they had been scorched. The damaged area fails to develop and distorted berries are formed.

Gooseberries grow in most soils, but if the soil is too poor growth may become weak, while heavy clays may cause a disease susceptibility. Also, although they have a great need for moisture, drainage must be satis-factory. The potting compost should therefore be enriched with humus.

Propagation is from hard-wood cuttings. For the best result, well-ripened, one-year-old wood should be taken from healthy, vigorous bushes just before the leaves fall. These cuttings should be trimmed into 12in lengths and any thin soft wood at the top of the shoots discarded. As they should be grown with a clear leg, the buds and spines are normally removed from the lower part of the cutting, leaving only four or five buds at the top part. This is the same procedure as with red currants. However, gooseberry cuttings do not root as readily as currants and it has been found

FRUIT SPURS

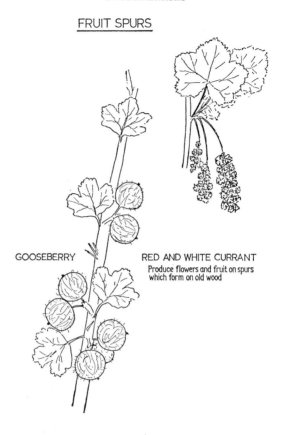

GOOSEBERRY

RED AND WHITE CURRANT
Produce flowers and fruit on spurs
which form on old wood

that they root more easily if all the buds are left. If all the buds are left, the lower shoots which form will have to be removed from the leg when the yearling is lifted. Cuttings should be inserted firmly into the soil, making sure that they are not in air pockets, and leaving 3–4in above the ground. Next autumn the yearlings should be lifted and potted. Any unwanted buds and suckers should be carefully rubbed off to give them good, clear legs. They can then be trained in the standard, bush or other artificial forms.

Once the desired shape has been attained, they can be pruned in two ways. They can be spur pruned and, although this reduces the crop, the size of the individual fruit is increased. Spur pruning may be used to prevent overcropping. Alternatively, they can be light pruned. By this method, the bush is merely thinned out and kept vigorous, in order to support a heavy crop with manuring; but pot restriction will tend to limit maximum results.

When spur pruning, the leaders are pruned hard, leaving about 4–8in of new wood, depending on vigour (the longer if vigorous). Annual leader pruning is essential to keep the bush growing vigorously, but this should not be carried to the extreme because excessive pruning results in strong unproductive growth. The side shoots should always be cut back to leave one good bud, thus gradually building up the fruit spurs. Some varieties are of a very drooping habit and the leaders of these should always be cut to an inward and upward pointing bud. Others have the habit of sending up suckers from the base and these must always be removed.

With light pruning, only a proportion of the side shoots are cut back to one bud, the others being left unpruned. The number of side shoots cut back to one bud will depend on the amount of new wood required for the next year. Fruit is borne along shoots formed in the previous year and also on spurs on the old wood. Leaders are only lightly cut back. The centre of the bush is kept fairly open to make picking easier. Crossing, crowded and weak shoots are cut and thinned out.

Potassium deficiency is the most common nutritional trouble and can be detected by a brown or grey marginal leaf scorch. Potassium is best given either in the form of wood-ash or potassium sulphate. Artificial fertilisers containing chloride should be avoided, as gooseberries can be damaged by them. Provided they have plenty of potassium, they will respond well to organic manure. Heavy applications of nitrogen, such as dried blood, fish manure, sulphate of ammonia, should be avoided as these cause excessive growth; the young shoots are then apt to break off in the wind and give a susceptibility to American gooseberry mildew. Magnesium deficiency may sometimes occur if a light soil is being used, particularly if the potassium level is too high. Symptoms of this deficiency are broad red marginal bands on the leaves, fading to pale yellow or cream. Epsom salts is a good source of magnesium.

The flowers of the gooseberry open a few days before those of the black currant. They are self-fertile, but cold winds hinder the activity of the honey bee and lessen the pollinating work of flies and other insects.

The first gooseberries can be picked when they are just over $\frac{1}{2}$in in diameter and still hard and green. These 'thinnings' can be used for tarts, jams etc. The berries should be picked with a quick jerk as this breaks off the stalk without damaging the spur. The colour of the berries does not develop until just before nearing maturity of ripeness and it is best to thin out the green berries in the centre of the bush which are unlikely to attain their full colour. The usual tendency is to pick gooseberries too early. Although if left on the bushes too long they will probably split, they

133

should, for dessert purposes, remain long enough to attain their full perfection. Their true colour and sweetness is seldom appreciated.

DISEASES

AMERICAN POWDERY MILDEW (*Sphaerotheca mors-uvae*)

This, the most serious disease of gooseberries, is called 'American' to distinguish it from European powdery mildew, which is much less destructive. American powdery mildew occurs in most countries of the north temperate zone, where the *Ribes* species are grown, as well as the south temperate zone. It is particularly troublesome in Britain and continental Europe.

The lower parts of the bush usually show the first symptoms from April onwards, when white fungal threads begin to completely cover small shoots. White powdery patches appear also on the leaves and berries, the production of large quantities of spores (conida) giving them a powdery appearance. These spores are readily dispersed and, under conditions favourable to their germination, fresh infection occurs on the growth throughout the season. The patches on the leaves enlarge and coalesce to form larger patches, but a more severe infection develops on the stems and berries where the white mycelium, as it ages, turns brown and felted. During the summer and autumn, black spore cases containing a second type of spores (ascospores) can be found in the felted mycelium. The disease causes the berries to remain small, and premature defoliation of the bush.

The spread of the disease is encouraged by moist stagnant conditions, as when bushes are planted close together in a plantation; also when soft, sappy shoots are produced, which is often because of excessive feeding with nitrogen. If the disease causes trouble, cut out the infected tips as soon as the wood is ripe in late August or early September, but do not do this too early otherwise new shoots particularly susceptible to mildew may commence to grow. Good control can be obtained with chemicals, but advice should be sought if using sulphur fungicides as some varieties (eg Leveller and Careless) are sulphur sensitive.

EUROPEAN GOOSEBERRY MILDEW (*Microsphaera grossulariae*)

This is more common in Europe than North America, but is not of economic importance. The fungus, much lighter than American mildew, occurs mainly on the upper surfaces of the leaves, and occasionally on the under surfaces and on the berries. It does not develop the brown felted appearance of American mildew.

The disease is found mainly on old bushes growing in heavily shaded conditions. If the attack is light, control may not be necessary, otherwise it is the same as for American mildew.

CLUSTER CUP RUST *(Puccinia pringsheimiana)*

This disease is not of great importance, but frequently occurs in very wet areas. Red or orange patches are first seen on the leaves and fruit. In a bad infection, the berries may be completely covered. The patches are usually observed as thickened cushions covered in tiny saucer-like depressions with frilled edges. If found before this stage, the cushions may appear to be covered in warts or pimples, the depressions occurring when the warts burst open to liberate spores. These spores, however, infect not gooseberries but sedges, where they produce a rust. Infection from the sedge to the gooseberry occurs in the spring when the life cycle of the fungus is completed. Thus the disease is of consequence only in badly drained soils or in places where sedges grow. Control consists of correcting soil drainage and elimination of the sedge.

PESTS

GOOSEBERRY SAWFLY (CURRANT WORM) *(Nematus ribesii)*

The adult moth has clear transparent wings about $\frac{1}{2}$in across, its body black in front and yellow-orange behind. It first appears in April or May when it commences laying its eggs, which are semi-transparent and pearly white or greenish in colour. The eggs are laid—usually a large number on one leaf—on the undersides of the leaves in the centre of the bush. After a week they hatch into caterpillars, with a black head and green body slightly speckled with black. For some days they feed together in colonies but, as they grow and become sage green in colour, they disperse over the bush eating the whole part of the leaves. Unlike the magpie moth, they reach their maximum size after about four weeks; their black spots disappear and the body becomes a pale green with an orange area behind the head and another near the hind end. At this stage they leave the bush to pupate. Within ten to twenty-one days, further adults emerge from the oval, brown cocoons. Usually there are three generations during the season so that their population may, if unchecked, show considerable increase by the end of the summer. Due to the overlapping of the generations, adults, caterpillars and eggs may all be observed at that time. The cocoons of the last generation remain in the soil during the winter and produce adults in the following spring.

The simplest method of control in a small potted orchard is to pick off the caterpillars by hand, but this must be done promptly before the colonies of young caterpillars have dispersed over the bushes. If an attack has been noticed at an early stage, the leaves on which the eggs have been laid should be picked off and destroyed. Otherwise control is with insecticides.

MAGPIE MOTH *(Abraxas grossulariata)*

The adult is on the wing at night during July and August. It has a black and yellow-orange body, and white wings with black and yellow-orange markings. Its forewings are about 1½in across. The female lays its eggs singly or in small groups on the undersides of the leaves. When first laid, the eggs are yellow, but they turn black later. After about two weeks, minute blackish caterpillars hatch. They move with a looping action and immediately commence feeding on the foliage. Their development is slow and they are still quite small in the autumn, when they hibernate amongst dead leaves and under loose bark. As soon as new foliage appears the following spring, they commence feeding again until about the end of May or early June. They are now quite handsome, being black and white with a yellow stripe down each side. When fully fed they turn into a shiny black-and-yellow banded chrysalis suspended in a cocoon among the leaves or twigs. The moth emerges about a month later.

Although only a minor pest, they may strip the bush of foliage if the attack is severe; consequently the season's crop may be lost and the bush so weakened that only a small crop is produced the following year. As the overwintered caterpillars commence their feeding very early, bushes should be examined for signs of injury during the blossom period in those districts where the pest is troublesome. At this time the caterpillars are almost black and should be picked off by hand. Otherwise control is by insecticides.

GOOSEBERRY BRYOBIA (GOOSEBERRY RED SPIDER) *(Bryobia ribis)*

The body of the adult gooseberry bryobia is about 1/30in long, is flattened and oval in shape, and bears a number of short, fan-shaped structures. They are red, grey and green in colour. The females are parthenogenetic, laying eggs that produce only females. These eggs, spherical and red, are laid under loose bark and do not hatch until the following year, starting in February or early March until about mid-April. Once hatched they take about seven weeks to reach the adult stage.

An infestation becomes evident from early spring until June, but subsequently little damage occurs. The attack starts on the lower branches and gradually spreads upwards. As a result of the sucking of the sap by the mites, the foliage turns pale green, then silver grey, eventually brown. When the attack is severe the young leaves are stunted and later many of these fall, while the fruit either drops or fails to swell properly.

Control is with chemicals, but these may also kill the natural enemies of the mites.

APHIDS   see under Black Currants.

CAPSID BUGS   see under Black Currants.

VARIETIES

Keepsake (Berry's Early Kent)—Very early. Medium, round to oval. Pale green, a little hairy. Flavour good if left to ripen. Useful for picking green for cooking. Vigorous, rather spreading, slightly drooping branches. Susceptible to mildew.

Careless   Early. Large, oval. Smooth, transparent, creamy white when ripe. Excellent flavour. Moderate vigour, upright when young, spreading habit later.

Broom Girl Mid-season. Large, round to oval. Dull yellowish green; long hairs scattered on the skin. Good flavour. Vigorous, spreading. Good cropper.

Lancashire Lad Mid-season. Medium to large, oblong to oval. Deep red, hairy. Not a good dessert variety, but excellent for jam or picking green. Moderately vigorous, upright when young, spreading later. Very heavy cropper.

Lancer (Howard's Lancer) Mid-season. Medium, oval. Greenish yellow, smooth. Useful for picking green or for dessert. Vigorous, forming suckers freely. Susceptible to mildew.

Leveller Mid-season. Large to very large, oblong to oval. Yellowish green, almost hairless. Good flavour. Hard pruning and careful manuring give very large fruits. Moderate vigour, spreading.

Whinham Industry Mid-season. Medium to large, oval. Ripens to dark red, hairy. Sweet, useful for jam or dessert. Vigorous, fairly upright with arching shoots. Tolerates some shade, but susceptible to mildew.

AMERICAN VARIETIES

The large-fruited English varieties are susceptible to mildew and therefore seldom grown in the USA. American species are resistant to mildew, but the fruit is smaller.

Fredonia Fairly large berried red variety.

Chautauqua Large fruited green variety.

Poorman Good red variety.

Downing Green variety.

Oregon Champion Another good variety. The berry is of medium size, light green to yellow, with a fairly good flavour. Vigorous, thornless.

Pixwell Considered to be of poor quality.

14

GRAPES

Grapes require long, warm, dry summers and a cool winter, also adequate moisture, preferably supplied by winter rain. In those areas where there is persistent summer rain the incidence of disease is increased; during the ripening season in particular excessive dampness may cause rotting of the berries. They are, though, very hardy and can withstand a temperature falling as low as $-4°$ F ($-20°$ C), but winters with persistent temperatures around $0°$ F ($-18°$ C) could eventually kill them. Although they flower late, they are susceptible to spring frost if it occurs after the new growth has commenced. High winds can also be troublesome in battering and bruising the ripening berries. A mobile potted vineyard therefore has several advantages.

Not that a glass house is necessary for grape cultivation, even in a cool climate. In Britain, the early varieties are successful outdoors anywhere south of a line from the Wash across to Wales and, with some of the very early varieties, the line can be pushed farther north. Of course, when grown under glass in a cool climate, they have longer to ripen their fruit and there is consequently a wider choice of varieties. Heat is not normally necessary in the house, but if a little warmth can be provided during the flowering period it ensures a better set. It is also very useful during the autumn ripening period if the weather outside is wet and will help to prevent mildew attacking the berries.

In the USA most of the European varieties can be cultivated in the hotter districts of interior valleys. In contrast, in the desert areas of Arizona and California, the temperatures may be too high for the production of good quality grapes. At low altitudes, European varieties are the most successful, but may require winter protection. In the north-west and in coastal areas, only the earliest ripening European varieties should be grown. Generally, the American varieties are better able to withstand wetter, colder conditions.

Grapes will do equally well on any kind of soil between one that is chalky and one that is clay. It is wise to choose varieties known to grow well in the locality as this may in part be due to the soil as well as climatic conditions. When grown outdoors in a cool climate the grape, if allowed to grow rampantly, makes too much wood which does not ripen properly, and this at the expense of fruit. Pot cultivation tends to check excessive growth.

A year-old vine should be potted in November, in a pot just large enough to take its roots. Whether the vines are grown under glass or in the open, the basic principle of training them will be the same. Grapes are mainly produced on the current year's shoots, which grow from wood formed the previous year. Because the wood which has finished fruiting is no longer needed, it can be removed but, on the other hand, one-year-old wood is required to replace it, so a combined system of pruning and training is required. Potted vines can be trained either on a circular wire fixed over the pot or on an inverted T made from canes. When training the young vine around a circular wire, the longest stem—or rod, as it is often called—is pruned down to about 3ft. Another stem is also selected, but this is pruned right down to form a short spur with only three buds left. All other growth is completely removed. The longest stem is pruned of all side growth and tied to the circular wire. Meanwhile, two new stems, selected from the short spur, are tied to the upright cane and allowed to grow vertically. The other stem from the short spur can be completely removed. At the end of the season the fruiting stem around the wire is cut right back, whilst the stems which were tied to the upright cane are reduced to one long and one short spur, as in the previous year. At this time the vine can be repotted, the procedure of training following as before.

With the inverted T method, the principle is the same. A 5ft cane is fixed horizontally to one that is upright and two stems, each no longer than 2ft 6in, are tied each way on the horizontal cane. This method requires that three stems should grow from the short spur and be tied up the vertical cane. Because of the shorter stems, this is more convenient for pot work, but the circular wire method may be considered more ornamental.

If the vines are to be grown in the orchard house, growth should be commenced as early as possible. If heat is available the house can be closed and warmth provided from the end of January. Minimum temperatures should be between 35° F (2° C) and 40° F (4° C). When growth commences, the temperature should be kept at about 40° F (4° C) and the house shut all the time. If the weather is warm, some ventilation can be given at mid-day as this will help to prevent soft, weak growth. During

TRAINING

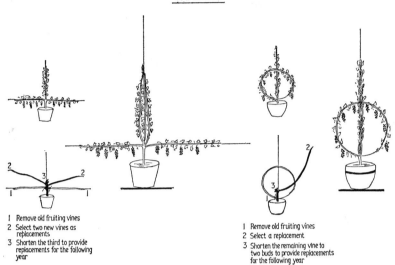

1 Remove old fruiting vines
2 Select two new vines as replacements
3 Shorten the third to provide replacements for the following year

1 Remove old fruiting vines
2 Select a replacement
3 Shorten the remaining vine to two buds to provide replacements for the following year

the flowering period the temperature should, if possible, be kept above 50° F (10° C), as cold conditions will cause a poor set and the resulting bunches of grapes will be imperfect. Grapes, however, are self-fertile and usually the 'set' is satisfactory. A warm, dry atmosphere will aid pollination but, to help shedding of the pollen, the stems can be given a sharp tap, preferably at mid-day. Any laterals not carrying flowers should be removed, so that more nourishment goes to those which will bear grapes.

They will need plenty of water when growth commences, but once the fruit has set care must be taken as an excess of water may cause the berries to split. A mulch of well-rotted compost or manure will help to retain moisture. When grown in a warm climate vines need plenty of feeding, but in a cool climate this should not be overdone. Excessive nitrogenous fertiliser will cause rampant growth. As the berries ripen, and if they are being cultivated in the orchard house, give as much ventilation as possible to maintain a dry atmosphere. High humidity and extremes of temperature may cause the skins to split.

If the grapes are to be used for wine it does not matter if they are small—whether they are thinned or not, the actual weight of the branch will remain the same. But when large table grapes are required it is desirable to thin them, and this should be done when they are about the size of small peas. The aim should be to remove grapes inside the bunch and any on the outside that are likely to spoil its shape. The ideal tool for this operation is a pair of nail scissors.

Grape bunches can be cut and eaten straight from the vine. The lateral should be cut with a pair of secateurs about 2in each side of the bunch. Most varieties can be kept for several weeks in a cool dark room, or even longer if one piece of the lateral is cut about 8in from the bunch and inserted in a bottle of water. For making raisins or currants, the grapes must be left on the vine as long as possible. They need to be very well exposed to the sun and picked when they are absolutely dry—the actual stem of the bunch being cut, not the bearing lateral.

DISEASES

DOWNY MILDEW *(Plasmopara viticola)*
This occurs in nearly all humid regions where grapes are grown, the European rather than the American grape being susceptible. Loss from the disease is not serious where rainfall and humidity is low. The vines will incur more loss than the berries, unless the infection occurs early in the season when bunches of young berries may be killed as well as the stems. Infection late in the season may cause defoliation and debilitation, so that the berries fail to ripen properly.

The symptoms first appear as patches of minute silvery white down but, as the fungus establishes itself on the leaves underneath, translucent yellow patches, later turning brown, appear on the upper sides. Control is by routine copper sprays.

POWDERY MILDEW *(Uncinula necator, Oidium Tuckeri)*
This occurs in all regions where grapes are grown. It is, like downy mildew, more serious to European than American grapes, but is a greater problem where relatively dry conditions occur during the growing season. For example, it is a very serious disease of European grapes in the Pacific Coast area of the USA, where it attacks both the foliage and fruit, destroying the entire crop if unchecked; in the eastern states, however, the attack is confined largely to the foliage.

The fungus makes rapid growth when temperatures are between 70° and 90° F (21–32° C), but above or below this optimum the growth is very much slower. Diseased leaves usually occur first on the shaded portions of the stems, and lesions in the form of circular areas of fine grey, grain-like masses are seen on the undersides of the leaves. The disease can be effectively controlled with routine sprays.

BLACK ROT *(Guignardia bidwelli)*
This is found in all countries where climatic conditions are favourable

for its development. It is more destructive in warm and humid regions than in drier cooler ones. In North America it is very destructive east of the Rocky Mountains, whereas in the dry grape growing regions of California it does not occur.

The principal damage caused is to the berries; loss of foliage is not severe and, although stem lesions weaken the vine, they seldom cause its death. Symptoms appear in late spring as red spots on the leaves, usually scattered over the surface, but sometimes grouped together. Later the spots become brown with black margins and minute black dots on their upper surfaces. Similar lesions also occur in the tendrils, leaf stems and veins. With the growth of the vine, the bark may split along the lesion. The disease is not seen on the berries until they are nearly half grown, then the whole berry soon becomes mummified and covered with numerous fruiting bodies, finally turning coal black.

All diseased berries should be removed and burned. Because of the drastic pruning necessary with pot cultivation, stems produced the previous year and which carry signs of the disease will in any case be cut out. Since the spores require a moist surface over a fairly long period in order to germinate, a free circulation of air and rapid drying of the foliage considerably reduces the risk of infection. When the disease is known to be prevalent in the area, European grapes should be protected with a fungicide during wet periods. When only a few vines are grown in pots, they can be taken under cover during a wet period, so that spraying may be unnecessary.

PESTS

PHYLLOXERA VITAFOLIAE

Severe devastation can be caused by this pest. American species are largely immune to it, and the most effective measure for European vines is to graft them on to American rootstock. This is a well-established practice on the Continent, where no vines are planted on their own roots.

Phylloxera vitafoliae are aphid-like insects which cause small galls in the leaves and small gall-like swellings in the roots. Their life cycle is rather complex. Their presence may be detected by small galls or blisters on the *undersides* of the leaves. The galls are 1–5mm in diameter, leaf-coloured or red, and similar to those made by red currant aphis. Each gall contains a single insect but, because it never emerges and lives entirely inside its burrow, ordinary chemical sprays are not effective against it. By means of a winter egg, the insects give rise to the root-dwelling *phylloxera*, which can only be detected in the first instance by the debility of the vine.

Established in the roots, the insect produces colonies of winged and sexed aphids which spread themselves throughout the vineyard, infesting other leaves. Should this pest be present, the vine should be ruthlessly destroyed.

OTHER PESTS

Aphid, grape berry moth, grape colapsis, grape leaf folder, grape leaf hopper, grape mealy bug and vine weevil all attack grapes, but with proper control should not cause too much trouble. The grape leaf hopper has been a serious pest of grapes in California, but is now under better control. The two most important mites are the two spotted mite *(Tetranychus*

telarius) and the Pacific mite *(T. pacificus)*. The grape colapsis or clover rootworm grubs, which are pale green and about ⅛in long, feed on the stems and foliage of grapes and other plants.

VARIETIES

Varieties best suited to the locality should be chosen, but all those listed under Northern Europe and the hybrids are suitable for cultivation in Britain.

NORTH EUROPE

Perle de Czaba   White, Dessert. Muscat. Small berries and bunches. Very good flavour.

Madeleine Noir (Pinot Noir Précoce)   Black. Wine. Medium berries, small bunches but prolific. Fair flavour.

Madeleine Royal   White. Wine or dessert. Medium berries, large bunches. Very thin skin.

Pirovano 14   Red to black. Dessert. Medium berries and bunches. Good flavour. Reliable cropper.

Précoce de Malingre   White. Wine or dessert. A very old French grape.

Siegerrebe   Golden. Wine or dessert. Muscat. Large berries. Sweet. Powerful bouquet when used for wine. German hybrid.

Muscat de Saumur   Golden. Muscat. Dessert. Medium berries and bunches. Well flavoured.

Gamay Hâtif des Vosges   Blue-black. Wine. Small berries, small bunches. Prolific, reliable.

Noir Hâtif de Marseille   Black. Muscat. Small berries. Very good flavour. Prolific.

Bacchus   White. Wine. Small to medium berries. Good flavour.

Faber   White. Wine. Medium berries. Rich flavour. Suitable for wide variety of soils but requires sheltered position.

Forta   White. Wine. Medium berries. Makes a Reisling-type wine.

Gagarin Blue   Blue-black. Wine or dessert. Oval, medium berries. Very good flavour. Russian hybrid, result of a cross between *Vitis vinifera* and *V. amurensis*

Tereshkova Purple-red. Dessert. Oval, medium berries. Delicate muscat flavour. Russian hybrid.

Mariensteiner White. Wine. Medium berries. Fairly hardy. Makes a rich wine with nice bouquet.

Muller-Thurgau White. Wine. Vigorous vine, susceptible to botrytis.

Reisling Sylvaner White. Wine or dessert. Large berries. A well-known hock grape, but being large with a good flavour is suitable for dessert.

Sevye-Villard 5/276 White. Wine. Heavy and regular cropper. Will ripen almost every year in southern England outdoors. A hybrid.

Oliver Irsay White. Dessert. Muscat. Medium berries.

Leon Millot Black. Dessert. Medium berries. Good flavour. Rampant grower. French hybrid.

Excelsior White. Dessert. Medium berries. Good flavour. Prolific. Usually ripens well in southern England outdoors.

Siebel 13053 Black. Wine. Very good cropper. Makes a good red wine.

Muscat Hamburgh Black. Dessert. Muscat. Medium berries and bunches. Very good flavour. The flowers are females, consequently needs another variety growing nearby.

White Frontignan White. Dessert. Muscat. Medium berries. Not suitable outdoors in England.

Golden Chasselas (Chasselas d'Or) Golden. Dessert or wine. Medium berries. Excellent flavour. Popular French dessert grape also grown extensively in France for wine. Susceptible to mildew.

Chasselas Rose Light red. Similar to previous, but berries pinkish.

Chasselas Vibert White. Similar to previous, but berries white and larger.

Chasselas 1921 Dessert and wine. Similar to three preceding varieties, but berries pale gold and large. Swiss grape used for Swiss Fendant wine.

Ascot Citronelle White. Dessert. Muscat. Very good flavour and quality. Vigorous vine, moderate cropper.

Traminer White with slight purplish tinge. Wine. Small berries and bunches. Famous Rhine grape.

Reichensteiner White. Wine. Small to medium berries.

Scheurebe Similar to previous.

Kolor Black. Wine. Noted for its colour rather than quality.

Pinot Noir Black. Wine. Medium berries. One of the best French varieties, used for famous Burgundy wines.

Pinot Meunier Similar to the previous, but ripens slightly later and has greater resistance to mildew.

Muscat Queen White. Dessert. Muscat. Large. Well flavoured.

Portugais Blue Blue-black. Wine. Large berries, medium bunches.

Black Hamburgh Black. Dessert. Medium to large berries, medium sized bunch. Fair flavour, sweet. Well-known grape commonly grown in greenhouses in England.

Madresfield Court Black. Dessert. Muscat. Large berries in very long bunches. Very good quality.

Royal Emile Black. Dessert. Large to very large berries. Very juicy, sweet, delicate flavour.

Leopold III Black. Dessert. Very large berries. Very handsome and excellent table grape. Very juicy, sweet, delicate flavour. Berries colour readily and before grape is properly ripe; for full flavour should not be picked too early.

White Muscat of Alexandria Pale gold. Dessert. Muscat. Oval berries, very large tapering bunches. Thick skin, but excellent table grape. Juicy, very sweet, pronounced muscat flavour.

Canon Hall Muscat Amber. Dessert. Muscat. Very large berries and bunches. Excellent quality, very juicy, pronounced muscat flavour.

Black Alicante Black. Dessert. Large berries, large and fairly long bunches. Very juicy, fairly sweet. Table quality only fair. In England, ripens satisfactorily in a cold glass house in a cold wet autumn.

Gros Colman Black. Dessert. Large to very large berries, large bunches. Juicy, sweet, pleasantly sub-acid, no distinctive aroma. In a heated glass house provides very late grapes.

NORTH AMERICA

Many of the varieties already described can be grown in North America and vice versa. The following *European* varieties are all table grapes.

Pearl of Csaba   White. Muscat. Suitable for north-west USA (see also under North Europe).

Delight   Pale golden. Dessert. Muscat. Medium berries, large bunches. Good quality. Seedless, suitable for raisins.

Thompson Seedless (Sultanina)   Medium berries, large bunches. Very sweet, but little flavour. Seedless, suitable for raisins. Requires winter protection in eastern Oregon and Washington. Suitable for hot valleys of California; unsuitable for cool coastal regions.

Ribier   Black. Large berries, large elongated bunches. Very good quality, sweet, agreeable flavour, slight vinous aroma. Very productive.

Red Malaga   Reddish-purple. Large berries, large bunches. Juicy, fair flavour.

Scarlet   Black. Large berries, fairly large bunches. Red juice, sweet, good flavour. Vigorous.

Flame Tokay   Red. Large to very large berries. Juicy, fair flavour.

White Muscat of Alexandria   see under North Europe.

The following American or American-European hybrids are unsuitable for hot summer climates. These are all table grapes.

Early Giant   Bluish-black. Large berries, medium bunches. Juicy, very good flavour.

Campbell's Early   Bluish-black. Large berries, fair sized bunches. Juicy, excellent quality.

Ontario   White. Small to medium berries, compact bunches. Exceptionally good quality.

Fredonia   Black. Medium berries and bunches. Juicy, good flavour. Vigorous, productive.

Schuyler   Black. Medium berries. Excellent hybrid grape.

Concord   Black. Medium berries, large bunches. Distinctive flavour.

Worden   Similar to preceding but sweeter.

Niagara   Similar to Concord, but white berried. Very hardy.

Pierce (Californian Concord)   Similar to Concord, but more suitable for warmer climates.

Seneca   White. Very large berries, excellent quality.

Agawan   Purplish-black. Medium berries. Distinctive 'foxy' flavour.

Delaware   Red. Large to medium berries. Very sweet, high quality.

Sheridan   Blue. Medium berries. Excellent quality when properly ripened.

15

MULBERRIES

Mulberries are naturalised in most parts of the northern temperate zone and individual trees are fairly common in some Mediterranean and Middle East countries. There are several species, principally: *Morus alba* (white mulberry), native of China and widely grown for its leaves to feed silkworm; *M. rubra* (red mulberry), native of North America; *M. nigra* (black mulberry), native of Persia and providing the best fruit. The black mulberry should be chosen for pot cultivation.

The mulberry tree is very long lived and, with age, becomes very spreading and large headed. When the tree has reached such a size, it is not easy to harvest the berries, which are readily eaten by birds. Fortunately, when growing it for its fruit, it is neither desirable nor necessary to have a large tree. The mulberry responds very well to pot cultivation and needs very little special treatment.

The easiest method of propagation is to take cuttings about 12in long in October or November. They should be inserted in a sandy soil and, by the autumn of the following year when they have rooted, can be repotted. From then on, they can be trained as dwarf pyramid or bush trees and repotted each year before new growth commences. As fruiting trees, they will need pots no larger than 10in.

Male and female flowers appearing in May are borne on the same tree—on wood of the previous year as well as on spurs of older wood. Because the fruit is borne on spurs and short jointed young wood, the shoots should be cut back in winter to four or five buds, only removing completely such shoots as are necessary to keep the shape of the tree and prevent overcrowding of the laterals. Lanky growing shoots should be cut right out. Summer pinching may be practised when necessary.

Under no circumstances should the soil in the pots be allowed to dry out during the summer months and, when the trees are fruiting heavily, they should be given a feed of weak liquid manure.

In cool climates the fruit ripens in August and September. The oblong-shaped berries, something like loganberries, should, if required for dessert, be allowed to remain on the trees until ready to fall. Bush or dwarf pyramids can be easily netted against birds and the fruit is easy to gather. The refreshing juice makes the berries very acceptable for all culinary purposes; when not thoroughly ripe, they are good for tarts and pies. The fruit ripens irregularly and is therefore available over a long period.

DISEASES AND PESTS

The mulberry is not prone to many diseases and pests.

CANKER *(Gibberella moricola)*

Pale brown spore pustules appear on cankers in damp weather. As the cankers may result in the death of young shoots, all such affected parts should be immediately cut out and burnt.

VARIETIES

Although a number of cultivars of the black mulberry have been produced, these are generally sold simply as Black Mulberry or Large Black Mulberry.

16

PEACHES

The peach, the most important deciduous fruit after the apple and pear, is grown throughout the temperate regions of both the northern and southern hemispheres. Greatest production is in USA, where peaches are grown from New York to Michigan and south-west to the Gulf States, with California the leading state. In Europe, the leading peach-growing countries are Italy, France, Spain and Greece, and there is considerable production in USSR, South Africa, Australia and Japan. In Britain, outdoor production is confined to southern England; farther north the protection of at least a south or south-west facing wall is needed. In Belgium and Holland there is some cultivation under glass.

The peach tree is as hardy as the plum but has an intolerance to severe cold. Unless really hardy varieties are available, it should not be grown where temperatures fall below $-10°$ to $-15°$ F ($-23°$ to $-26°$ C). Flower buds are as hardy as those of the apple and plum but, because it flowers some days earlier than plum, there is a greater danger of injury by frost. This is the main limiting factor in peach cultivation. The tree needs plenty of warmth and sunshine to ripen and mature its wood, yet it is not successful where the winters are too mild, because it requires a chilling period to induce a complete dormancy. In warm areas, only those varieties known to grow successfully locally should be chosen.

The peach will grow on various soils, from gravelly loams to silt loams, but does best in a well-drained medium loam. It dislikes a very high lime content, but one that is acid needs the addition of a little chalk or mortar rubble. It needs to make good new growth annually, so for pot trees a rich soil should be provided, consisting of two parts medium loam, one part manure or humus, one part burned earth, a little mortar rubble, chalk or sand and a good dressing of coarse bone meal.

Varieties are normally budded on to plum or peach seedling rootstock.

Plum rootstock: Common Mussel and Damas C will both produce a small tree; Pershore gives a tree of moderate size, while Brompton makes a strong fertile tree. Peach seedling rootstock: the advantages are that it produces a healthy fertile tree which stands up to heavy pruning, and with fewer suckers than the plum.

Whether the tree is a maiden or already trained to the form required, it should be potted in October. A maiden can be trained, as preferred, into a bush, pyramid, short standard or fan tree. The dwarf open centre bush on an 18in leg is a good form to choose. In alternate years, during September or October, it should be repotted, using the same pot for up to five or six years, after which a 15in size will be required.

Fruiting is produced on new wood, so that some of the old needs to be removed to encourage fresh growth. If the tree is allowed to grow vigorously and remains unpruned, it will overcrop and bear only small fruits. A balance should be aimed at between obtaining a satisfactory crop during the current season and producing new wood for the one to follow. Some growers prune their trees during or just before blossom time. Thus, if there is a heavy blossom the amount of fruit can be reduced and the size increased, while at the same time stimulating production of new wood to bear fruit the following year. The drawback with pruning at this time is that the peach is susceptible to certain fungus diseases, so that it is safer to leave pruning until after the tree has fruited. At this time all dead and broken shoots can be removed, and those crossing and crowded thinned out. Twigs which bore fruit should be cut out, but at the base of this twig will be found a new shoot which should be left as a replacement. About one-third of the laterals should be cut back to basal shoots so that new laterals grow and this should be done evenly over the tree so that it keeps its shape. Leaders can also be pruned where further extension growth is required.

When growing a peach tree in the orchard house it is important not to coddle it, but one of the most common mistakes is not to provide sufficient water and ventilation. By the end of January the temperature should be about 40° F (4° C) rising to 50° F (10° C) in February. If necessary the house may be shut down from early afternoon to late morning to trap the sun's rays, but ample ventilation should be given whenever climatic conditions are suitable. By March the temperature should have risen to 50°–55° F (10°–13° C), when the tree is in flower. During these early months it should be kept well watered. Over-dry conditions are detrimental to a vigorous bud break and growth. Trees should be syringed once or twice a day from the commencement of bud break up to flowering, at which point it must stop.

153

Most varieties are self-fertile, but some, mainly American, are only partly so. When trees are outdoors, bees will normally assure adequate pollination but if the weather is windy and cold—and when trees are under glass—it is advisable to hand pollinate. This can be done by lightly dusting a small piece of cotton wool over the flowers.

Trees outdoors as well as under glass need to make plenty of new growth, therefore a high nitrogen content in the soil as well as adequate moisture are required. A mulch of manure or compost in early spring helps to reduce loss of moisture from the soil as well as feeding the tree when watered. Liquid fertilisers should also be given from spring onwards. When flowering has ended and the fruit set, syringing should be recommenced and the temperature raised to 65° F (18° C). When the fruit approaches the ripening period, syringing should again cease. The fruit should now be fully exposed to the sun. It may be advisable to lightly shade nectarine fruit which is sometimes susceptible to sunscorch. A drier atmosphere is needed during the ripening period, so the house should have all the ventilation possible.

The tree may often set an excessive crop, so the fruit should be thinned gradually, starting when they are small fruitlets which can be easily rubbed off. Thinning should be spread over a period of two or three weeks. When the tree first commences fruiting, it should not be allowed to carry more than fifteen fruits.

The fruit should be allowed to hang on the tree as long as possible before

being eaten. It has its richest flavour when fully ripe and ready to fall naturally. A daily check for readiness for picking should be done with care, as continual handling bruises the soft flesh. Cup your hand around the fruit; do not press it with your fingers, but with gentle overall pressure try to ease it from its twig. If it does not come away, leave it for another day.

NUTRIENT DEFICIENCIES
AND PHYSIOLOGICAL DISORDERS

Apricots, cherries, peaches and plums may all suffer from nutrient deficiencies. The following applies to all stone fruits.

NITROGEN

The most common and important disorder is caused by a deficiency of nitrogen. Leaves become yellowish green. Red to purple spots often appear on the blade of the leaves, in severe cases becoming brown and necrotic. Growth of twigs is checked and they remain thin. Defoliation of basal leaves may occur during mid-season, while leaf fall is usually several weeks in advance of trees which have an adequate supply of nitrogen. Fruit will be small unless excessively thinned.

PHOSPHORUS

Symptoms of this deficiency are more likely to be seen on the peach than other stone fruits. Old leaves will have light green areas between dark green veins, giving a mottled effect, while a purplish pigmentation will develop in the stems and leaf petioles. Progressive defoliation of mottled leaves, from base to tip of the twigs, occur as the season advances.

POTASSIUM

Necrotic areas appear on leaves of peach trees suffering from potassium deficiency. These areas vary from very small spots to large irregular patches. Twigs will often be slender and fruit buds sparse. In spring the foliage is usually much lighter in colour than on trees with an adequate supply of potassium. On cherry trees the lighter green of the foliage is more noticeable while the leaves have a tendency to curl upwards. With plum trees, symptoms appear later in the season. It is usually July or August before the leaves begin to lose their dark colour; as they turn lighter, they roll inwards on the upper surface. Ripening of fruit may be delayed and young trees become dwarfish.

MAGNESIUM

Light grey or fawn spots appear on leaves. In severe cases the spots may develop into large areas, including the margin of the leaves, and the leaves fall from the base of the twig towards the tip where only a few may remain.

ZINC

Although peaches, plums and apricots can suffer from a zinc deficiency, the sweet cherry is most seriously affected. Symptoms are irregular splashes of yellowing between the veins on young leaves and, in general, foliage is lighter than normal. Leaves at the tips of new growth are small and wrinkled, and there is progressive defoliation from the base to the tip of the twig. Sometimes, especially with the sweet cherry, there is a dying back of shoot terminals.

MANGANESE

All stone fruits are susceptible to manganese deficiency. Symptoms will be observed on the leaves. The mid-rib and main veins with adjacent bands of tissue remain green, but interveinal areas are chlorotic.

IRON

A deficiency of common occurrence. Chlorotic symptoms first appear at the tips of growing shoots and the condition develops during succeeding years. Symptoms are often confused with potassium or manganese deficiency but because an iron deficiency can be quickly corrected—with, for example, Sequestrene—it can soon be ascertained if this is the cause of the trouble.

BORON

Peaches, plums and apricots are most likely to suffer from this deficiency. In British Columbia severe symptoms have been observed; the buds fail to break in the spring, and there is dying of twigs, branches and even of entire trees. Other symptoms are brown sunken areas on the fruits, with the flesh below being brown and firm. The fruits ripen earlier than normal and drop.

Boron—excess In some areas water is high in boron. In California, for example, where stone fruits are irrigated, injury can be caused. The shoots die back at their tips and the bark cracks and becomes corky. Lateral buds on the injured shoots start to grow but are later killed.

DISEASES

PEACH LEAF CURL *(Taphrina deformans)*

Peach leaf curl occurs almost everywhere the peach is grown, but is less prevalent on trees under glass. It is important in the USA in all the peach-growing regions except the semi-arid regions of the south-west. Occasionally it attacks apricots. The intensity of an attack varies year by year; in seasons which favour the development of the fungus, it can be destructive. It is easily recognised. Infected leaves are puckered, curled and thickened, these symptoms appearing shortly after the leaves emerge from the buds. Diseased leaves are yellowish with a tinge of red and, as they become older, the curling and puckering becomes more pronounced. The thickened parts become bulbous, fleshy and more red, with a delicate whitish bloom appearing on the upper surface as the fungus begins to produce its spores. Eventually the leaves turn brown, wither and die. In severe attacks, the tree may be completely defoliated and, although new leaves develop, the tree suffers a severe check. The injury caused by this disease therefore saps the vitality of the tree by causing it to produce a second flush of leaves and, in severe cases, the immature fruit falls.

The fungus also attacks young shoots, which become swollen and twisted. The tips of laterals frequently die back. During summer and autumn some of the spores produced on the leaves reach the surfaces of the stem and twigs. The spores immediately germinate and produce yeast-like colonies, which remain in the bark or bud scales throughout the winter to provide a further source of infection the following spring. Infection of leaves in spring takes place at the time the buds are expanding. Cold, wet weather favours development of the disease, while in a warm dry spring it is much less prevalent.

Affected leaves should be removed before the characteristic bloom occurs on them. All infected leaves should be collected and burnt. The most effective control is by spraying just before the buds begin to swell.

PEACH SCAB *(Cladosporium carpophilum)*

This occurs wherever the peach is grown. Circular, dark lesions up to $\frac{1}{8}$in in diameter occur on the fruit; on the upper part they are numerous and may merge together, on the sides they are more scattered, and on the lower part entirely absent.

VIRUS DISEASES

Several known virus diseases affect peaches, two of which are peach yellows and peach mosaic. The first occurs in the eastern United States and Canada, and losses from it can be severe; the second is limited to south-western USA.

PEACH YELLOWS

Usually symptoms do not occur in the first year of growth following the infection, and in the early stages the tree is not greatly different from normal, though it may appear to be suffering from malnutrition. In time the tree develops bunches of slender, willowy shoots which quickly branch giving a broom-like effect. The leaves on these shoots are narrow, yellowish and red spotted. Buds set very early in autumn and, in spring, both the flower and leaf bud break earlier than in a normal tree. Although infected trees sometimes bloom in autumn, this in itself should never be taken as evidence of the disease, as abnormal growth conditions may cause similar blossoming in a healthy tree. Fruits of a diseased tree ripen from four days to three weeks earlier than normal and are often larger than usual. Reddish blotches or specks are, in most cases, to be seen on the fruits but the most reliable indications are reddish streaks in the flesh and a deep red colour around the stone pit. The flavour is insipid. Infected fruit may appear on one branch only, but in time the tree will become completely diseased. The willowy growth will occur on more branches and within three or four years the entire tree dies. When the disease is diagnosed the tree should be burnt. It is known that the plum leaf hopper *(Macropsis trimaculata)* can transmit the disease. Aphids can also be suspected and should be kept in check.

PEACH MOSAIC

There are thought to be a number of strains of this virus so that symptoms vary. Those described may be observed in the variety J. H. Hale, which is very susceptible to the disease. In the first year of infection, leaves may wither and fall although quite young, or they may be irregular in shape with a yellow and green mottled effect. Because of a shortened growth of the twigs, the dwarfing of the tree soon becomes apparent. By the second year of infection the disease is chronic. Shoot growth will be very reduced and the mottling more pronounced, although there will be less defoliation. With some infections the fruit will show small bumps, while in others, caused by different strains of the virus, the fruit is normal. Infected trees should be destroyed.

ROOT KNOT

This has a world-wide distribution but is most severe in areas with warm climates and mild winters. In the northern peach growing areas of North America, for example, it causes little trouble. Root knot is found also on plums and cherries, but apricots are rarely affected. Damage to the peach tree is more likely in light, sandy soils. Heavily infected trees are stunted and foliage is lighter in colour than normal. The tree may be so weakened that it finally dies. When infection is slight, no definite symptoms appear above ground and may only be noticed during repotting. Root knot galls may be spindle-shaped enlargements or irregular globular growths of variable size; in peach trees they may be as much as 1in across. The infection is caused by *Meloioogyne* sp. (nematodes), and in mild areas where nematode infestation is known to be heavy it may be advisable to sterilise the potting compost.

PESTS

ORIENTAL FRUIT MOTH (*Grapholitha molesta*)
The adult moths are nocturnal, but during the day may be found resting on dark parts of trees. About $\frac{1}{2}$in long, the moth has a dark grey body with tinges of bronze. When the forewings are folded there is a distinctive band of silver grey forming an inverted V across the middle of the wings. Each female lays from 125 to 150 eggs on the leaves, twigs and fruit. In a warm midsummer these eggs hatch in from three to six days, but in cooler weather they take up to fourteen days. Newly hatched larvae are about 1/16in long; they are almost transparent but have black heads. They burrow into new twigs causing them to die. Fruit is also attacked, the larvae burrowing and entering through the stem, although the hole is almost undetectable. When fully grown they leave the twigs and fruit to find a concealed place to spin their cocoons. Control is by chemical sprays.

PEACH TWIG BORER (*Anarsia lineatella*)
The pest overwinters in the larvae stage in little cells beneath the bark. In spring the larvae burrows down through the tips of the growing twigs, killing them from 3 to 4in back. A second brood emerges in early summer and attacks the fruit and other twigs. Late varieties of peach may be attacked by a third brood. Apricots are also affected.

GREEN PEACH APHIS (*Myzus persicae*); LEAF CURLING PEACH APHIS (*Anuraphis amygdali*)
These and other aphis often cause trouble when they feed on young leaves and shoots in spring.

RED SPIDER *(Tetranychus telarius)*
This can be a troublesome pest of peach trees grown under glass. In spring the mites become active and commence feeding on the underside of leaves, causing a very fine and regular speckling on the upper surface of the foliage. As the attack develops, the foliage becomes silvery brown. New leaves are small and the edges often curl upwards. The vitality of the tree is reduced causing the crop to be small both in quantity and size. Once the mites become established in the orchard house, they are sometimes difficult to eradicate. Control is by mitecides (acaricides), applied as sprays or as aerosols or smokes.

SAN JOSE SCALE *(Quadraspidiotus perniciosus)*
This and other scales, such as brown apricot scale, white peach scale, affect peach trees (see under Apples).

VARIETIES

1 Peach varieties are continually changing and being improved in many ways.

2 No one variety is satisfactory in all peach growing areas. This, to some extent, is due to the chilling requirements of the tree.

3 Not only will varieties ripen at different times in different areas, but there can be some variation in the sequence of ripening. They are listed here in order of ripening. In the North American list a ripening time will apply only to the area stated.

4 In Britain, at the beginning of the season, fruit under glass will ripen about two weeks earlier than on a tree having only the protection of a warm wall and about four weeks earlier than on a tree completely in the open. As summer proceeds these differences will decrease, so that by the end of August there may be no more than a week between a tree indoors and one in the open.

5 The nectarine is a natural 'sport' or mutation on the peach, but the fruit is smaller, and smooth in contrast to the velvet-like skin of the peach. It is also a little less hardy, but cultivation is the same.

BRITAIN AND NORTH-WEST EUROPE

Alexander Ripens beginning July. Medium. Stone clinging.

Amsden June Mid-July. Medium. Carmine red; greenish yellow on shaded side. Flesh yellowish white, sweet, juicy. Stone partially clinging, but comes away when fully ripe.

Duke of York Mid-July. Large. Flushed deep crimson. Flesh white, tender, sweet. Suitable for forcing in a glass house.

Early Rivers Nectarine. Mid-July. Large. Greenish white, flushed red. Flesh white, juicy.

Hales Early (Early German) Late July. Medium to large. Apricot-coloured, flushed purplish red. Flesh white, sweet, delicately aromatic. Free stone. Suitable under glass; also hardy.

Charles Ingouf Late July. Large. Yellowish green, flushed dark carmine. Flesh greenish white, juicy. Stone partially clinging.

Early Rivers Late July. Large. Flesh white, sweet.

Peregrine Early August. Large. Flushed bright crimson. Flesh greenish white, juicy, excellent flavour. Long season.

Delespaul Early August. Large. Skin yellowish green, flushed dark purplish red. Flesh creamy white, greenish tinge. Slightly sub-acid, faintly aromatic. Stone clinging. Vigorous.

Erle Redfre Early August. Large. Creamy yellow, crimson flush. Flesh white, rich.

Lord Napier Nectarine. Early August. Greenish white, flushed red. Flesh white, juicy.

Madeline Rouge Second half August. Large. Pale yellowish, suffused purplish red. Flesh white. Very juicy, sweet, faintly perfumed, excellent flavour. Stone free. Susceptible to mildew. Unreliable outdoors.

Rochester Mid-August. Medium to large. Yellowish, mottled red. Flesh yellow, rich, sweet, juicy. Suitable indoors or out.

Dryden Nectarine. Mid-August. Medium to large. Flesh white. Juicy, good flavour.

Humboldt Nectarine. Mid-August. Large. Dark red and yellow. Flesh yellow, juicy. Good cropper.

Noblesse End August. Large. Greenish yellow, flushed crimson. Rich. Only slightly hardy.

Elruge Nectarine. End August. Medium. Pale green, flushed dark red, Flesh white, juicy, good flavour. Good cropper.

161

Hardwicke Nectarine. End August. Fruit similar to Elruge but larger.

Viotette Hâtive Nectarine. End August. Medium. Flesh white. Ripens over long period, crops well.

Royal George End August. Large. Pale apricot, speckled red. Good flavour. Good cropper, susceptible to mildew.

French Mignonne (Gross Mignonne) Early September. Large, sometimes irregular in shape. Attractive carmine and brownish red; greenish white on shaded side. Flesh white, slightly greenish. Very juicy. Stone small and free. Vigorous.

Bellegarde Early September. Large. Flushed dark crimson. Flesh yellow, firm, rich. Very hardy.

Orchard Queen (Reine des Verges) Early September. Large to very large. Very markedly flushed carmine or deep purplish red. Flesh greenish white, juicy, moderate quality. Stone fairly large but free.

Dymond Early September. Large. Pale yellow, flushed scarlet. Flesh yellow, very good flavour. Reliable under glass.

Madame Gaujard First half September. Large. Deep carmine red, yellowish green on the shaded side. Flesh creamy white, greenish tinge. Juicy, pleasantly sweet, no distinctive aroma. Stone free when fully ripe.

Barrington Mid-September. Large. Flesh yellowish green, excellent flavour. Late outdoor variety.

Belle Imperiale Mid-September. Large. Carmine and purplish red, yellowish on shaded side. Flesh yellowish white, juicy. Free stone.

Sea Eagle End September. Large. Pale coloured; outdoors in dull weather it does not colour very well. Under glass, a useful variety to extend the season.

Baltet Beginning October. Large. Flushed with light red, creamy white on shaded side. Flesh yellowish white. Juicy, sweet, perfumed. For cultivation under glass.

USA AND CANADA

Springold Ripens about mid-May in North Louisiana. Small to medium. Bright red, streaked light yellow. Flesh pale yellow, juicy, good quality. Clingstone. Vigorous, highly productive.

Armgold. About same time as Springold. Small. Yellow and bright red. Flesh yellow, light red staining. Good flavour. Small stone. Very vigorous, good cropper.

Fillette Few days after Springold. Medium to small. Mainly dark red. Flesh yellow. Fairly vigorous. Not very satisfactory in warm climates.

Cardinal About two weeks after Springold. Medium. Yellow and bright red. Flesh yellow, firm, good quality. Clingstone.

Redcap Small to medium. Yellow and deep red to rose. Flesh yellow, juicy, good quality. Ripens unevenly.

Collins About two weeks after Springold. Medium to large. Light yellow with green shading, flushed and streaked brilliant red. Flesh pale yellow. Good flavour. Semi-freestone. Vigorous, highly productive.

Garnet Beauty Last half July in Michigan. Golden yellow, much red shading. Flesh yellow, good quality and flavour. Semi-freestone. Vigorous, hardy.

Harbelle Just after Garnet Beauty. Large. Bright red over yellow. Flesh rich yellow, very good quality. Freestone. Very hardy.

Merrill Gem Free First week July in Kentucky. Medium. Red with light purple. Flesh rich yellow. Semi-freestone. Moderate vigour, medium productivity.

Earlired Overlaps previous. Medium to large. Red over golden yellow. Flesh rich yellow, much red near stone. Juicy, good texture, good flavour. Semi-freestone. Vigorous, highly productive.

June Gold Overlaps Earlired. Very large. Yellow and green, with light red shading. Flesh deep yellow to light orange. Rather coarse, mediocre flavour. Very vigorous with high productivity.

Nectared 1 (Nectarine) Last week July in Michigan. Large. Yellow and red. Flesh yellow, no red at the stone. Good quality. Semi-clingstone.

Maygrand (Nectarine) Mainly red. Flesh yellow, very good flavour. Vigorous.

Crimson Gold (Nectarine) Medium. Yellow and bright red. Flesh yellow, juicy. Very productive.

Red June (Nectarine) Small to medium. Intense red, very attractive. Flesh yellow, stained red. Good flavour, slightly acid. Vigorous and fertile.

Morton (Nectarine) Small to medium small. Yellow background with intense red, attractive. Flesh white, acceptable flavour. Good resistance to bruising. Exceptionally fertile.

Nectared 2 (Nectarine) Last week July in Michigan. Medium to large. Yellow and red. Flesh yellow. Good quality, handles well.

Dixired Beginning June in North Louisiana. Medium. Bright yellow to dark red. Flesh yellow, firm, good quality.

Rubired Medium to large. Larger than most early ripening peaches. Light yellow and red. Flesh pale yellow. Very good flavour. Moderately vigorous, somewhat spreading.

Winblo Large fruits, $2\frac{1}{2}$in diameter when properly thinned. Attractive with predominant red blush. Flesh bright yellow. Very firm, excellent flavour. Freestone when ripe.

Early Sungrand (Nectarine) Medium to large. Yellow and deep red. Flesh yellow, with red staining. Good flavour. Large stone which is semi-free.

Independance (Nectarine) Medium to large. Dark red. Flesh yellow with red staining. Large, freestone.

Silver Lode (Nectarine) Medium to small. Red. Flesh white, juicy, good flavour. Resistant to Monilia infection.

Stark Sunglo (Nectarine) Medium to large. Yellow and brilliant red, very attractive. Flesh yellow, good quality and flavour. Freestone. Very fertile.

La Gem Medium to large. Mainly red. Flesh bright yellow, good quality. Semi-freestone. Heavy cropper, usually needs heavy thinning. Fruit and foliage have good resistance to bacterial spot.

Redhaven Second week June in Louisiana; mid-July, Kentucky; first half August, Michigan. Medium. Golden yellow, with deep red overcolour. Flesh yellow, very good flavour. Freestone.

Comanche Medium to large. Yellow flesh. Freestone.

Raritan Rose Large. Attractive red colour. Flesh white, high quality. Freestone. One of the best white peaches. Vigorous and hardy.

Harbrite Matures one to two days after Redhaven. Medium to large. Yellow and bright red. Flesh rich yellow, firm, good quality. Freestone. Hardy, resistant to bacterial spot.

Harken About same time as Harbrite. Large—$2\frac{1}{2}$in diameter. Brilliant red. Flesh yellow, exceptionally good quality. Freestone. Hardy, highly resistant to bacterial spot.

Sentinel Medium to large. Yellow with some bright red overcolour. Flesh yellow, slightly soft. Semi-freestone. Fairly resistant to bacterial spot.

La Gold Medium. Bright golden colour with bright red flush. Flesh golden yellow, little red pigment, slightly soft. Freestone. Resistant to bacterial spot.

Enboy Medium. Red, flushed yellow. Flesh yellow, good quality. Freestone. Fruit drops when fully ripe. Resistant to bacterial spot.

Velvet Mid-July, Kentucky; mid-August, Michigan. Medium. Red over yellow. Name aptly describes its smooth appearance. Flesh yellow, firm, deliciously flavoured. Freestone. Slightly susceptible to bacterial spot.

Reliance Medium to large. Mainly red, attractive. Flesh yellow, high quality. Freestone. Hardy.

Nectar Medium to large. Mainly red. Flesh white, high quality. Freestone. Productive, fairly hardy.

Sunqueen Medium to large. Golden yellow, with bright red. Flesh rich yellow. Good flavour. Freestone. Fairly vigorous, good productivity.

Glohaven Mid-August, Michigan. Very large. Mostly red, with deep yellow. Flesh yellow, good quality. Freestone. Fairly hardy, productive and resistant to bacterial spot.

Sunhigh Large. Highly coloured. Flesh yellow, excellent quality. Freestone. Good mid-season variety in eastern locations.

Harmony Last two weeks August, Michigan. Large. Yellow, flushed red. Flesh yellow, good quality. Freestone. Productive, hardy.

Golden Jubilee Small to medium. Golden yellow, flushed bright red. Flesh bright yellow, very soft, good quality. Freestone.

Wildrose Medium size. Greenish yellow with bright red. Flesh white with red flecks throughout, soft, good quality. Freestone.

Redglobe Large. Yellow to dark red. Flesh yellow, excellent quality. Freestone. Fruit hangs on tree quite well without becoming overripe.

La Red Medium to large. Yellow with bright red. Flesh yellow, mottled red, excellent quality. Freestone.

La Premiere Medium to large. Bright yellow with bright red. Flesh bright yellow with very little red. Freestone. Good resistance to bacterial spot.

Loring Second week July, Louisiana; last two weeks August, Michigan. Large. Yellow, flushed deep red. Flesh yellow, firm, good quality. Freestone. Heavy cropper with adequate winter chilling.

Somerset Large. Yellow, flushed bright red. Flesh yellow, very firm, good flavour. Freestone. Vigorous, highly productive, very susceptible to bacterial spot.

Babygold 5 Medium to large. Yellow, flushed red. Flesh yellow. Clingstone.

Babygold 7 Similar to preceding.

Nectared 6 (Nectarine) Small. Yellow to full red. Flesh yellow. Freestone. Very productive.

Suwanee Large. Yellow to deep red. Flesh yellowish orange. Very good flavour. Freestone. Fairly vigorous. Suitable warmer climates.

Nectared 8 (Nectarine) Medium. Yellow to dark red. Flesh yellow, very good flavour. Freestone.

Flamekist Medium to large. Rich yellow, flushed red. Flesh yellow. Clingstone. Productive, but fruit sensitive to Monilia infection.

Suncrest Large. Yellow with deep red blush and streaks. Flesh rich yellow, very red near stone. Freestone. Vigorous, highly productive.

Early Coronet Medium. Yellow with light red blush and streaks. Flesh pale yellow, light red staining, good quality and flavour. Semi-clingstone.

Stark Earliglo Medium to large. Yellow with bright red. Flesh pale yellow, good texture, good flavour. Semi-clingstone. Vigorous, very productive.

Early Redhaven Medium. Yellow with light red to bright red. Flesh pale yellow with light red stain; greenish near the stone. Semi-clingstone.

Sunshine Medium to large. Golden yellow with light red blush and streaks. Flesh yellow with some red staining, good texture and flavour. Freestone. Very productive.

Suncling Beginning September, Michigan. Large. Mostly golden, flushed bright red on side exposed to sun. Very smooth. Flesh orange-yellow, fine texture, very firm. Clingstone.

M. A. Blake Large. Bright yellow with red blush. Flesh yellow, good quality. Tree fairly tender.

Cresthaven Beginning August, Kentucky; beginning September, Michigan. Medium. Golden flushed bright red, very attractive. Flesh yellow, firm. Freestone. Hangs well on the tree. Hardy.

Olinda Medium. Mainly red. Flesh yellow, firm, good quality. Freestone. Ripens over fairly long period. Leaves subject to bacterial spot.

Redskin Mid-July, Louisiana; second half August, Kentucky; second week September, Michigan. Large. Colours well with deep blush even in shade. Flesh yellow, good quality. Freestone. Good cropper even under frosty conditions because of long flowering period.

Jersey Queen Large. Highly coloured. Flesh yellow, firm, excellent quality. Freestone. Susceptible to bacterial spot.

Elberta Old variety. Fruit drops when ripe, flesh browns badly. The Barden Elberta, a superior strain in colour and quality, retains the productiveness of the original variety.

Dixiland Second half July, Louisiana. Medium to large. Yellow with light to medium dark red. Flesh yellow, firm, excellent quality. Freestone. Fruit and foliage have good resistance to bacterial spot.

Tyler End August, Virginia. Medium. Orange-yellow with red. Flesh orange-yellow. Superior quality to other varieties ripening at same time. Moderate vigour, hardy.

J. H. Hale Mid-September, Michigan. Very large. Highly coloured, attractive. Good quality.

Marhigh (Late Redskin) Closely resembles Redskin, but ripens few days later.

VARIETIES FOR WARMER CLIMATES

These varieties can fruit well, although subjected to very little winter chilling.

Flordared Second half April, south central Florida. Medium. Heavy red blush. Flesh white, good quality. Freestone.

Early Amber First half May, central Florida. Small to medium. Red blush covers most of surface. Flesh yellow, firm. Clingstone.

Desertgold Small to medium. Attractive red blush. Flesh yellow. Clingstone.

Sunred (Nectarine) Medium. Almost completely red. Flesh yellow, firm, excellent flavour. Semi-freestone.

Flordabelle Late May, central Florida. Large. Yellow. Flesh yellow, firm. Freestone.

June Gold Late May. Yellow, blushed red. Flesh yellow, good texture. Clingstone. Suitable for north Florida.

Maygold Late May, north Florida. Medium. Yellow blushed red. Flesh yellow, firm. Semi-freestone. Principal commercial variety in north Florida.

Rio Grande Early June, north Florida. Large. Yellow, heavily blushed red. Flesh yellow, firm. Freestone.

Suwannee Large. Yellow, with light green shading and red blush. Flesh yellow, good flavour. Fairly vigorous, highly productive.

VARIETIES FOR WET, COLD CLIMATES

Wet and cold conditions during the flowering period causes poor setting of the fruit. The following varieties have been recommended for areas such as western Washington: *Redhaven, Ranger, Fairhaven, Redglobe, Cardinal, Herb Hale, Veteran, Early Elberta* (Gleason strain). Their harvest season extends from about 20 July to 10 September in south-western Washington.

17

PEARS

Pears prefer a slightly acid soil; one that is excessively alkaline should be avoided as it suffers badly from iron deficiency. Although pears are better able than apples to withstand poor drainage, they do not contend so well with a dry soil. A very light sandy soil must be liberally enriched with moisture-holding humus. What is required is a warm rich loam, so a good compost would consist of turf loam to which has been added a small quantity of decayed manure. Pear trees in pots must have a good supply of moisture. They need slightly more nitrogen and less potash than apples, but will not respond to inorganic fertilisers. However, a small amount of sulphate of ammonia (say, 1 oz to a bushel of compost) may be added when a good proportion of the compost is humus. In all cases the amount of nitrogen given should depend on growth and cropping.

The choice of rootstock for pears is more limited than for apples. It is unsatisfactory to obtain trees on seedling pear rootstock, as these will grow to an unmanageable size and not come into production for perhaps twelve years. There are several varieties of quince, two of which are: Malling Quince A (Angers Quince) which produces good bush trees that maintain their vigour; Malling Quince C which induces slightly less vigour. Some varieties of pear (eg Dr Jules Guyot, Merton Pride, Williams Bon Chretien) are incompatible with quince, so that, even if the bud 'takes', the union is brittle and the scion is liable to break away from the rootstock. Because of this, it is necessary with some varieties to resort to double grafting, using an intermediate variety compatible to both the rootstock and the required scion.

The recommended form of tree is the dwarf pyramid because it comes into cropping early and is convenient for pot work. Or the single cordon can be used and in this way the maximum number of different varieties may be grown. In France the extensive use of pyramid, espalier, fuseau and various forms of cordon in the open orchard is made possible by the fact that pears stand harder pruning than apples and generally form spurs more freely. Tip-bearing varieties should be avoided in a potted orchard. For training trees to the dwarf pyramid form, strong maidens should be purchased; the method to be followed is outlined in chapter 2.

The pruning of pear trees follows the same pattern, basically, as for apples. Once the framework of the tree has been attained, all side shoots should be pruned to four leaves during summer. When the trees have started cropping, the spurs should be thinned out, either in summer or winter, to encourage new wood growth. A difficulty with dwarf pyramids is to prevent them becoming bare at the base, so it is of benefit to cut back branches, causing them to produce new growth.

Certain varieties (eg Doyenne du Comice) have a more erect habit than apples; when pruning branch leaders to a bud for extension growth, it is better to prune to a bud *above* the outward pointing bud required. The result will be that the outward pointing bud will grow at a wider angle or more horizontal position and the unwanted part of the stem above can be removed later.

Because of the root restriction in the pots and with summer pruning, the growth of the tree is checked; if manuring is satisfactory, plenty of fruit buds but few shoots will be formed so that in some years fruit thinning will be necessary. Some varieties have a tendency to produce a heavy crop one year and a light one the next. If this happens, the pruning of new wood should be very light and the spurs reduced before the next year. About a third of the blossom should also be removed in spring to further reduce a heavy crop.

The pear blossoms just before the apple. The honey bee is particularly useful as a pollinator. Pear buds are almost as hardy as the apple and plum, and if pollination has been satisfactory a good set is usually obtained. Most pears are diploids, so two varieties are needed to pollinate each other; a few are triploids, which means that two other varieties will be required. Several diploid varieties are unable to pollinate each other although they may be in bloom together. For example, the very fertile Conference is unable to pollinate Beurre d'Amanlis, though the reverse pollination is effective. However self-fertile a pear may be, it is always good practice to have one or more other varieties in the vicinity.

In some seasons, Conference sets a full crop of fruit which carry no seeds in them. This is more noticeable in years of frost when, although the ovules or seeds are killed, the receptacle that forms the fruit continues to grow. Thus a full crop of fruit may be obtained from this variety when others fail, which helps to give it a good reputation for regular cropping.

As the fruits develop, they should never be allowed to touch one another and those varieties which bear small fruit should be thinned more than others. As the fruit ripens, protection may be necessary from birds and wasps. Pears must be harvested with more care than apples. They bruise more easily and early varieties quickly deteriorate if left to become overripe. The correct time to pick early varieties is when, if they are lifted level with the stalk, they just—but only just—part from the tree. Mid-season and late season varieties should be picked when, if lifted, they readily part from the tree. This lifting test is a more reliable guide than the colour of the skin. For example, the early variety Laxton Superb should be gathered and eaten while still pale green in colour; if allowed to remain on the tree until it becomes yellow, it will have lost its flavour. When picking the fruit care must be taken not to pull them off roughly as this will break or damage the spurs. They should be lifted and at the same time twisted sideways.

Early fruits should be laid out and allowed to ripen for a few days only before being eaten, because few of them keep and they soon become mealy and tasteless. Mid-season varieties can be stored in a cool, slightly moist room and used as required, or they can be kept in the open in boxes, provided they are protected from rain, birds, mice etc. Late varieties are not ready for eating when first picked and will need similar storage conditions as for apples but with a slightly higher temperature to continue their ripening. They are best stored in single layers in trays, standing upright with stalk uppermost and not touching one another. Preferably they should be kept in an even temperature between 40° F (4° C) and 45° F (7° C). If it is lower than this, the ripening is delayed and breakdowns may develop in the flesh, causing brown patches. The fruit should be inspected from time to time, any decayed pear being removed before it affects others near to it.

DISEASES

FIREBLIGHT *(Erwinia amylovora)*

This bacterium originated in North America but now affects pears and apples almost everywhere they are grown.

First symptoms are dead blossom or dark brown leaves hanging from a truss or branch. Numerous blighted twigs with clinging dead leaves give the tree the appearance of having been scorched by fire, hence the name fireblight. On branches the bark of diseased areas is dark green or dark brown, often water soaked, and with an indistinct margin between healthy and infected tissue. During warm, humid weather a glistening whitish bacterial slime may ooze from affected shoots, branches and fruit, but in dry weather this appears as a silvery film. Leaves on infected branches turn dark brown, as do the infected fruits which remain attached to the tree after leaf fall. During summer the disease spreads very rapidly through the tissues of spurs and shoots, and into the branches which are quickly killed. Once the disease reaches the trunk, it invades other branches and the tree soon dies. After leaf fall the disease usually becomes dormant, the canker extension ceases and cracks appear on the branches at the margin between diseased and healthy branches. The onset of winter does not always check the disease and, in the case of pears, the cankers may continue to extend and exude slime even in mid-winter. When less vigorous trees are infected the symptoms are similar, but the disease spreads more slowly, produces smaller cankers and, in general, causes less damage to the form or framework of the tree. Also a typical reddish-brown discolouration under the bark may be less apparent.

In warm, humid weather the bacterial slime from the diseased branches is carried to the blossom by insects or rain and, under suitable conditions, the bacteria multiply very rapidly and the infection is again transmitted, not only by insects and rain but by wind-blown contaminated blossom. Epidemic infection can occur under these conditions when there are daily maximum temperatures higher than 65° F (18° C) at blossom time. Thus in countries, such as England, where blossom time normally occurs in much lower temperatures than this, blossom infection is less likely to occur. Branches can be infected directly through wounds.

If death of part of a tree is thought to be due to fireblight, a slanting cut should be made into the bark of the twig or branch, well below the external signs of the disease. Further cuts should be made towards the canker or discoloured part to ascertain whether the typical reddish-brown staining of the bark is present. If it is visible in the bark of the trunk, the tree should be destroyed. Twigs or shoots 1in or less in diameter which show symptoms should be cut off not less than 12in below the stain. Affected branches 1in or more in diameter should be cut off not less than 2ft below the stain. If three or more points of infection are found, the tree should be destroyed. Knives and secateurs should be disinfected between examining one twig or branch and the next. If a saw is used, it should be swabbed thoroughly with disinfectant. All cut surfaces on the tree should be painted immediately with white lead paint. In the USA, spraying with copper sulphate just before bud-burst reduces the amount of infection from the bacterial slime.

PEAR SCAB *(Ventura pirina)*

This is of much greater importance in Europe than North America, partly owing to climatic conditions and also because of cultivation of more resistant varieties in America. Although of world-wide distribution, it is not prevalent in dry conditions.

Apple scab and pear scab have much in common, but are distinct biologically; apple scab cannot affect pears and pear scab cannot affect apples. Symptoms of the two diseases are similar, but with pear scab the fruits are usually affected before the leaves; until blossom time these are tightly rolled and offer little surface on which the spores can alight. Compared with apples, infection of young shoots is often more severe and the individual pustules are much larger and more open, providing easier access for canker.

Most varieties of pear are susceptible to the disease, but some are more resistant than others. However, because there are distinct races of the fungus, varieties which are resistant in one region may be susceptible to a different race in another region. For example, in Denmark the variety Clapp's Favourite is recorded as resistant while in England it is considered susceptible. (See also under APPLE SCAB.)

CANKER see under Apples.

PEAR LEAF BLIGHT (FRUIT SPOT) *(Fabraea maculata)*

Leaf blight occurs in most countries of the world where pears are grown. Symptoms may be seen on leaves, fruit and shoots. Small purple dots appear on leaves, later extending to purple or dark brown lesions about ¼in in diameter, with a small black pimple in the centre of the spot. When the leaf spots are numerous extensive defoliation takes place. On the fruit the spots are black in colour and become slightly sunken, otherwise they are similar to the spots on the leaves. When the spots are grouped together, which is often the case, cracking of the fruit occurs. On twigs the lesions may be seen on the current season's growth in midsummer or later. They consist of purple or black areas with an indistinct outline which merge together and form small cankers. Many of these will later heal, but some will be found on the shoots in the spring of the year following infection.

Sometimes the infected tree may be defoliated by mid-summer, it will carry dwarf fruit, and fruit buds will be reduced. Leaves should be gathered in order to prevent primary infection. Chemical sprays will control the disease, preventing canker development.

SOOTY BLOTCH (SOOTY SMUDGE) *(Gloeodes pomeigena)*
This disease of pear and apple occurs in North America, Europe and Australia. It spoils the appearance of the fruit and will be seen as small black, often glistening, spots which resemble flyspecks. At the same time larger spots will appear, varying in size and indefinite in outline, with a smudged, sooty appearance. The fungus is superficial and can be removed by scrubbing, but underneath where it has occurred there might be a slight pitting. It may be confused with the growth of fungi or honeydew deposited by aphids.

The fungus is often more prevalent in low or shaded areas, so a better movement of drying air around the trees may provide a remedy.

PESTS

PEAR MIDGE *(Diplosis pyrivora)*
Sometimes this pest is a nuisance in gardens, occurring year after year. An attack can be easily diagnosed soon after the fruit has set. The infected fruitlets swell to about twice their normal size, sometimes becoming deformed, and within a few weeks they begin to crack, decay and fall from the tree. The large, round fruitlets will consist of wet, black debris in which are a number of small, white, legless maggots. When the fruitlets fall to the ground the maggots leave them and burrow into the soil. They are able to travel short distances with curious jumping movements. They pupate in the soil and the following April emerge as small inconspicuous midges which commence to lay their eggs in the pear blossom.

As a control measure all infected fruit should be collected and burnt or buried. Birds and poultry will quickly pick up the maggots.

PEAR LEAF BLISTER MITE *(Eriophyes piri)*
The mites, close relatives of the big bud mite, which attacks black currants, are less than 1/100 in in length. During winter they spend their time under the outer scales of the buds, but in spring move out on to young leaves where they commence feeding. At this time their presence is easily recognised by the blisters and puckering of the leaves which they cause. When the foliage of an infested tree opens in spring, small pink or yellowish green pimples or blisters will be seen on the upper surface of an attacked leaf. As they age the blisters turn brown and then black. Sometimes in late summer the entire leaf blackens and dies. In severe infestations the fruitlets may become deformed and die.

Breeding takes place within the blisters and the young mites, after feeding within them for a time, move on and cause fresh blisters elsewhere.

Reproduction continues throughout the summer, but before the commencement of leaf fall the mites move back into the shelter of the bud scales. Infested leaves should be hand-picked and burnt. The mite can also be successfully controlled with chemicals.

PEAR AND CHERRY SLUGWORM *(Caliroa cerasi)*
This slugworm is the larva of the pear slug sawfly. In the adult stage, the sawfly is a small, black insect about $\frac{1}{3}$in long with two pairs of wings. It first appears in early summer when it lays its eggs on the undersides of the leaves, each egg being inserted into a slit made in the leaf. After about two weeks the eggs hatch and the young larvae make their way to the upper surface of the leaf and commence feeding. At first the slugworms are whitish, but soon become dark green or black and exude a dark green slime. When fully fed, usually in early July, they lose their slug-like appearance and become yellow with a dry, wrinkled skin. They then descend to the ground and burrow a few inches below the surface, eventually turning into the chrysalis stage. After about a fortnight a second generation of adult sawflies emerges and eggs are again laid on the foliage. The majority of the resulting slugworms do not change into pupae when fully fed but remain throughout the winter as larvae within their cocoons until the following spring. The pest can be very serious on small trees but is easily controlled with chemicals. Almost any kind of dry powder, such as Derris (rotenone), will kill the larvae.

CODLIN MOTH *(Cydia pomonella)*
The habits of this pest are much the same as on the apple, except that there is a greater tendency for the larvae to enter at the eye rather than at the side of the fruit. Sometimes it can be a serious pest of pears but its general occurrence is less than with apples (see further under Apples).

ITALIAN PEAR SCALE *(Epidiaspis piricola)*
This is an important pest in the western districts of USA, if moss and lichen are present. Other scale such as San Jose may occur in other parts (see also under Apples).

PEAR APHIS *(Yezabura pyra)*
In appearance and habits this very much resembles the rosy apple aphis. Various other aphis may infest the pear, but generally are of less importance than on the apple tree.

PEAR SUCKER *(Psylla simulans)*

An important pest in North America and Europe, it appears to transmit a virus causing 'pear decline'. Adult suckers, green in colour, may be seen in winter resting on shoots and spurs, but many may also shelter amongst dead leaves or other places offering protection. They appear to be unaffected by cold and often make short flights on bright, sunny days. They commence laying eggs on spurs and shoots from mid-March until full bloom. At first the eggs are almost colourless, but later become a deep lemon colour. Hatching usually begins at bud-burst and continues until the end of flowering. Newly hatched suckers are very pale with prominent pinkish-red eyes. Maturity is reached by summer, when a second batch of eggs are laid on the leaves. There are usually three generations a year, peak populations being reached about early June, late July and mid-Octo-

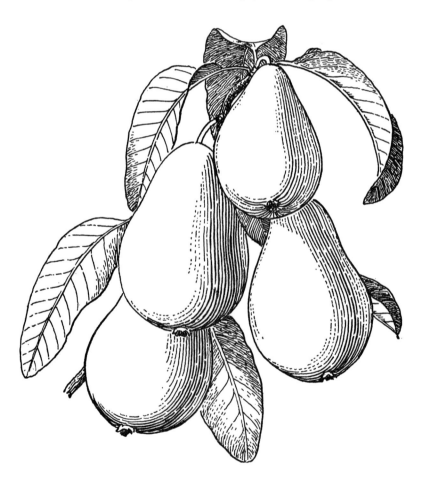

ber. In the absence of any control measures, even small numbers of adults surviving the winter can result in very large populations by the end of the following summer.

VARIETIES

For pollination purposes, the varieties are set out in their periods of flowering. Colour applies to when they are fully ripe.

Précoce de Trevoux Medium to small, conical. Bright yellow. Sweet, slightly sub-acid, juicy. Ready for picking beginning August, keeps in natural store for only very short time. Small to medium tree. Prone to scab but very productive, coming into bearing early and cropping regularly. Flowering early. Incompatible with Louise Bonne and Williams Bon Chretien.

Passe Crassane Large, round to conical. Orange-yellow, spotted russet when ripe. Agreeably sub-acid with slight aniseed flavour, juicy. Keeps well in natural storage if picked as late as possible. Moderate vigour. Crops well and regularly, not suitable for exposed positions. Resistant to scab. Flowering early.

Comtesse de Paris Medium, pyriform. Yellow with russet spots. Fair texture, juicy, sweet. Good dessert pear. Ready for picking October, as late as possible. Keeps well in natural storage. Weak growth. Resistant to scab. Bears early, crops well. Flowering early. Self-compatible.

Louise Bonne de Jersey Small to medium, pyriform. Pale green, yellow flushed carmine on sun side. Sweet, slightly sub-acid, very juicy, pleasant aroma. Good dessert pear. Ready second half September. Weak growth. Prone to scab, bears well and regularly. Flowering early. Incompatible with Précoce de Trevoux and Williams Bon Chretien. Vulnerable to spring frosts.

Durondeau Medium to large, pyriform. Yellow, tinged with carmine. Fair texture, juicy, sweet, sub-acid, refreshing. Very good dessert pear. Ready for picking second half September. Weak to medium growth. Prone to scab, crops well and regularly. Early flowering. Tendency to parthenocarpy.

Conference Medium to medium-large, pyriform. Pale yellow when ripe. Tender, juicy, sweet. Very good dessert pear. Ready end September, deteriorates rapidly in natural storage. Weak vigour. Prone to canker,

M

resistant to scab. Bears early, crops well and regularly. Flowering semi-early. Tendency to parthenocarpy.

Doyenne de Merode Medium, round to oval. Yellow, flushed carmine, with brown-grey mottling. Sweet, sub-acid, juicy. Good for dessert or cooking. Ready end August. Vigorous growth. Crops well but often biennially. Flowering semi-early. Compatible with Beurre Hardy.

Legipont Medium, pyriform. Light green, shaded pale yellow, covered with large grey spots when ripe, sometimes slightly tinged red. Good texture, sometimes a little coarse around core. Sweet, sub-acid, aromatic. Good for dessert, canning or bottling. Ready end September, should be picked while still green and ripened in store. Medium to strong vigour. Prone to scab, crops well. Flowering semi-early. Tendency to parthenocarpy.

Emile d'Heyst Medium, oval. Bronze, stippled with brown. Flesh firm, juicy, sweet, refreshing, perfumed. Weak growth. Crops well. Flowering semi-early. Self-incompatible.

Merton Pride Medium to large, conical to pyriform. Golden yellow, almost covered with brown russet. Fine texture, excellent flavour. Ready last half September. Moderately strong growth, light cropper. Flowering mid-early. Triploid.

Beurre Superfin Medium, conical. Yellow with much russet. Sweet, delicately perfumed. Good for dessert, canning and bottling. Ready for picking October. Moderate growth, moderate cropper. Flowering mid-season.

Doyenne d'Eté Small, conical. Yellow with brownish red flesh. Very juicy, sweet. Excellent flavour for an early fruit. Ready end July, beginning August (one of the first to ripen but lasts only a few days). Moderate growth. Flowering mid-season.

Trout Pear (Forelle) Medium, pyriform. Skin covered with pinkish red dots like a trout. Good texture, tender, well flavoured, rather sweet. Ready for picking late November. Medium growth. Erratic cropping. Flowering mid-season.

Thompson's Medium, conical. Yellow with light brown russet. Juicy, richer flavour and sweeter than Doyenne du Comice. Good dessert pear. Ready for picking late October—early November. Weak growth. Moderate cropper. Flowering mid-season.

Souvenir de Congres   Large, conical. Yellow with bright red flush. Juicy, sweet, musky flavour like Williams. Ready September, ripens very quickly and needs watching. Vigorous growth, upright. Heavy cropper. Flowering mid-season.

Merton Star   Medium, conical to pyriform. Greenish yellow with patches of golden brown russet. Fine texture, firm, juicy. Superior flavour to Conference, ready about same time during last half September. Weak growth, sparse branches spurring freely. Flowering mid-season.

Williams Bon Chretien (Bartlett)   Medium, turbinate to oval. Golden yellow with russet dots, streaks and patches of fawn, sometimes tinged with light red on sun side. Juicy, sweet, faintly sub-acid, highly aromatic with muscatel flavour. Popular dessert variety, good also for canning or bottling. Ready end August, beginning September. Keeps only short time in natural storage. Medium vigour. Prone to scab, crops well. Flowering semi-late. Incompatible with Louise Bonne and Précoce de Trevoux.

Beurre Hardy   Medium, turbinate. Dull yellow, stippled all over with fawn. Fine texture, buttery, very juicy, sweet, aromatic. Excellent dessert. Ready for picking second half September. Vigorous growth. Very hardy, succeeds in most places. Heavy cropper, slow to come into bearing. Flowering semi-late.

Beurre d'Humboldt   Medium to large, calabash, rather long. Fawn-yellow or yellowish brown, covered with patches of russet and greyish white spots, colour deeper on sun side. Very juicy, sweet, refreshing. Good for dessert, excellent for cooking and canning. Ready for picking end September, beginning October. Keeps fairly well in natural store. Moderate vigour. Good and regular cropper, but sometimes biennial. Flowering late.

Jean D'Arc   Medium, pyriform. Lemon yellow when ripe. Fine texture, very juicy, sweet, sub-acid, distinctive flavour, faintly perfumed. Good dessert pear, if picked as late as possible. Weak growth, upright. Bears early and crops regularly. Resistant to scab. Flowering semi-late to late. Self-incompatible.

Bristol Cross   Large, calabash. Resembles Conference. Yellow with thin, patchy russet. Good texture, juicy, good flavour. Ready for picking beginning October. Moderate growth. Resistant to scab. Heavy cropper. Flowering semi-late.

Doyenne du Comice Large, turbinate. Straw yellow, stippled with small greyish dots and mottled with fawn, sometimes slight red flush. Juicy, very sweet, rich, sugary agreeable flavour, delicate aroma. The best of the dessert pears. Good for canning and bottling. Ready for picking first half October. Keeps in natural store until Christmas. Vigorous growth, fair cropper. Intolerant of lime-sulphur sprays. Flowering late. Self-incompatible, compatible with Williams, Conference, Jean d'Arc.

Gorham Medium, conical. Pale yellow, streaked russet. Tender, juicy, sweet with muscatel flavour. Ready end September, lasts about two weeks. Medium vigour. Resistant to scab. Moderate to heavy cropper. Flowering late.

Winter Nellis Small, conical. Yellowish green turning to dull russet. Sweet, very juicy, good flavour. Good quality. Keeps till late January, should be eaten while still yellowish green. Weak growth. Resistant to scab. Flowering late. Useful as pollinator of Doyenne du Comice.

Moonglow Large. Very attractive. Good flavour and quality. Ready early August ahead of Bartlett. Heavily spurred, very productive. Resistant to fireblight.

Howell Medium to large. Bright golden with red flush. Fairly good quality. Useful as good pollinator for Bartlett.

Box Large. Deep yellow overspread with cinnamon russet. Tender, very juicy, aromatic. A good late pear.

18

PLUMS

Plums are the most widely distributed of the stone fruits. There are several species of Prunus, commonly called plums, damsons and gages, the three most important being *P. domestica* (European plums), *P. insititia* (damsons, bullaces, mirabelles), *P. salicinia* (oriental plums). Mirabelles and bullaces are small round fruits usually ripening later than damsons, which can be eaten raw but are excellent for cooking. Gages are a type of plum with a more characteristic and delicious flavour. They are all cultivated in the same way as plums.

The European plum does not adapt itself very well to regions with hot dry summers or dry cold winters. In North America they do best in the irrigated regions of the inter-mountain states, Pacific coast states, north-eastern United States and sheltered areas around the Great Lakes. The oriental plum is far more tolerant of soil and climatic conditions and, as a consequence, has been introduced into North America. Throughout Europe many varieties of the European plum are cultivated, from Italy in the south to southern Norway and Sweden in the north.

Plums require a medium to heavy soil which is moisture retentive yet not water-logged. They do best in districts where the rainfall is between 20 and 35in. A high rainfall area is not a disadvantage, except at blossom time or when the fruit is close to ripening, because certain varieties, such as gages, may tend to split. They flower after the peach, before the apple and pear, and about the same time as the bush fruits. A frost-free site is therefore essential. Sometimes a crop is poor because pollinating insects were discouraged by cold winds and dull weather. During blossom time, trees should, if possible, be given a sheltered site so that bees are encouraged to work among the blossom. Plums do not require so much sunshine as pears and, once the blossoming period is finished, they can be moved into a more open position.

Trees should be potted up as early as possible from November to March, using a rich garden soil with plenty of humus to hold moisture. A very acid soil should be limed because pears need calcium, but at the same time do not need one with a high degree of alkalinity, otherwise they will suffer from lime-induced iron deficiency. The soil should be rich in nitrogen so that, when established, the tree makes plenty of healthy young shoots. Each spring a mulch of well-rotted manure, if available, or garden compost can be given.

There are many named plum rootstocks, but only two which can be described as 'semi-dwarf': Common Plum and St Julian 'A'. Characteristics of some of the rootstocks are as follows:

St Julian 'A' (Semi-dwarf) Produces fertile trees and is compatible with most varieties. For pots, choose this rootstock in preference to others.

Common Plum (Semi-dwarf) Incompatible with many varieties and sometimes infected with bark-split virus.

Pershore (Semi-vigorous) Produces medium-sized, heavy-cropping trees.

Common Mussel (Semi-vigorous) Compatible with most varieties, produces heavy-cropping, medium-sized trees.

Mariana (Vigorous) Slow to crop, but very heavy when in crop. Incompatible with many varieties.

Myrobalan B (Vigorous)   A commercial stock. Produces the largest and heaviest cropping trees. Compatible with most varieties.

Brompton (Vigorous)   Produces trees comparable in size to Myrobalan B, but not quite so heavy cropping. Compatible with most varieties.

The plum, like the cherry, produces fruit spurs on one- and two-year-old wood. Its best form is, therefore, one which allows plenty of new shoots to grow full-length each year without crowding the tree. The choice should be the bush or dwarf pyramid. Although plums are not so amenable to training as the apple and pear, the artificial forms may be tried if fruit size and quality is the first consideration.

Once the desired form has been established, the plum should be pruned as little as possible in the winter as it is susceptible to silver leaf disease. Pruning should be done after the fruit has been picked. To keep the tree well supplied with plenty of new fruiting wood, a few laterals can be cut back or entirely removed each year. Shoots arising vertically on the lower laterals should be tipped as for a leader, so that if necessary they can replace the drooping ends of the lateral on which they are growing. Young trees, however, may be pruned in winter so as to get a good response in spring from the selected buds. Such pruning of young trees during the period of dormancy is less liable to cause an infection of silver leaf because they should be healthy and vigorous, and the wounds are relatively small.

One of the greatest troubles with plums is their continual formation of suckers. If possible, these should be removed immediately they are noticed. The soil should be carefully scraped away up to and around the scion, as the suckers usually arise from roots just below the point where the scion has been grafted on to the rootstock. The sucker should then be pulled from the root, which will soon heal. Suckers can also be removed when repotting, but if they are cut off the cut should be clean with the root, otherwise, although only a small fraction of the sucker is left, buds will form from which more suckers will arise.

A few varieties, such as Pershore (Yellow Egg), are sufficiently self-compatible to give a heavy crop without a pollinator, but generally it is desirable to grow more than one variety. When partially self-fertile varieties are grown, adequate cross-pollination must be provided by other varieties which flower at the same time and are not more than 40ft away.

The fruit of the potted plum tree should be thinned. Quality is improved and biennial bearing minimised. Thinning should be spread over several days when the stones have just formed. Diseased and mis-shapen fruits must be removed whenever they occur. Fruit should be spaced out and, when a young plum tree first commences bearing, say, at three years old, it can be allowed to keep about twenty of its fruit. When thinning, snap the stalk with a twist of the thumb and fingers close to the fruit. The stalk should be left on the shoot; if pulled from it, this may injure the shoot and so affect the next year's crop.

Birds will spoil ripening plums, and wasps will be attracted to pecked fruit, but small potted trees can easily be protected with netting. The trees can be moved in succession into the orchard house as their fruits ripen. Choice dessert plums of a very high quality will be obtained, unmatched by commercial varieties. The fruits should be left on the tree until thoroughly ripe. They should be handled as little as possible so that the 'bloom' is not spoiled, being snipped off with scissors with the stalk attached, care being taken not to damage the shoot or spur. The season can be extended slightly by gathering some a few days before they are dead ripe, wrapping them individually in paper and storing them in a cool, airy place. It is possible to keep them for about two weeks. Gages ripen unevenly and, by careful picking, one variety can be made to last up to two weeks. Cooking plums are gathered as soon as they begin to turn colour, the largest fruit being taken first.

DISEASES

BACTERIAL CANKER (LEAF SPOT) *(Pseudomonas mors-prunorum)*

This is a serious disease of young plum trees. Symptoms are similar to those of cherry infections (see under Cherries), but there are a few important differences. With the plum, the stem is usually more cankered than individual branches. Gumming at the side of the canker is not so copious and the leaf spot phase does not normally appear to any extent before summer. When the tree stem is attacked, provided it is not girdled in one season, it will probably recover, although its vigour will be curtailed for a time.

SOOTY BLOTCH *(Gloeodes pomigena)*

This can spread rapidly in wet weather, but is not of common occurrence in dry summers. It can occur in the orchard house when air is stagnant and the atmosphere humid. Affected fruits have blackish circular areas on the skin and look as if they have been handled with sooty fingers. However, the fungus is entirely superficial and the spread of the disease can be prevented by allowing a free circulation of air around the trees to promote rapid drying after rain or spraying.

SHARKA (PLUM POX)
This is a very important virus disease in south-eastern Europe and isolated
cases have been found in Britain. An infected tree may appear little different from a healthy one as regards vigour of growth but the leaves will
show various types of mottling, depending on the season and variety. In
general, the mottling is indistinct and consists of light green to yellowish
green blotches. It may be first seen when the leaves are fully expanded
and is more easily visible on dull days or when the sunlight is behind the
leaf. Symptoms are more obvious on the fruit, the disease causing it to
drop thirty to forty days before ripening, leaving very little on the tree.
Most of the fruit is poxed, with the flesh below being dark red or brown
and rotten. The stones may have dark red lines and rings on their surface,
while the fruit is tasteless or sometimes rather bitter. Fruit which remains
on the tree ripens ten to fifteen days before the normal ripening period.

The virus is spread by aphid vectors and a regular spray programme will
help to give protection. Once infection occurs, there is no alternative but
to eradicate the tree.

SILVER LEAF *(Stereum purpureum)*   see under Apricots.

BROWN ROT   *(Sclerotinia laxa)*   see under Apricots.

PESTS

PLUM CURCULIO *(Conotrachelus nenuphar)*
A troublesome pest in North America, where it not only damages the
fruit of the plum, cherry, peach and apricot, but is a vector of the brown
rot fungus. The adult is a dark brown weevil, about $\frac{1}{5}$in long, with two
prominent tubercles on its back and a head drawn out into a long snout.
During winter it hibernates beneath rubbish under the tree, emerging in
early spring to feed on the buds and young leaves. The female lays its eggs
in little holes chewed in the developing fruit, using its snout to push the
egg deep into the hole, and then cuts a crescent-shaped slit just below.
Perhaps hundreds of eggs are laid in the one fruit. The spots and crescents
are a clear sign of the infestation. In about two weeks the eggs hatch and
the grubs feed their way through the flesh towards the stone. Usually the
fruit drops before the larvae are fully grown. Later, when they have
reached full growth, they leave the fruit and burrow into the soil to pupate.
A new generation of adults appears in mid-summer, feeding on fruit on
the ground until the onset of cold weather when they hibernate under

rubbish. An obvious method of control is to break the life cycle by removing all fallen fruit from the ground.

APHIDS

Several species of aphids are commonly found on plums, the most important being leaf-curling plum aphid *(Brachycaudus helichrysi)*; mealy plum aphid *(Hyalopterus pruni)*; damson-hop aphid *(Phorodon humuli)*.

The presence of the leaf-curling aphid is recognised by the tightly curled leaves which occur on infested spurs and shoots. After a bad attack the leaves may turn yellow and fall prematurely, while the new growth is checked and fruit is undersized. Eggs are laid in autumn on twigs and at the base of buds; unlike the eggs of most species of aphids, these hatch within a month of being laid. The hatch is usually completed by the middle of January. The young aphids feed on the dormant buds and reach maturity before bud-burst. Successive generations of wingless aphids appear until May and from then until July winged forms are produced which migrate and form colonies on herbaceous plants. In September, aphids return to the plum trees to lay eggs.

The mealy plum aphid is less harmful. Eggs are laid in autumn on twigs and at the base of buds, but do not hatch until April. The pest is abundant in mid-summer and produces a white, sticky secretion on the leaves and fruit. Colonies often persist on plum trees until August, although some may begin to migrate to water grasses and reeds in June. A closely related species with a similar life cycle lives on the peach, but will not survive on the plum; conversely the mealy plum aphid cannot live on the peach.

The damson-hop aphid causes damage and distortion of leaves very early in spring. Its feeding cripples leader growth and saps the strength of the tree. Eggs are laid on plum, damson and blackthorn in autumn, hatching in early spring. The first two generations are wingless but subsequent ones are winged, migrating to hops where their offspring cause hop blight. Wingless aphids are born on hops until September, when winged aphids are produced which return to plum trees.

Control is with chemical sprays.

FRUIT-TREE RED SPIDER MITE *(Panonychus ulmi)*
This mite is often very serious on damsons, particularly the prune types, while certain plums and gages do not seem to attract it.

PLUM MAGGOT *(Cyoia funebrana)*
The adult moths are very closely related to the codlin moth. Eggs are laid

on fruit stalks in June and July. Tiny pink caterpillars hatch out and tunnel into the green fruit where they feed around the stone. In late summer they emerge and then hibernate in cocoons under rough bark and similar places. Usually no evidence of the pest is apparent until the fruit is eaten, when a brown frass will be found near the stone and usually a large red maggot. However, affected fruits ripen prematurely, so these can be collected and destroyed when they drop. Otherwise sprays, such as Derris, are effective in July and August, provided they catch the caterpillars as they hatch and before they tunnel into the fruit.

PLUM SAWFLY *(Hoplocampa flava)*
In appearance and habit this is similar to the apple sawfly. Some varieties, such as Victoria and Czar, may in some seasons be badly infested when many of the fruits will be found to contain a maggot near the stone with a consequent gumming and distortion. Fruit will often fall and the grubs then pupate in the soil. All fallen fruit should therefore be immediately collected and destroyed.

ORIENTAL FRUIT FLY   see under Peaches.

PEACH TWIG BORER   see under Peaches.

VARIETIES
Most plum varieties which are grown commercially are self-compatible and will crop successfully when planted on their own. However, some varieties may not set a good crop unless pollinated by another suitable variety. A suitable variety is one which is self-compatible and will flower at about the same time as the one to be pollinated. This selection of varieties is, for flowering purposes, classified into three groups—early, mid-season and late. When the spring is warm, the flowering period of all varieties is shortened and all three groups may overlap, resulting in very effective cross-pollination.

EARLY FLOWERING

Victoria   Large. Typical plum red but yellowish on shaded side, slight bloom. Flesh golden, translucent. Fairly juicy, fair dessert flavour when fully ripe. Excellent for cooking and preserving. Ready second half August. Heavy cropper, tends to overcrop. Moderate growth, drooping, prone to silver leaf disease.

Ariel   Medium, oval. Yellowish green, flushed light pinkish red. Flesh golden, firm, moderately juicy, rich. Stone partially clinging. Ready mid to late September. Vigorous, upright.

Bonne de Bry   Medium to medium small, round. Deep reddish purple when fully ripe. Flesh greenish yellow, juicy, good flavour. Stone almost free. Ready late July. Very vigorous, rather spreading, with open habit and few laterals.

Merton Gem   Medium to large, oval. Light gold with bright red and dark red patches. Flesh yellow, very juicy, slightly rich. Ready second half August. Moderately vigorous, round headed, drooping, crops regularly.

Opal   Medium. Yellow almost covered with purplish black flush when fully ripe. Flesh pale gold, partly transparent, moderately firm, good flavour. Stone almost free. Ready beginning August. Moderately vigorous, round headed, dense. Regular cropper.

Edwards   Large to very large, oval. Reddish purple, becoming blue black, with heavy bloom. Flesh pale creamy yellow, sometimes tinged purple, transparent, firm, juicy, sweet to sub-acid, pleasant flavour when fully ripe. Stone clinging. Ready first half September. Moderately vigorous, spurs freely.

Early Laxton   Medium, round to oval. Pale yellow with slight flush and dots of bright, rosy red. Flesh yellow, sweet, juicy, good gage flavour. One of the earliest plums, ready late July. Good for cooking. Small growth, moderate cropper.

Prune Monsieur   Medium. Dark purplish red on sun side, greenish on the other. Flesh greenish yellow, moderately juicy, medium firmness. Stone free. Good for cooking or dessert. Fairly vigorous, pendulous branches. Variable cropping. Self-incompatible.

Jefferson   Medium. Greenish yellow, flushed and mottled pink, slight bloom. Flesh yellow, firm, juicy, sweet, excellent gage flavour. Stone semi-clinging. Excellent dessert. Ready early September. Moderately vigorous, fairly resistant to diseases, variable cropping. Self-incompatible.

Black Prince   Medium. Deep blue-black, heavy bloom. Flesh greenish, but dull, reddish brown when cooked, good flavour. Stone large, clinging. Cooker. Ready early August. Strong, upright. Heavy cropper.

Coe's Golden Drop Large, oval. Golden yellow with red dots. Flesh yellow, firm, rich, juicy. One of the finest dessert plums and cooks well. Ready late September; if gathered carefully, keeps in cool place into October. Stocky, well spurred.

Comte d'Althann's Gage Large to very large, oval. Purplish red, but purplish pink on yellow background on shaded side. Flesh yellowish, juicy, rich flavour. Very good dessert fruit. Ready first half September, but ripens unevenly. Straggling.

Denniston's Early Gage Medium, oval to round. Yellowish, marked with very characteristic green stripes. Flesh golden yellow, fairly juicy, slight gage flavour. Stone small, almost free. Ready mid-August. Good dessert plum. Straggling, hardy, reliable, good cropper.

Monarch Large, very round. Deep blue purple with russet dots, some bloom. Flesh greenish yellow. Rather flavourless, but cooks well without the skin becoming tough. Free stone. Ready late September. Upright, moderate, irregular cropper.

Severn Cross Large, oval. Pale yellowish green with purple dots, heavy bloom. Flesh yellow, sweet, juicy, moderate flavour. Cooking and dessert. Ready late September. Upright, moderate growth. Prone to brown rot.

Warwickshire Drooper Medium, oval to oblong. Deep yellow. Flesh yellow, mealy but cooks well, good for preserving and jam. If left to hang as long as possible, it has refreshing flavour acceptable for dessert. Ready mid-September. Compact growth.

Farleigh Damson Small, roundish. Purple. Yellow flesh, excellent damson flavour. Ready mid-September. Cooking only. Compact, heavy cropper.

Merryweather Damson Small, roundish. Purple. Yellow flesh, moderate damson flavour. Ready late September. Heavy cropper. Self-compatible.

Ontario Medium. Greenish yellow. Yellow flesh, juicy, fair flavour. Ready mid-August. Dessert. Moderate vigour, good cropper.

MID FLOWERING

Czar Medium. Purplish blue, heavy bloom. Flesh greenish yellow, juicy, moderately firm. Free stone. Fairly good for cooking, cooks with red juice. Moderate to strong vigour. Fruit susceptible to brown rot if touching one another and not thinned. Self-compatible.

Reine Claude Verte   Medium. Green with slightly yellowish tints, spotted purplish pink on sun side. Often cracked near the stem. Very slight bloom. Flesh greenish, juicy, sweet, good flavour. Excellent dessert. Ready end August. Medium to strong growth. Cropping variable, often light. Fairly resistant to red spider.

Belle de Lourain   Medium. Dark purplish red with bloom. Flesh yellowish, juicy, fair flavour when cooked. Stone partially free. Ready late August. Vigorous, heavy cropper. Partially self-compatible.

Mirabelle de Metz and *Mirabelle de Nancy*   Two similar varieties. Small. Uniform yellow, flecked with red on sun side, with bloom. Flesh yellowish, not very juicy, distinct flavour, sweet. Free stone. Ready September. Mirabelle conserves have world-wide reputation, but fruit too small for dessert. Weak to medium vigour, good, regular cropper, prone to red spider.

Bryanston Gage   Medium to large, oblong. Greenish yellow, sometimes with some red dots. Flesh greenish yellow, good gage flavour, less pronounced than Reine Claude Verte. Very good for jam. Ready early September. Straggling, good cropper.

Cambridge Gage   Small, round. Green to yellow, some russet dots. Flesh yellow, translucent, exceptionally rich, juicy, true gage flavour. Small stone, free. Good for dessert, cooking, preserving. Ready late August. Ripens unevenly. Vigorous growth, fair crop, regular.

Early Prolific (Early Rivers)   Small, roundish oval. Dark purple red, heavy bloom. Flesh yellow, cooking to excellent dark red, damson flavour. Makes good red plum jam. Stone small and free. Ready late July. Moderate to weak growth, fairly good cropper. Self-compatible. Prone to red spider.

Early Transparent Gage   Medium, round. Pale yellow, some red dots. Flesh golden yellow, sweet, rich gage flavour. Stone small, very round, free. Excellent dessert plum. Ready mid-August. Fairly vigorous, tends to make many twigs. Heavy cropper which repays thinning.

Italian Prune (Fellenberg)   Largest of prune types, oval. Dark violet blue, heavy bloom. Flesh yellow; if left to hang on the tree becomes streaked with reddish brown. Rather dry but, when cooked, rich in flavour and good dark colour. Dries well. Stone fairly free. Ready late September. Moderate vigour, drooping, good, regular cropper.

German Prune (Early Russian) (Quetsche Commune) Medium, oval. Purplish red, heavy bloom. Flesh yellowish green, moderately juicy, pleasant sub-acid flavour. Excellent cooker, medium as dessert. Stone free. Ready September. Vigorous, hardy. Grows well in wet and cold situations. Good cropper.

Oullins Gage (Reine Claude de Oullins) Medium to large, roundish. Greenish yellow, sometimes red dots, slight bloom. Flesh pale creamy yellow, not true gage quality except in dry, warm summers. Stone clinging. Good for jam. Ready first half August. Fairly strong growth, straggling, spurring well. Reliable cropper, leaves break first, helping protect flowers from frost.

Pershore Golden Egg (Yellow Egg) Medium, oval. Dull yellow. Flesh yellow, mealy but excellent when cooked. Makes one of best jams, if picked green. Good for bottling or canning. Ready late August. Moderate growth, drooping. Heavy cropper, tends to become biennial if allowed to crop too heavily.

Reine Claude Violette (Purple Gage) Small to medium, round. Dark purple. Flesh yellow, very juicy, rich, sweet. Ripens unevenly, if carefully stored keeps for a few weeks. Ready end August. Fairly vigorous, fairly good cropper.

Transparent Gage (Reine Claude Diaphane) Medium, round. Greenish yellow with purple dots and flush. Flesh golden yellow, juicy, rich, sweet. Stone free. Ready early September. Strong growth, good cropper. Fairly free from cracking common with many gage varieties.

Wyedale Small, round to oval. Reddish blue. Flesh yellow, mealy but cooks well. Stone free. Useful because of its lateness. Ready end October, hangs well into November. Moderate growth, good cropper.

Washington Medium. Yellow. Flesh yellow, juicy, sweet, delicious. Excellent dessert plum. Ready late August. Moderate growth, irregular cropper.

President Large. Deep purple. Flesh greenish yellow, sweet, good flavour. Cooker, but can be eaten as dessert. Vigorous growth, irregular cropper.

LATE FLOWERING VARIETIES

Kirke's Blue Gage Large, round. Deep reddish blue, heavy bloom, handsome. Flesh greenish yellow, rich flavour. Stone large, free. Ready mid-September. Moderate growth, rather straggling, irregular cropper.

Laxton's Gage Medium, roundish. Golden yellow, slight bloom, shows bruise marks. Flesh deep yellow, very juicy, rich gage flavour. Free stone. Ready mid-August. Small, compact, good, regular cropper.

Belle de Louvain Medium, oval. Dark purplish red, with bloom. Flesh yellow, juicy, fair flavour when cooked. Stone partially free. Ready late August. Fairly vigorous, pendulous. Fairly good cropper, slow to come into bearing.

Burbank (Giant Prune) Large. Deep red. Flesh golden, little flavour when cooked. Ready mid-September. Moderate growth, good, regular cropper.

Marjorie's Seedling Large, oblong to oval. Blue black, with bloom. Flesh yellow, sweet, mealy but cooks well, can serve as very late dessert. Ready first half October. Very vigorous, upright, good, regular cropper.

ORIENTAL PLUMS

Methley Medium. Reddish purple with red flesh. Juicy, sweet, distinctive flavour. Ripens middle July in south-western Michigan. Very vigorous, upright. Flowers self-fertile and numerous, buds hardy.

Shiro Medium to large. Yellow. Ripens end July. Very productive.

Santa Rosa Large. Dark crimson. Exceptionally good flavour. Ripens first half August. Self-fertile.

Frontier Large. Bluish-black. Flesh red, firm, good flavour. Vigorous, very good cropper in California, needs a pollinator (Santa Rosa).

19

RED AND WHITE CURRANTS

Cultivation details given here apply to both red and white, even if red currants only are referred to by name, white currants being a variation of the red.

Red currants are very hardy. Although not such a popular fruit as black currants, they are grown throughout the cool temperate regions. In Britain the commercial crop is grown mainly in Kent, Norfolk, Suffolk, Isle of Ely, Essex, Worcestershire and Sussex. Although they will grow in most of the USA they do best in cool, moist climates as in western Oregon and Washington and in the central and northern coastal areas of California. In California it is possible to grow them in the foothill areas of the Sierra Nevada, while in the warmer areas of California they can be tried in the shade along the north side of a wall or fence. In the USA, however, it may, in some places, be illegal to grow the currant because of white pine blister rust (see under Black Currants).

Red currants will tolerate shade. They flower a little before black currants and have a long flowering period. Because the flowers are not resistant to frost, however, they should be kept in a frost-free area during the blossoming period. Also they must not occupy exposed positions during times of strong wind in summer, as leaders and tender shoots of some varieties can be broken off. Almost any soil is suitable, particularly one that is slightly acid or neutral.

Propagation is fairly easy with hard-wood cuttings, if taken at leaf fall or soon after; it is usual for 90–100 per cent of them to take root. Cuttings should be from healthy shoots which have grown during the summer and are well ripened, strong and straight. Any soft wood at the tips must be removed, the cut being made just above a bud and the lower cut just below a bud. The cutting, after this preparation, should be 10–12in long. The red currant is grown on a leg, so all buds except the top four are rubbed off

with the fingers to prevent sucker growth. The cuttings should be planted as quickly as possible, about 6–8in deep, with the base of the cutting firmly pressed against the soil and not in an air pocket. Only about 4in of the top of the cutting should be above soil level. Three to four strong shoots grow out from the top buds and, in the following autumn, they can, as yearlings, be lifted. Before potting, the upper roots are cut clean away in order to prevent suckers from growing. (See diagram page 77.)

Red currants fruit on spurs growing on wood one to ten years old, and because of this they can be grown in the standard, bush and cordon forms. When the bush form is used, it should be allowed a leg or stem of at least 5in as this makes it easier to keep the open goblet-shaped bush free from suckers. The number of leading shoots should be strictly limited and all sucker growth prevented. Annual routine pruning, once the bush has been formed, is fairly simple. All laterals arising from the main branches should be cut back to about $\frac{1}{2}$–1in of the branch or removed entirely if strong. Leaders should be cut back by about a third depending on their vigour, the weak being cut back more than the strong. Fruit buds are formed in clusters at the base of new shoots, which should be pinched back in summer to four or five leaves just as the fruit is beginning to colour. If this is done early, secondary growth is stimulated; if too late, there is no check to the stronger shoots. Spur pruning helps to ripen the fruit earlier. Summer pruning must not be too vigorous at one time and a little should be done each day. Leaders must not be summer pruned.

With cordons, the leader is pruned by about 6in each year and the resulting side shoots cut back to one bud to form spurs. Hard spur pruning will encourage semi-permanent spurs, which will eventually resemble gnarled knobs of dark wood. The leader should be tied to a cane to get good straight growth and not be allowed to grow taller than 5ft, otherwise the lowest spurs will begin to die.

Potash is an essential requirement of the red currant; deficiency will become evident in the leaf margins having a scorched appearance. Potash can be added to the compost when repotting, but fertilisers containing chloride (eg muriate of potash) should not be used, otherwise damage may occur. Wood ash makes a good addition to the compost; failing this, sulphate of potash is best. The supply of nitrogen should not be excessive, and phosphate requirements are low. Red currants are also not very susceptible to trace element deficiencies.

All varieties of red currants are self-fertile, but require the attention of bees, flies and other insects. The flowers are rather small and unattractive to the honey bee. Serious damage can be done by birds, when the bushes are grown in the open. Bullfinches and sparrows, for example, attack not only the ripening fruit but buds and flowers as well.

The berries colour rapidly but should be left a few days to acquire their full flavour. The majority of varieties will hang well for up to a fortnight. They should be picked on the strig to avoid crushing the berries and without injuring the spurs from which will come the next year's crop.

DISEASES

CORAL SPOT (DIE BACK) *(Nectria cinnabarina)*
This attacks not only currants but many kinds of trees and shrubs. The fungus is readily recognised by the orange or flesh-coloured spots or spore pustules scattered thickly over the surface of dead and dying branches. In damp weather they are more or less waxy and salmon-coloured, but in dry weather firmer and rather paler.

Infection usually occurs through wounds or small snags of dead wood left after pruning. The fungus spreads from the infected parts into the main healthy branches, causing them to wilt in May and June. Death of the infected branches follows sooner or later. Wood that has been destroyed by the coral spot fungus turns first dark green or black and then brown.

All dead shoots and branches should be removed during pruning. Unnecessary injuries and 'snags' should be avoided when pruning. Diseased branches must be cut out cleanly, the cut being made right back into healthy wood. Dead wood and sticks should never be left lying around in an orchard—potted or otherwise.

CANE BLIGHT (BLACK PUSTULE) *(Botryosphaeria ribis)*
This is very similar to coral spot in action, but the pustules formed on the infected wood are black rather than red. It occurs in the United States in all areas where currants are grown, but is most prevalent in the eastern and northern states. It is most commonly found on the red currant but can occur in other *Ribis* species, including gooseberries.

Black, wart-like pustules arranged in parallel rows appear on the diseased wood and there is sudden wilting of infected branches. Scattered branches or whole bushes may die.

Control is by good sanitation in the orchard, cutting out and burning diseased parts of the bush, and by careful pruning.

CURRANT MOSAIC
This is one of a number of virus diseases which affect red currants and reduce cropping and vigour. The most striking symptoms of currant mosaic is the chlorotic pattern to be seen on the leaves. Irregular light green spots appear, mainly along the midrib and larger veins, which become larger and merge into an irregular band along the vein. It is unusual for the entire leaf to become chlorotic. The light green areas gradually turn white. Stunting of the bush occurs in advanced stages of the disease and it loses its vigour and fruitfulness. After several years it may die.

LEAF SPOT   see under Black Currants.

CURRANT RUST (WHITE PINE BLISTER RUST)   see under Black Currants.

PESTS

BIG BUD MITE (BLACK CURRANT GALL MITE)
This pest is usually associated with black currants, but does attack red currants. Instead of producing swollen gall-like buds, the mite causes red

currant buds to become dry and fall off. It is not a severe pest and can be kept under control in the same way as with black currants.

CURRANT CLEARWING (CURRANT BORER) *(Aegeria tipuliformis)*
Although not generally widespread, this is troublesome in some localities.

The adult is a slender, quick flying, dark blue, wasp-like moth; ½in long and ¾in broad. It has three yellow bands across the body. It lays its eggs at the end of May and beginning of June. The caterpillars which hatch bore into the stem and tunnel up through the pith into the main framework of the branches. This tunnelling often results in coral spot, causing severe damage. The caterpillars are very hard to find in the early stages. They live and feed inside the branches throughout the winter until April, when they pupate as chrysalids usually near to the entrance hole. Whilst the caterpillars are feeding, the shoots begin to wilt and die. If the branch is removed it will be found to be hollow, with the caterpillar, white with brown head, in its tunnel. Control is with chemicals.

AMERICAN CURRANT BORER *(Psenocerus supernotatus)*
This pest occurs in North America. In its life cycle it is very similar to the currant clearwing, but belongs to an entirely different order. When mature, instead of being a moth, it is a small narrow brownish beetle, varying in length from ⅛ to ¼in. The grub is small, white, round and wrinkled. Control is with chemicals.

CURRANT SAWFLY   see under Black Currants.

CAPSID BUGS   see under Black Currants.

APHIDS   see under Black Currants.

VARIETIES

Jonkeer Van Tets (Early)   Medium-sized berries, thin but tough skin, deep red, sub-acid flavour. Good quality. Strig of medium length, carrying eight to fourteen berries. Moderately vigorous, fairly upright, spurring freely, heavy cropper.

Earliest of Fourlands (Early)   Good, but uneven sized, bright-coloured berries on fairly long strig. Vigorous, upright bush, reliable cropper, useful because of its earliness.

Cherry (Early)   Large, bright red, juicy, well flavoured. Short strigs make them difficult to pick. Vigorous, stocky, compact bush. Suckers less than some kinds.

Fay's New Prolific (Early mid-season)   Large, dark red, slightly acid, fairly tolerant to humidity, berries do not split easily. Medium to long strigs. Medium vigour. Branches brittle, liable to be broken by wind. Good cropper, unreliable some seasons.

Laxton's No 1 (Mid-season)   Medium, with small seeds, very bright red, thickly bunched. Strigs moderately long. Upright to slightly spreading, strong vigour, heavy, consistent cropper.

Laxton's Perfection (Mid-season)   Exceptionally large, very dark red. Strig long. Good berries for show purposes, but not always a good cropper. Large, straggling bush, liable to wind damage.

Red Lake (Mid-season)   Very large, even-sized, bright red, juicy, seeds moderately large. Strig very long. Upright, moderately vigorous. Most productive variety for California, Washington and Oregon.

Minnesota (Mid-season)   Good sized berries. Long to medium strig. Strong growth, very heavy cropper.

Wilder (Late)   Large, lighter colour than Fay's Prolific, remaining bright and attractive until late in season, mildly sub-acid. Fairly long strigs carrying ten to twelve berries. Vigorous, upright. Does well in eastern Washington.

Wilson's Long Bunch (Late)   Medium, bright red, good quality, will hang late. Strigs about 4in long, crowded on the spurs. Semi-erect, moderately vigorous. In England, several stocks are sold under this name, but the true stock is a distinct variety usually recognised by late ripening of berries

Rondom (Late)   Medium, almost pear shaped, light red turning to dark red. Fair flavour. Generally good quality. Strigs 2–3in long, bearing ten to twenty berries. Moderately vigorous, cup shaped, spurring freely, heavy cropper. Good variety because of its lateness and resistance to leaf spot.

Rivers Late Red (Very late)   Medium, pale to bright red. Long strigs. Vigorous, upright. Useful to prolong season.

WHITE VARIETIES

White Versailles (Early)   Large, pale yellow, sweet. Medium length strig. Upright, strong vigour, very heavy cropper.

White Grape (Mid-season)   Medium berries. Strigs difficult to pick without crushing some berries. Compact, well spurred, moderate vigour.

Transparent (Late)   *Large*, yellow. Long strigs. Upright, strong vigour, good cropper.

White Leviathan (Very late)   Large, deep yellow. Medium strigs. Vigorous, good cropper.

20

STRAWBERRIES

Strawberries, which are essentially woodland and meadow plants, thrive in a loam rich in humus. The soil can be slightly acid, and in woodland soil they make very strong plants. Their liking for a rich soil can be more easily met in pots than, normally, in an open plantation. Where soil can be obtained from pasture land, the top 5–6in can be taken and chopped up fine, but not sieved. Or alternatively a good compost can be made up of one part medium loam, one part compost, one part peat. If available, well-rotted manure can be added; otherwise about 1lb of fine bone meal can be added to each barrow load of potting soil. Avoid a heavy or sticky soil and, if necessary, add some brick rubble or lime to make it more friable.

Horticultural pots are not essential; any kind of container can be used provided it is at least 9in deep, about 7in in diameter and permits drainage. Bottomless pots of the kind used for ring culture are suitable if it is intended to keep them in one place for the season. Pots can be made from old floor covering cut to a rectangle 9in by 2ft, the longest side being bent round and fixed with a wire or plastic string.

Plants should be potted up in August as early as possible, so that they are growing well before the end of the season and have already formed a good crown. The level of soil should be about 1in below the top of the container. Make a shallow depression in the soil to take the full spread of the roots and make sure the crown will stand just above the soil. Plant firmly but never bury the crown. Once established, they will normally grow very fast, maximum growth being towards the end of September. During August they will need plenty of watering, but in autumn this may be lessened. By the middle of October, when growth has finished, heavy watering will serve no purpose.

If the plants are to be taken into the orchard house in order to obtain early fruit, they must first be thoroughly rested. An adequate period of

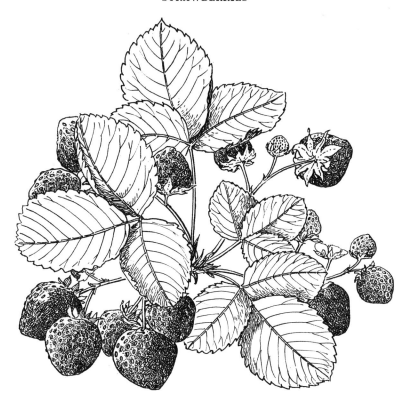

dormancy is essential and up to 10° of frost at the end of October or early November is of great benefit. As the roots are protected only by the thin sides of the pots, however, they must be protected with litter etc if left standing out in a severe winter.

To force strawberries in pots in a glass house, bottom heat is not required and they will thrive best in a cool house. When taken into the house at the beginning of January, a day temperature of 50° F (10° C) and a night temperature of 45° F (7° C) should be the maximum for the first two weeks. During the next two weeks the temperatures should rise by about 5° F, remaining at that level until the plants commence flowering when the aim should be a maximum day temperature of 69° F (16° C) and 55° F (13° C) at night. If the sun is shining, 70° F (21° C) can be allowed, but the house must be given plenty of ventilation.

The atmosphere should be reasonably moist and no effort made to keep a dry atmosphere during the pollination period. Once the fruits begin to swell, the plants should be fed weekly with weak liquid manure, but as soon as the fruit commences to turn colour the feeding must stop. As the fruit ripens, the temperature must be gradually lowered by giving as much ventilation as possible.

When plants are kept entirely outdoors, a good plan is to put them in different parts of the garden—some in a warm place, others in a cooler place—so that the fruiting season is lengthened. However, during the flowering period, they should not be unprotected from frost; nor should they be exposed to bitter cold winds, as this will check growth. The colour and quality of the fruit depends very much on temperature, as well as the supply of moisture. If the fruit develops too slowly because of low temperatures and an inadequate supply of water, it will lack a bright colour, be of poor flavour, and 'woody' in texture.

Although a young plant when first potted will benefit from a good supply of nitrogen, which will cause good growth, it should not be given in excess. Nitrogenous fertilisers will produce a large amount of leaf growth and fruit which tends to be acidic and of poor flavour. As the plants develop they should be given a good supply of potassium and phosphorus rather than nitrogen.

In the open plantation, it is normal practice to replant with new stock every three years. Some growers, however, are now treating the plants as annuals—taking fruit the first year after planting; immediately fruiting has finished, setting new plants from the runners, and then destroying the old ones. This should certainly be done with potted plants which have been forced into early fruiting. As soon as they have finished fruiting, remove the old leaves and dead fruiting stems, then peg the strongest runner with its small plantlet into a 3in pot and remove all other runners. If you want to increase the number of plants several runners from one plant can be used, but the aim should be to get good strong new plants growing as quickly as possible. In any case runners must only be taken from healthy parent plants free from virus disease.

VIRUS DISEASES AND THEIR VECTORS

The strawberry is subject to a number of widespread virus diseases. There are many different viruses, some of which cause only slight symptoms or even none at all, but the presence of more than one virus within a plant often causes serious disease. These viruses are spread by different kinds of vectors, and are grouped according to their carriers: aphids, leafhoppers (frog flies) or nematodes (eelworms).

The principal aphid vector is *Pentatrichopus fragaefolii* which, in itself, is not a serious pest. The viruses transmitted by it commonly occur together as complex infections and often produce very severe symptoms, but the effect on the plant depends not only on the number or strains of viruses involved but on the variety of strawberry. No variety is resistant to infection, but some show no symptoms when infected by a particular virus or a complex of viruses. These varieties are classed as *tolerant*. Varieties which show symptoms are classed as *sensitive*, but here again the reaction depends on the strain of the virus as well as the extent of any complex infection. The usual complex infections are as follows:

YELLOW EDGE
Symptoms are most obvious from August onwards in sensitive varieties. There will be yellowing of the margins of the younger leaves and plants will be stunted.

SEVERE CRINKLE
Symptoms will be seen in early summer. Leaves will bear numerous chlorotic spots which become brown and dead. Growth stops in these areas on the leaf, causing the foliage to become wrinkled and distorted.

MILD CRINKLE
Symptoms are more pronounced in early summer and autumn. Leaves bear only faint chlorotic spots which are less numerous than with severe crinkle. Leaf distortion may be absent or only slight.

DEGENERATION COMPLEX
This causes both stunting and severe leaf crinkling. Only stock certified free of virus infection should be purchased. Spraying established plants with an insecticide shortly before the flowering period will lessen the possibility of infection by aphids.

Leafhopper diseases are transmitted principally by *Aphrodes bincinctus*. Adult leafhoppers are winged and pale yellow; the larvae, apart from being smaller and wingless, are similar. Their presence is shown by dry, white, cast-off skins on the lower surface of leaves. Control is by spraying with insecticides. Leafhoppers transmit the following diseases:

STRAWBERRY GREEN PETAL
Symptoms may be seen in spring. Young leaves are chlorotic and reduced in size. Petals are smaller than normal and sometimes green. When the flowering period ends, mature leaves become red or bronze. The main symptom is the failure of the fruit to develop. When plants are infected

early in the season they wilt and die during summer. This disease can be transmitted from infected clover plants.

STRAWBERRY BRONZE LEAF WILT

Symptoms are very similar to green petal disease, but there are no flower symptoms and plants die more rapidly.

Nematodes or eelworms are of many types and have different habitats. In the soil, a great many kinds are harmless to plants; indeed many are beneficial in that they kill and feed upon harmful kinds, while others feed upon micro organisms and decaying organic matter. Those that transmit virus diseases obtain their food from plants by piercing living cells with their stylets and sucking out the contents. Strawberries can be attacked by several species of nematodes, some of which live in the soil and cause root lesions, while others live above the ground on the foliage or stems.

The main nematode-transmitted viruses are caused by *root feeding* nematodes. These usually live for two to four years and reproduce by laying eggs which, on hatching, release larvae ready to begin feeding immediately. The range of host plants is very wide, but the absence of a host does not reduce their population, as they can live through many months, even years, of starvation to resume breeding when food again becomes available. Apart from being vectors of virus diseases, root damage causing severe stunting or the death of plants may occur when large numbers of the worms feed on roots. Nematodes transmit the following diseases:

ARABIS MOSAIC

No varieties are immune to this disease. When infected, many varieties show chlorotic mottling on leaves and there will be severe stunting. Other varieties may show only a slight infection. This disease also affects raspberry, black and red currant and cherries. It is transmitted by the nematode *Xiphinema diversicaudatum* which occurs mainly in hedgerow and woodland soils, but may also be found in pastureland. After feeding on a diseased plant it may remain infective for several months.

RASPBERRY RINGSPOT

Symptoms are leaf mottling and a reduction in both growth and crop. No variety appears to be immune to the virus, which is transmitted by *Longidorus* species. These nematodes may be as much as 10mm in length, but despite their large size they are difficult to see, being transparent and threadlike.

TOMATO BLACK RING

When this virus infects strawberries it is usually combined with raspberry ringspot and its actual effect is uncertain. It is transmitted by the *Longidorus* species of nematodes.

Leaf or foliar nematodes *(Aphelenchoides* sp.*)* also cause disease in strawberries. However, these are not virus diseases but are incited by the nematodes. Invisible to the unaided eye, they spend their lives among the leaves of the crown of the plant and runner buds, unless washed off or otherwise removed. Small colonies are carried out on the buds of runners and propagation from infested plants is one of the chief means of spreading the parasites.

SPRING DWARF

Symptoms are most obvious during early spring. Diseased plants have an abnormal character to the crown. Buds are small and poorly developed, and the hairs covering them are greatly reduced in number. Development of foliage is retarded and, as the leaves unfold and elongate, they are seen to be distorted and abnormal. Leaflets are sometimes reduced in numbers and size, and may even be absent so that only very short, tapered leafstalks remain. In severe cases, the main crown is usually killed and weak secondary crowns are formed. Flowering and fruiting are seriously affected.

SUMMER DWARF

This hot weather disease is confined mainly to southern regions, such as the south-eastern and Gulf states of the USA. Summer dwarf symptoms do not appear until July to September. Because of this, the older leaves are more or less normal in winter while the younger and inner ones are crinkled and distorted.

Another nematode *(Ditylenchus dipsaci)* lives mainly within the tissues and may invade all parts of the plant except the roots. Infested plants become stunted. Effects will be more noticeable during spring and autumn when growth is relatively slow and the worms are breeding rapidly. Leaves will be crinkled, with their margins turned down towards the under surface and, in severe attacks, the leaves have fewer marginal teeth and become more roundish in outline. The leaves are usually brittle and may be a darker green than normal. Lower parts of the main veins near the junction with the stalk are generally pale, enlarged and puffy. When ripe fruits are infested, they have pale patches, are soft and easily squashed.

When young stock is infested, nematodes can be eradicated by treating the plants in a hot water bath, which will control mites, weevils and other insect pests at the same time. No damage will be done to the plants if they are put into hot water with a temperature of 115° F (46° C) for ten minutes, but they should be plunged into cold water immediately after removal and planted as soon as possible. However, there is little point in planting treated plants in infested soil. When infestation is suspected the soil should be treated with a fumigant.

OTHER DISEASES

GREY MOULD *(Botryitis cinarea)*
This is very common in regions where rainfall and dews occur during the fruiting season. Heavy losses of fruit may result and in some years it is particularly troublesome in England. The fungus attacks many kinds of plants and also occurs on dead growth. At first the strawberry fruit usually becomes soft, followed by blackening and later a greyish, fluffy growth or mould. Control is by ensuring good air circulation so that plants and fruit dry quickly. All decaying leaves should be cleared. Flowers of sulphur can be dusted or puffed into the crown of the plant and under the leaves from April onwards, stopping when the fruit begins to ripen. An alternative is to spray with Karathane during May

STRAWBERRY MILDEW *(Sphaerotheca humili)*
This is often confused with grey mould. Dark patches appear on the upper side of leaves, while greyish white patches occur on the underside. The fungus spreads to the berries causing a grey powdery growth. To control, dust frequently with flowers of sulphur, or spray with lime sulphur just before the blossom opens and again several times, at fortnightly intervals, after flowering.

VERTICILLIUM WILT *(Verticillium albo-atrum)*
This widespread, soil-borne fungus becomes more prevalent when potatoes, tomatoes, peppers, aubergines, raspberries and strawberries are grown year after year on the same land. It can cause wilting and death of strawberry plants, its effects being usually seen in July and August. Outer leaves become wilted and later begin to dry at the edges. As the season progresses they collapse and turn brown, sometimes partially recovering as the weather becomes cooler in September.

Provided it is not necessary to take soil from sick land there is no reason why this disease should give concern in a potted plantation. Soil suspected of carrying the fungus can be fumigated.

RED STELE (RED CORE, RED ROOT ROT, BLACK STELE ETC.) *(Phytophthora fragariae)*

This is serious in most of USA where strawberries are grown commercially, except in the extreme south. It is also common in Scotland and in parts of Kent, Sussex and Hampshire. It usually occurs on poorly drained soils and destroys plant roots. Losses are not great when the soil is first infected, but the disease builds up and can remain in the soil for many years.

First signs of the disease are stunted plants in spring. Leaves barely extend over the surface while those of healthy plants may be as much as several inches above the soil. If a plant is only lightly infected, the leaves and fruit stem may develop normally until the berries begin to ripen then, in a warm spell, the leaves will show a definite droop. If a suspected plant is dug up and the roots are dead and 'rat-tail' in appearance rather than fibrous, the disease is confirmed. The most characteristic symptom, however, is the red colour of the core of the root. This will be seen as a red streak if a thin root is cut down its length with a sharp knife. Where this disease is prevalent, the soil should be fumigated before being used for pot grown strawberries.

BLACK ROOT ROT

This occurs in most parts of the world and is caused by several soil fungi. Small fibrous rootlets of the plant become infected and are killed back to the main roots. Once the entire root system is infected, the plant shows symptoms above the soil. Leaves will be small and yellowish and, following a hot dry period, may become withered or brown around the margins. Fruit stems will remain short and berries, if formed, will remain small and often wither before ripening. As a control, the soil can be fumigated. The fungi causing this trouble increase and become dangerous to the plant in conditions creating an unbalanced biotic equilibrium, so the answer is to provide well-drained fertile soil, rich in organic matter.

PESTS

WEEVILS

Several species of weevils attack strawberries. The strawberry blossom weevil or elephant beetle *(Anthonomous rubi)* cuts through blossom stems, after laying eggs in the buds. The strawberry leaf weevil *(Caenorhinus germanicus)* chews stems of fruit and leaves. Both can be controlled with insecticides. The strawberry root weevils *(Brachyrhinus sp.)* may be troublesome in some parts of Washington, but can be eradicated by the hot bath treatment and fumigation of the soil.

STRAWBERRY MITE *(Tarsonemus pallidus)*

These pale brown mites are similar to red spiders. They are hardly visible, but may be discovered between unopened young leaves. A small number of adult female mites overwinter in the crowns of the plants and commence laying eggs from late April onwards; these take about eleven days to hatch. Each generation, from egg to adult, takes about three weeks and the mite population builds up to a peak about the end of July. They spread from plant to plant, where these are touching, and along runners; they may also be transported by other insects or by humans on clothes, tools etc.

Injury is caused when very large numbers of mites penetrate surface cells of young plants and commence feeding. Infected leaves develop a down curling of the leaf edges, so that the symptoms may be confused with those of the leaf nematode. The difference is that leaf nematode damage is more evident in spring while mite damage does not appear until the end of July. With the attacks continuing throughout August and September, the plants become stunted and young leaves often turn brown and die. Severe attack can reduce flower-bud formation and so reduce the following year's crop. One-year-old plants are not severely attacked, unless already heavily infested when planted. Miticides are available for the control of this mite. With pot cultivation, one-year or maiden cropping will lessen the damage from this mite, as well as from other pests and diseases of the strawberry.

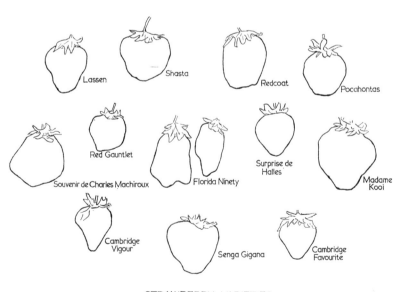

STRAWBERRY VARIETIES

VARIETIES

Varieties of strawberries are so numerous, with new ones constantly appearing, that only the best known can be mentioned here. Growers should buy stock certified free from virus disease.

Cambridge Prizewinner Early, useful for forcing under glass. Bright red, attractive fruits, fair flavour and texture. Crops well over short period. Resistant to grey mould. Fairly resistant to red stele.

Cambridge Vigour Very early in maiden year, thereafter mid-season. Good for forcing. Good quality, juicy. Large growing. Virus tolerant. Resistant to red stele.

Senga Precosa Early. Medium to small, firm, orange-red, white flesh. Fairly sweet. German.

Surprise des Halles Early. Medium to small, orange-red turning scarlet, orange flesh. Moderate, acid flavour. Crops heavily. Fairy resistant to grey mould and mildew. French.

Merton Herald Early. Medium, good flavour, attractive. Fairly good cropper.

Tamella Early. Very large, wedge shaped, firm, juicy. Good flavour. Very heavy cropper. Dutch.

Cambridge Rival Early. Medium, dark red, firm, very good flavour. Good cropper. Suitable wet districts and acid soils. Resistant to red stele. Very susceptible to strawberry mite.

Cambridge Favourite Second early. Large, firm, attractive. Little flavour. Fairly resistant to red stele. Very susceptible to strawberry mite.

Senga Precosana Second early. Medium to large. Orange-red turning scarlet, orange flesh. Fair flavour, rather acid. Fairly resistant to mildew. German.

Gorella Second early. Large, dark red, juicy. Fair flavour. Heavy cropper. Dutch.

Royal Sovereign Second early. Large, excellent flavour. Likes good soil with plenty of humus, but not a heavy cropper. Susceptible to disease and strawberry mite.

Crusader Mid-season. Medium, bright red, good flavour.

o

Emperor Mid-season. Medium to large, attractive, medium red, evenly shaped, very sweet, juicy. Flavour considered better than Royal Sovereign. Suitable for acid soils.

Senga Gigana Mid-season. Very large, scarlet to dark scarlet, pale orange flesh. Fair, slightly acid flavour. Very susceptible to grey mould. German.

Marieva Mid-season. Medium to small, orange-red turning scarlet. Very good flavour, slightly aromatic. Resistant to grey mould. German.

Madame Kooi (Madame Moutot) Mid-season. Large, red. Fair flavour. Very productive. French.

Grande Mid-season. Exceptionally large, up to 3in diameter and 3oz weight. Dark red, with juicy red flesh. Good flavour.

Souvenir de Charles Machiroux Mid-season. Very large, bright red, rather irregular shape. Red flesh, rich flavour. Very productive in second year. Belgian.

His Excellency Mid-season but will fruit again in the autumn when berries may weigh up to 2oz. In a heated glass house fruit can be available at Christmas from plants potted in the previous July. Very good flavour. Prefers acid soil but lime soil suitable if plenty of humus added. Has good resistance to virus and mildew.

Merton Dawn Mid-season. Large to medium, pale orange to orange-red, pale orange flesh. Moderate flavour. Resembles Cambridge Favourite. Heavy cropper, fairly susceptible to grey mould.

Merton Princess Mid-season. Large, good flavour, sweet, juicy. Very heavy cropper. Susceptible to red stele.

Elista Late mid-season. Medium, orange-red becoming scarlet, red flesh. Good flavour, slightly acid. Compact, crops well. Resistant to grey mould and mildew. Dutch.

Jurica Late mid-season. Medium to medium small, deep red, orange-red flesh. Good flavour, slightly acid. Heavy cropper. German.

Cambridge Late Pine Late. Medium to large, crimson, excellent flavour, very sweet. Fairly good cropper. Frost resistant.

Red Gauntlet Late. Large, scarlet, white flesh tinged red. Poor flavour, very heavy cropper.

Templar Late. Large, dark red when ripe. Firm, juicy, rich flavour. Heavy cropper.

Talisman Late. Large, bright red, good quality and flavour. Heavy cropper, prone to grey mould. Resistant to red stele.

Domanil Late. Large, orange to orange-red, orange flesh, firm, rather acid. Heavy cropper. Belgian.

PERPETUAL FRUITING VARIETIES

In average weather conditions, these will continue cropping into mid-October, or later under glass. They are well flavoured and equal in size to ordinary varieties. They yield their heaviest crop in the first season after being planted and should therefore be treated as annuals. So that fruiting follows on after normal varieties have finished, blossom should be removed when they come into flower. Because of their sustained fruiting, they will need more moisture and plenty of organic matter.

Christopher York Medium to large, good flavour. Very good cropper from July onwards.

Hampshire Maid Medium, bright red. Good flavour. For best results, remove all blossom until late June; they will then commence cropping from the end of July onwards.

Rabunda Medium to large, bright red, moderate flavour. Crops heavily during August and September.

Gento Very large, excellent flavour. Heavy and continuous fruiting from August until October. Even when potted in spring, a full crop can be expected in autumn.

September Glow Medium, attractive, orange-red, one of the best flavoured. Crops from August to October. A variety for quality rather than quantity. In late autumn, berries should remain on the plant a day or two longer than most other varieties to acquire their full flavour.

Merlin Large. Good flavour. Crops heavily from August to October. Very resistant to diseases, except verticillium wilt.

Saint Claude Variable size. King fruits large, with numerous small berries on same truss. Sweet, very good flavour. Crops from August onwards, ripens very quickly.

Sans Rivale Medium, glossy red, good flavour. Crops heavily and continuously from September; for best results remove all blossom until late July. Fruits until very late in the year and very suitable for cropping under glass.

NORTH AMERICA

Earlydawn Early. Large, bright red, firm, tart. Large, very productive plant. Susceptible to verticillium wilt and powdery mildew.

Sunrise Early. Medium, light bright red, good flavour. Very vigorous and productive. Some resistance to red stele and verticillium wilt.

Midland Early. Medium, red flesh, tart flavour. Good cropper.

Gala Early. Large, moderately firm, good flavour. Very productive.

Cavalier Early. Large, attractive, good quality. Highly resistant to verticillium wilt. Fairly susceptible to powdery mildew.

Veestar Early. Large, attractive, moderately firm, very good flavour. Fairly resistant to verticillium wilt. Susceptible to leaf scorch.

Raritan Second early. Large to medium, bright red, excellent quality and flavour. Not resistant to red stele.

Redcoat Second early. Specially suitable for eastern Canada and northern New England. Large to medium, bright red, attractive, very firm, good flavour. Very productive. Susceptible to verticillium wilt and leaf spot. Fairly resistant to powdery mildew.

Vibrant Second early. Large, firm, attractive. Red flesh, good quality. Susceptible to verticillium wilt in Southern Ontario.

Catskill Mid-season. Popular commercial variety in the north-east. Large, soft, attractive red with bright green cap. Excellent flavour. Vigorous, prolific. Fairly resistant to verticillium wilt, powdery mildew, leaf scorch and leaf spot.

Jerseybelle Mid-season. Very large, fairly good quality. Vigorous, prolific. Susceptible to red stele and verticillium wilt.

Midway. Mid-season. Large, deep red, firm, good flavour. Vigorous, prolific. Susceptible to verticillium wilt. Some resistance to red stele.

Surecrop Mid-season. Medium, bright red, firm, excellent flavour. Very vigorous. Some resistance to red stele, fairly resistant to verticillium wilt, leaf scorch and leaf spot.

Redchief Mid-season. Large to medium, red flesh, firm, sub-acid. Moderate vigour. Some resistance to red stele, resistant to leaf scorch and mildew. Susceptible to leaf spot.

Garnet Mid-season. Large, medium red, attractive, moderately firm, fairly good flavour. Vigorous, very prolific. Some resistance to foliage disease.

Guardian Mid-season. Large, light red, very good flavour. Some resistance to red stele and verticillium wilt.

Robinson Mid-season. Large to medium, bright red, pleasant flavour. Vigorous, good cropper. Resistant to verticillium wilt.

Fulton Mid-season. Medium. Red, attractive with conspicuous seeds. Flesh red, firm, good flavour. Vigorous, productive.

Holiday Mid-season. Large, bright red, attractive. Firm, good quality, distinctive aromatic flavour. Vigorous, productive.

Pochahontas Mid-season. Medium small to small. Orange-red to red, with orange-red flesh. Good flavour, somewhat tart. Moderately vigorous, very productive. Susceptible to verticillium wilt.

Suwanee Mid-season. Medium, long and conic, light bright red, attractive. One of the best flavoured. Vigorous, moderately productive. Resistant to foliage diseases.

Grenadier Mid-season. Medium, dark red, firm, excellent flavour. Good for jam. Good cropper. Fairly susceptible to powdery mildew.

Sparkle Late. Medium, dark red, attractive. High quality, excellent flavour. More adaptable than most to a wide range of soil and climate. Resistant to powdery mildew.

Fletcher Late. Medium to large. Medium red, good quality, somewhat tart. Vigorous.

Ozark Beauty Ever-bearing. Large, elongated, deep red, fairly good flavour, sweet. Vigorous, prolific.

Streamliner Ever-bearing. Medium to large, bright red, very good flavour. Productive.

Gem Ever-bearing. Medium. Rather acid but very good flavour.

Rockhill (Wazata) Ever-bearing. Medium, attractive, excellent flavour. Resistant to leaf spot. Makes few runners.

Arapahoe Ever-bearing. Medium, firm to soft, glossy red, very good flavour.

Ogallala Ever-bearing. Medium to large, richly flavoured. Hardy, resistant to leaf spot.

Geneva Ever-bearing. Large, deep red, soft, richly flavoured.

Klondyke Medium, deep red, rather acid, good flavour. Withstands heat of southern summers. Susceptible to leaf scorch and leaf spot.

Blakemore Very early. Medium, bright red, rather acid, firm. Good for jam. Suitable for southern states and has largely replaced Klondyke. Virus tolerant. Susceptible to verticillium wilt and foliage diseases.

Shasta Large, roundish, bright red, attractive, fair flavour. Fruits all summer on the California coast.

Lassen Large. Medium to large, dark red, soft, fair flavour. Suitable for southern California coast.

Goldsmith Large, glossy red, fair quality, only fair flavour. Very productive along California coast during summer and early autumn.

Fresno Large, bright red, good flavour. Suitable for southern California.

Torrey Similar to Fresno, but berries more squat.

Tioga Very large, bright red, good flavour. Suitable for California coast.

Solana Medium, bright red. Very rich flavour. High tolerance to virus diseases. Suitable for southern California.

Northwest Medium to large, medium red, firm, very good flavour. Susceptible to red stele, mildew and leaf spot. Suitable for Oregon, Washington and British Columbia.

Siletz Medium, deep red, excellent flavour. Resistant to red stele. Suitable for Pacific North-West.

Dabreak Large, very attractive, sweet, excellent flavour. Resistant to leaf spot.

British Sovereign Large, very attractive. Excellent flavour. Susceptible to red stele and mildew. This and Northwest are principal varieties grown in British Columbia.

AUSTRALIA

Richmond Red Medium, dark red, firm, fair flavour. Susceptible to leaf spot.

Ettersburg Medium, bright red, fairly good flavour. Susceptible to leaf spot.

Phenomenal Medium, bright red, very good flavour. Productive.

Majestic Large, bright red, very good flavour. Susceptible to mildew and leaf spot.

Bountiful Large, light red, soft, fair flavour. Very productive. Resistant to leaf spot.

Kendall Medium, dark red, firm, fair flavour. Highly resistant to foliage diseases. Susceptible to grey mould.